JENNI CALDER was born in Chicago, educated in the United States and England, and has lived in or near Edinburgh since 1971. After several years of part-time teaching and freelance writing, including three years in Kenya, she worked at the National Museums of Scotland from 1978 to 2001 successively as education officer, Head of Publications, script editor for the Museum of Scotland, and latterly as Head of Museum of Scotland International. In the latter capacity her main interest was in emigration and the Scottish diaspora. She has written and lectured widely on Scottish, English and American literary and historical subjects, and writes fiction and poetry as Jenni Daiches. She has two daughters, a son and a dog.

By the same author:

Chronicles of Conscience: A Study of Arthur Koestler and George Orwell, Secker and Warburg, 1968

Scott (with Angus Calder), Evans, 1969

There Must be a Lone Ranger: The Myth and Reality of the American West, Hamish Hamilton, 1974

Women and Marriage in Victorian Fiction, Thames and Hudson, 1976

Brave New World and Nineteen Eighty-Four, Edward Arnold, 1976

Heroes, from Byron to Guevara, Hamish Hamilton, 1977

The Victorian Home, Batsford, 1977

The Victorian and Edwardian Home in Old Photographs, Batsford, 1979

RLS: A Life Study, Hamish Hamilton, 1980

The Enterprising Scot (ed, with contributions), National Museums of Scotland, 1986

Animal Farm and Nineteen Eighty-Four, Open University Press, 1987

The Wealth of a Nation (ed, with contributions), NMS Publishing, 1989

Scotland in Trust, Richard Drew, 1990

St Ives by RL Stevenson (new ending), Richard Drew, 1990

No Ordinary Journey: John Rae, Arctic Explorer (with Ian Bunyan, Dale Idiens and Bryce Wilson), NMS Publishing, 1993

Mediterranean (poems, as Jenni Daiches), Scottish Cultural Press, 1995

The Nine Lives of Naomi Mitchison, Virago, 1997

Museum of Scotland (guidebook), NMS Publishing, 1998

Present Poets 1 (ed, poetry anthology), NMS Publishing, 1998

Translated Kingdoms (ed, poetry anthology), NMS Publishing, 1999

Robert Louis Stevenson, (poetry, ed), Everyman, 1999

Present Poets 2 (ed, poetry anthology), NMS Publishing, 2000

Scots in Canada, Luath Press, 2003

Not Nebuchadnezzar
In Search of Identities

To Twin & Trevor with all best wishes Jenni Calder

JENNI CALDER

Luath Press Limited

EDINBURGH

www.luath.co.uk

First published 2005

The paper used in this book is recyclable.
It is made from low-chlorine pulps produced in a low-energy,
low-emission manner from renewable forests.

The publisher acknowledges subsidy from the Scottish Arts Council

 Scottish
Arts Council

towards the publication of this volume.

Printed and bound by
DigiSource GB Ltd, Livingston

Typeset in 10.5 point Sabon
by Jennie Renton

Acknowledgements

My grateful thanks to Faith Pullin, for reading this with such sympathetic attention, for hugely helpful and constructive comment, and for all the hours we have spent talking about issues of identity over red wine and cappuccino.

Thank you to Rachel, Gowan and Gideon.

And thank you to Gavin MacDougall of Luath Press who suggested what became Chapter 2 and piloted the way to publication, and to Jennie Renton for thoughtful and supportive editing.

Contents

Prologue

THERE WERE TWO reasons for writing this book. Identity – national, ethnic, tribal, religious, cultural – is a prominent issue as the twenty-first century gets under way. More and more people see themselves as uprooted, displaced or marginalised. More and more people lead migratory lives and are exiled from some area of existence, geographical or cultural, that is important to them. By undertaking a personal search for identities I hope to throw some light on what identity means and how it affects the way we lead our lives and interpret the world. But I was also motivated by the biography sections of libraries and bookshops. How many memoirs and biographies of women are there? And how many of these are not about women in the world of theatre, style or entertainment? We need to know more about women's lives, and if women themselves don't tell their stories how will we achieve this?

For some, parentage and place and time of birth provide an identity which remains a fixed point throughout their lives. But for many, identity is much more fluid and elusive. This may be because they are transported in space or time from the things that shape and colour that identity. Or it may be the product of a more general malaise, a sense that vital connections and continuities have been fragmented. In the twentieth century millions were forced to abandon their homes and were subjected to shifting borders and changing national labels. The country where my grandfather was born was, then, Poland but under the control of Russia. It is now Lithuania. He was born in the city he knew as Vilna, but is now Vilnius. He went to school in the German city of Königsberg which is now the Russian city of Kaliningrad. I have never been a refugee, never had to flee persecution or deprivation, or to learn to survive in a language not spoken by my parents. But, like increasing numbers of people, I have, for reasons which this book I hope explains, experienced uncertain identities and an unsettled sense of place.

This book tracks some of these elusive identities. My starting point is my family inheritance. My grandparents were born in the Black Isle, Banffshire, Liverpool and Vilna. My parents were born in Aberdeen and Sunderland. I was born in Chicago. I inherited a mix of identities, which have stayed with me, but not as constants. Their shape and influence have changed, subject to cultural and physical environments, and to the pressures of experience. This process provides the context of my search. Its content is autobiographical, but it is not an autobiography. It includes those aspects and stories which I believe are relevant to my overarching theme. While this covers most of the key phases and episodes of work, marriage, family, friends and children, and also the influence of literature and history, film and music, landscape, icons of identity ranging from tartan to the Star of David, there are people, places and events that are not here. It is necessarily selective and possibly – for memory notoriously plays tricks – inaccurate.

How does Nebuchadnezzar enter the story? He was a king of Babylonia whose extensive empire included Palestine. When the Jews rebelled, he captured Jerusalem and deported large numbers to Babylonia: 'by the waters of Babylon we sat down and wept'. The episode has become an icon of dispersal and exile, not only for the Jews. I knew nothing of this when as a child I played a family game, often round the supper table, called 'I'm not Nebuchadnezzar' (some know the game as 'Botticelli'). The game goes like this: if I am 'it' I kick off by saying 'I'm not Nebuchadnezzar and I'm not Macbeth.'

This provides the clue to the initial letter of the person I am – M for Macbeth. The others have to guess who I am by asking identity questions, for example, 'are you the author of a book about a whale?' I, in turn, have to guess who this is: 'no, I am not Herman Melville'. If I get this wrong, the others can ask me a direct question to which I have to answer yes or no, perhaps: 'are you a man?' 'No,' I say. Gradually through question and answer information emerges until I am asked 'are you the woman who helped to rescue Bonnie Prince Charlie?' 'Yes, I am Flora Macdonald.'

The game is a constant trading of identities, negative and positive, providing clues but not too many, guessing from insufficient information, jumping to conclusions, building up a picture. In other words, it's what we do all the time in our ordinary dealings with people. We trade not just on verbal information, but appearances, gestures, expressions. It's the currency of communication, and it's endlessly fascinating. It's how we express and evade who we are, and assess and respond to who others are. But Nebuchadnezzar, I now know, has a particular resonance in relation to my own background and experience. These are reasons why 'Not Nebuchadnezzar' gives me the title for this book.

The negative in the title implies two things. The first is that it is often easier to know what you are not than what you are. This is perhaps especially true of those who have a mixture of prominent, sometimes conflicting, identities. The second is reticence. National identity is most often dominated by male images and utterances. This book, while not intended as a piece of feminist polemic (though I am a feminist), offers a woman's words on issues of identity, including gender. It is not only women who have inherited a culture of reticence. It belongs to all whose voices have customarily been excluded from government and public debate, for reasons of class or occupation or education.

I am writing at a time when the United Kingdom is going through a process of re-examining its histories and the sources of its cultural make-up and differences. This is always a crucial part of any country's cultural life. Scotland's cultural energy has been at its most depressed when the spirit and challenge of enquiry has diminished. As the world becomes simultaneously increasingly complicated and increasingly uniform, the need for enquiry intensifies on every level, intellectual, political and personal. And we need to take the debate about identity beyond conventional frontiers, whether of nation or language, race or gender. Nationality may be fixed by defined borders, parentage and the official issue of passports, but identity is protean. Identity is personal and resists formalisation. It changes shape and significance according to circumstances.

I have links with two of the world's most influential democratic traditions, the Scottish and the American (which are themselves linked) and with another tradition which has, more often than not, been excluded from the main political and cultural currents of Europe. These strands have influenced not just what I am exploring here, but the fact that I feel the need to set out on this particular journey in the first place. My approach is thematic. The themes reflect my own life, but also some of the issues that are at the centre of the way we present ourselves to the world. Much of my experience I share with millions of women in the developed world: gender stereotyping, marriage and the end of marriage, raising children part of the time alone, work in male-dominated environments, sustaining friendships and disappointing love affairs. The fabric of my life matches that of many others. But it is the particulars that make each life unique, and which inform the issues that I raise.

The very act of writing is a statement of identity, especially for one who has for over half a century labelled herself as a writer, however hesitantly. In these essays I have, consciously and perhaps unconsciously, left out a great deal and I am aware of contradictions in what I have written. Contradiction is inevitable; it is part of the human condition. We look for certainties amid ambiguity and paradox. We create religious and political belief to resolve this and it leads so often to rigid and exclusive definitions which are full of danger. While I have some respect for those who believe in gods, I find both faith and certainty disturbing. Ritual, however, can be rich with cultural and historical resonance and I often find it moving, even when it relates to nothing in my own heritage or experience. Writing itself is a kind of ritual, and so is reading.

It is a feature of modern life to talk of roots and attempt to trace them; it is part of what I am doing here. But locating roots is not the same as becoming rooted. I believe it is important to know where we come from, but almost impossible to go there ourselves. Yes, we can go to the places of our ancestors but what we find can never be the place that helped to make us what we are. We cannot experience it as our ancestors did. When I visited Vilnius nearly a century after my grandfather left the city I did not meet his ghost walking the streets, or find, except in a museum, echoes of what had once been Northern Europe's most vibrant Jewish community, 'the Jerusalem of the north'. There are reasons for that, of course, other than the erosions of time.

The hero of George Orwell's *Nineteen Eighty-Four* (1950) tries to recover memory and reconstruct the past, which the State is continually obliterating and manipulating. For Orwell, and for his protagonist Winston Smith, retrieval of a connection with the past is essential to identity. The emblem of this is the glass paperweight Winston finds in a junk shop. 'What appealed to him about it was not so much its beauty as the air it seemed to possess of belonging to an age quite different from the present one.' *Nineteen Eighty-Four* remains one of the twentieth century's most powerful statements of the necessary survival of individual identity for the continuation of a collective humanity. Primo Levi's *If This is a Man* (1960) is another. This is bound to be, and should be, a continuing preoccupation. Issues of identity have negative connotations too, of course, as conflicts all over the world demonstrate. But identity is about being the same as well as about being distinctive. When Robert Louis Stevenson voyaged in the South Seas he was quick to acknowledge what he shared with the exotic islanders he encountered. Most contemporary Europeans registered only difference.

How do we achieve a balance between the individual and the collective? How can we simultaneously maintain our own personal and distinctive connection between ourselves now and the people, places and events that have formed us, and ally ourselves with the often multiple communities in which we live, and avoid excluding those who ally themselves differently? I don't know the answer, but I do believe we can make some small steps towards an answer by a continuing exploration of ourselves and the world we occupy, whether at the centre, on the edge or somewhere in between.

I have been thinking and writing about these issues for all of my writing career, which began formally in 1968 with the publication of my first book, *Chronicles of Conscience: A Study of Arthur Koestler and George Orwell*. I have been reading books for much longer. These activities are inseparably linked. I cannot disentangle the way books have informed my ideas and understanding from the impact of experience. For a start, books are a part of experience. The printed word, whether poetry or prose, fiction or non-fiction, is not a separate area of reality, still less a realm of fancy. The printed word has been woven through my life from my earliest awareness. My worst fear is to be deprived of it. Books have been essential in enabling me to describe where and what I think I am. So throughout what follows books and my reading of them appear as reference points and signposts, to remind me, and I hope my readers, of where I am going. They are also lurking in the shadows, where I don't always detect or recognise them. I suspect that without them I would not have known where to begin my search.

CHAPTER ONE

American Child

IN MY TENTH year, everything changes. I know it is changing, and I feel excited at the prospect of new places and new experiences. But I don't know that something is ending which will never be recovered.

I see myself as small for my age, with hair long, dark and thick, usually plaited into two pigtails with a few unruly wisps escaping round my forehead. In snapshots I sometimes have a bright-eyed grin but just as often I am a solemn-looking child. I have a slightly crooked leg, though no one has noticed yet.

I am a middle child. My brother Alan is nearly three years older, my sister Elizabeth four and a half years younger. The shape and spacing of the families we grow up in must surely stay with us for the rest of our lives. The imprints of siblings and where we fit into sibling relationships can be as deep as those of parents. As a child, they are a part of who and what I am: a younger and an older sister. It is not something that can be questioned or changed, but there are ways of escaping: these, also, are a part of who I am.

I admire, envy and resent my brother. He is rather distant, especially now, for he has been away at school on the other side of the Atlantic, and this summer, the summer of 1951, I am going to see him again after a ten month absence. Since he has been away I have become friendly with two brothers whose family moved into our apartment block in Cayuga Heights, part of a small American university town in upper New York State. They are called George and Billy. They don't believe I have a brother: they think I've made him up. I play football with them. Neither do they believe that my family comes from Scotland. One evening in the dusk they pin me to the grass and demand that I 'say something Scottish'. Another time they employ the same tactic to get me to sing. Lying on the damp grass I tentatively produce in a small voice my favourite song.

As I walked out in the streets of Laredo,
As I walked out in Laredo one day,
I spied a young cowboy all wrapped in white linen,
Wrapped in white linen as cold as the clay.

Earlier we had lived downtown, and Alan and I had gone to the movies on Saturday afternoons. I can only remember the cowboy films. My first hero was Roy-Rogers-and-Trigger. The inseparability of man and horse – 'as if they'd traded souls' – was profoundly part of the appeal. The movie-going ritual included sharing a box of Good and Plenty and afterwards cantering home across the park. I must have been about six when I was given a splendid rocking horse which I called Tom. Later, I prevailed upon my father to buy me toy pistols with a wonderful white holster belt.

In 1951 my sister is very much the baby, not yet at school, pretty, her heart-shaped face dominated by huge grey eyes and framed by Botticelli curls. My mother dresses her in pretty clothes. I see her in pastel colours, a pink sundress. I'd rather be in jeans than frills, but notice the care that seems to go into my sister's clothes. Perhaps my parents want a more feminine daughter. At the age of six or seven I battled with my mother to be allowed to wear jeans to school, and at least once perpetrated an elaborate subterfuge to achieve my wish, much to her annoyance. When I was seven we moved house and I went to a new school. There, other girls wore jeans, and I won my battle. By my tenth year my favourite outfit is blue jeans, sneakers, T-shirt, beige windcheater with a leather thong attached to the zipper (a much treasured item of clothing) and baseball cap. In 1951 this is not the way little British girls are dressed. I am an American child.

And yet, I am not. I wear a baseball cap and sing cowboy songs, but home is Scotland. 'When we go home' is a refrain that has been with me from my earliest awareness. And every other summer we do go 'home'. We make a momentous journey – at first by ship, later by plane – to the country where, one day, we will stay, and after two or three months we return to Ithaca, New York. I am vaguely aware of my father's efforts to go back to Scotland for good. When he had arrived in Chicago with my mother, to take up a post at the university, he had never intended to stay for more than a few years, but war intervened. I am vaguely aware that we are not part of the American melting pot, that I am not quite as American as George and Billy, whose Irish surname I have forgotten, or Petey, whose family are from the Philippines, or the Abrams or the Larsens or the Guerlacs or the Rintouls.

In 1946 we crossed the Atlantic in the battle-scarred *Queen Mary*. For me the ship was an enormous playground and in my memory, which surely cannot be correct, I ran about unsupervised. I was four years old. In the summer of 1951 my mother, sister and I fly across the Atlantic in a BOAC stratocruiser. At the end of the previous summer we had flown the other way. On that trip the captain, who had a daughter called Jennifer, singled me out for a visit to the flight deck. I sat in the co-pilot's seat and gingerly touched the controls and looked out at an awe-inspiring expanse of sky and cloud. I had never felt so special. This time, the flight from New York is delayed. Much loved friends, Ged and Esther Bentley, have come to see us off. And my father is there, though he will stay behind to teach summer school at Cornell University where he has been teaching since 1946. I know he is doing this because we need the money. I know he is going to a new job which will pay him less. I am a quiet listener to the grown-ups' talk.

There is a farewell hug from Ged in a New York street. The particular timbre of his voice and his gentle laugh and the tweedy feel of his hug remain. Memory tells me it is dark and raining. But the plane is delayed and we do not go to the airport but to the apartment of other friends, Marshall and Betty Sterns, where I am put to bed in a room with a television set. I have never seen television before, and lie in the dark watching little black and white cowboys, Indians and horses. It's the Lone Ranger.

We leave finally in the early hours of the morning. In Scotland, my brother awaits us. The previous September we had left him at night on the wet tarmac of Prestwick airport as we boarded our flight back. He was in the safe care of relatives, but nevertheless that image has stayed with me during the intervening months. Big brother, maybe, but small and wet, in a borrowed raincoat, and vulnerable. Rainy night departures from airports, with the lights reflected on the glistening tarmac, have ever since raised spectres of sadness and loss. Yet memory is probably playing tricks. We must have said goodbye not on the tarmac at Prestwick but at the coach terminal. He was going to school in the north of Scotland. I know I cried as we moved off into the night, but they may have been tears of envy as well as of parting. Though I missed him painfully.

My only memory of my mother crying belongs to the months before we left Ithaca. I have no idea what the circumstances were: she sat on the sofa in tears, and I was puzzled rather than upset. It can't have been easy for her to say goodbye to her son, or to my father in New York before making that transatlantic crossing with two young children. She had lived in the United States since 1937. She had many friends there. The only member of her immediate family still living was her much older sister Ethel, with whom we would stay in Glasgow. Her aunt and uncle and assorted cousins lived in Banffshire. As a child she had spent summers at Nethermills, the farm tenanted by Uncle Dode and Auntie Lizzie. Nethermills becomes an icon of my childhood, at the heart of which is Auntie Lizzie, the cracked veins of her rosy cheeks, the warmth and gentleness of her language which I barely understand. There she is on the doorstep wiping her hands on her apron: 'Come awa in.' Eleanor, the unmarried daughter, beaming at her elbow, Uncle Dode moving slowly in his huge farm boots or seated in his chair by the fire, with his pipe and his dram. The smells. Hay and nettles and cows. Horse sweat and dung. Milk and warm scones and oatmeal. Hot tea and barn dust. Eleanor in the kitchen in her flowered apron with a huge brown kettle. Farm workers at the table, dipping their spoons first into hot porridge, then into a bowl of milk.

We will go to Nethermills that summer of 1951. But now we are arriving at Prestwick. In the coach which takes us to Glasgow I look out at the extraordinary green, a lush, rich, wet green unlike anything to be seen in a New York State summer. It had been hot in those last few weeks before we left. I play my favourite road and rail travelling game. (Recently I have discovered that it is not my own, unique toy of the imagination.) In the game, I am on horseback, keeping pace with the coach, galloping across fields, leaping walls and ditches, overcoming all obstacles at a flying speed, unstoppable, dauntless. It is wonderfully exhilarating, but better on trains than on buses.

It is something like sixteen hours since we left New York, and we must have stopped en route. Nine months before, going the other way, we came down at Shannon and at Gander in Newfoundland. We were allowed off the plane in Gander, little more than a landing strip, as I remember it. There was a family of blue-jeaned, check-shirted children looking out at our plane. How foreign they seemed after my months in Scotland, how strange their accents to my unaccustomed ear.

I was usually airsick on takeoff and landing, and probably was this time. I am glad to be on the ground. I think it is afternoon. Were we met at the Glasgow terminal by Auntie Ethel? Certainly, we stayed with her. Was it then, or another time that Liz and I sat in her large but gaunt and gloomy and, in my eyes, intriguingly old-fashioned, kitchen in Keir Street, Pollokshields, and had boiled eggs and toast and empire biscuits before being bundled off to bed? There were not meals like that in America.

Liz is five years old, small and slight with thin, long legs which are always folding under her, like the legs of a foal. I am sure that summer she is never without skinned knees. We play on the pavement, as I learn to call it, in front of the street's dark terrace. Hopscotch, bouncing balls, one-two-three aleary, which I may have absorbed from my parents. We play roly-poly – an American game? – rather like hopscotch but with a ball that is rolled from square to square. We have skipping ropes. It is frustrating playing with Liz, as she is too small to be a good partner in my games. We watch Glasgow children pass with their school bags and curious uniforms, and are stared at in return.

When it rains Auntie Ethel lets me play with her bridge cards. She is a regular bridge player. Among those she plays with is a married couple: he is a teaching colleague. He and Auntie Ethel have been in love for years, though I don't yet know this. Was it an 'affair' as we would understand the word? There were five fiancés and she broke it off every time. At least, that's the story. I find photographs of her as a young woman; she looks like a film star. But she is about thirteen years older than my mother, who already has grey hair, and looks, to a nine-year-old, beyond middle age. Auntie Ethel teaches me how to play patience. I make card houses. I play bagatelle with addictive concentration and clock up enormous scores. I read my aunt's school books; she is a teacher of English and History at Hutcheson's Girls School.

Do we go out? Does she show me Glasgow? Does she take me to Kelvingrove Museum or the Botanic Gardens? I don't think so, although I remember Glasgow orange and green trams and Glasgow streets and crossing the Clyde and gap sites where the bombs fell. But she does take me to Hutchie, where I sit in on an English lesson. The Glasgow girls are surprised at how well I can read.

From Glasgow we go north on the train, to Cullen on the Banffshire coast. We have already had three holidays there, in the same house, Kinnaird, Victoria Street. Ethel is with us, I think. We arrive at the little yellow and green station. Victoria Street isn't far, but there is probably a car to take us and our baggage there. It doesn't seem quite right to call it a taxi. I love the house. Compared with our small Ithaca apartment, it is spacious. There is a big kitchen, a living room and a dining room, with four bedrooms upstairs. The stair divides, with a bathroom on a half landing, and steps going in one direction to the back bedroom which Liz and I share, and in the other to the remaining bedrooms. Liz and I sleep in a double bed. When things are really bad I insist on positioning the bolster, something met only in Scotland, between us. From our window we can see the sea. At its best, the view is a square of two shades of blue, sea and sky, though both were often grey.

We settle in to a pattern of life in Cullen which is perhaps so memorable because it is different. We go for the messages in the morning, to Mr Ingram the grocer where there are big square glass-covered tins of loose biscuits – in America, cookies. I know that cookies in Scotland are what we buy at the baker, along with warm pan loaves wrapped in thin paper, and softies and butteries. Alan has developed a taste for cream buns. Sometimes we have an ice cream at Ingrams, a pale cylinder wrapped in paper which fits in to a cone. It is nothing like American ice cream. In Ithaca my favourite flavour is 'bittersweet', shavings of dark chocolate mixed through creamy vanilla. For three years we lived in Cayuga Street. There was a drugstore at the corner and sometimes Alan and I were sent out to buy ice cream cones for dessert, which we brought back in a little cardboard tray with holes for the cones. I loved drugstores. A great treat was to have a root beer, poured over a glass full of crushed ice. I can still feel on my tongue the grittiness of the ice and the sweet, herbal taste of root beer.

There is nothing like that now, only big bottles of lemonade and cream soda which we take on beach picnics. Over the Cullen summers routines are established. In the morning, when the messages are done, father and three children often go to the little beach, while mother is at home, doing the housework (there is a young woman called Cathy to help) and making lunch. At the end of the morning we climb the path up the cliff from the harbour, which takes us to the sea-end of Victoria Street. On at least one occasion I go straight up the cliff, in the wake of Alan, who perhaps takes this route habitually. This introduces me to the word 'fuck', scratched on a rock near the top. I know it's a rude word and by the age of eight or so I have a vague notion of what it means. My parents have supplied us with sex education books which I find interesting but odd. I can't imagine myself ever engaging in any of the activities described. But I do imagine myself having my own family, though even at the age of eleven, when at school we did 'reproduction' in biology, I wondered if there was a way of having a baby without going through the messy preliminaries with a man.

Cullen is part of what defines my childhood. And I understood that it was important to both my parents, but particularly to my mother. This part of Scotland contributed to her make-up, and I recognised that even though she always seemed to me separate from it. Perhaps it was the way she spoke. Although she never lost a Scots flavour in her accent and used Scots words, she did not sound like Auntie Lizzie and Uncle Dode. She did not seem to me to belong to a farm, although she told us about her summers at Nethermills, met off the train with a pony and trap and trotting through the village of Cornhill. She told the story of the curly-haired cousin who died of lockjaw as a small boy. She told of the traditional meal of 'tatties and herrin', always called that even when times were hard and there was no herring. But she was a city girl, born in Aberdeen, growing up in Edinburgh when her father's career as an agricultural correspondent took him from the *Aberdeen Free Press* to become eventually editor of *Farming News*. She was separate, but I could still see the line that tied her to rural Banffshire and the Moray coast. The line that tied *me* was much more elusive.

But I am tied to Cullen and its particular magic. The place itself is enough to explain the enchantment. It had once been a thriving fishing village, with many of the men either running their own boats or employed on trawlers out of Banff or Buckie. Mr Mair, who owned Kinnaird and whose wife lived in the back premises with her old father when the house was rented out, was a trawlerman. But even in the late 1940s there wasn't much fishing out of Cullen's small, neat double harbour with its white rusting lighthouse at the end of the main pier. Sometimes a boat went out, and sometimes it came back with only mackerel which wasn't considered fit to eat. I would watch mackerel being sliced up to use for bait. I often caught snatches of talk about the problems of the fishing. There were always little groups of navy-jerseyed old men leaning over the cliff rail or puffing their pipes at the harbour wall.

I didn't know then that Cullen had once been much more than a fishing village. There had been boat building, too, and trade. A hundred years earlier the Moray Firth had been 'bespangled with trading vessels and fishing boats'. There was good agricultural land. There were mills on the burn – the surviving names Lintmill and Mill of Towie are reminders – and a distillery at Tochieneal. The post road between Banff and Elgin ran through Cullen, and in the nineteenth century there was a daily stagecoach. Gas lighting came to the town in 1841, and the second *Statistical Account* (1857) tells us that 'there are probably few places in Scotland more conducive to health and longevity'.

The original village, Old Cullen, was demolished in the eighteenth century to make way for a newer, grander Cullen House for the Marquess of Seafield. A planned, spacious new town went up nearer the shore. The main street, sloping down to the sea, is still wide and handsome, with a spacious town square. Looking down from the top of the street you get the impression that it ends abruptly in the sea, just beyond the railway viaduct. In fact, the main street bends sharply to the left with a narrower street leading down to the harbour. There seemed then, and still seems now, something clean and bright and fresh about the little town. Below it is the more crowded Seatown, built for fishermen, narrow lanes of low-roofed cottages with gables towards the sea.

We came first to Cullen in 1946, when I was four years old and visiting Britain for the first time. I named the three beaches. The Little Beach, which we went to in the mornings, was in the harbour itself. My father would dig himself a sand chair and settle into it with his newspaper, while Alan and I, and later Liz, busied ourselves with buckets and spades. The games were endless. We made not just castles, but elaborate fortifications, whole towns with houses and shops, networks of highways on which we drove Dinky cars. The Horrible Beach came next, so called because it was stony and seaweedy. We never went there. Then, a long walk it seemed, the Big Beach, a glorious stretch of sand that swept round the curve of Cullen Bay to Portknockie, the next village. The Big Beach was for afternoons. It was for swimming and picnics. We'd pack sandwiches and flasks and go to the tiny shop next door for bottles of lemonade. Swimming costumes, buckets, spades, my parents' paperbacks, extra sweaters... then off on the long march to the Big Beach. Down to the end of Victoria Street, along the cliff path that took us down to shore level, past the harbour, along the sea front past the Horrible Beach and on to the golf club house (immediately behind the beach are golf links) and past the changing huts, which we spurned, and the three upstanding rocks known as the Three Kings. All along the edge of the sand dunes the wartime concrete blocks still remained and we had a favourite corner beside them which offered shelter from the wind. If it rained, my father rigged up a tent of plastic macs which we crouched under. A little further on, a bold backdrop to our play, was a jutting cliff called Scarnose.

Part of the magic lay in being a family together. Most of my sense of 'being a family' is associated with Cullen or with special occasions – birthdays, celebrations, perhaps especially Christmas. What was special about Cullen was that it wasn't special. I took it for granted.

Cullen meant the family. It meant my father, participating in the lives of his children in a way that was otherwise rare. It meant, precisely because we were more together as a family, more awareness of my mother's role. She did not often take part in our morning activities. If she came down to the Little Beach she left before us to return to the house and make lunch. In Cullen, she was more separate from us than my father, although sometimes Liz, as the youngest, shared that separateness. Father and children bathed in the sea: my mother never did. Alan and I and my father went fishing. Not my mother. Sometimes in the evenings my father took Alan and me out for a walk after tea, which we always tried to steer in the general direction of the little chip shop with a low doorway down a step. If our luck was in, we would stand on the pier watching the grey evening sea and eating vinegary chips out of the poke which warmed our hands.

Liz did not share in our more adventurous ploys, but this must have been sometimes because she wasn't interested. I caught my first fish when I was four. I don't remember Liz fishing, ever, though she was five in 1951 and we were to return to Cullen in subsequent years. Alan and I caught geeks off the pier end; Alan planned opening a sardine factory. Sometimes he and I went off on our own. There were sunny evenings spent scrambling on the cliffs. There was always an ambivalence in time spent with Alan. I was the little sister tagging along. In Ithaca, in Cayuga Street, there was Alan's friend Steve a few doors away. We played cowboys. I was always the sheriff, forlornly pursuing the two outlaws in and out of neighbours' backyards. They had more hideouts than the Hole-in-the-Wall Gang. I remember once Steve's mother taking pity on me when I knocked on her door and giving me a cheese and mustard sandwich.

I was seven when we moved from Cayuga Street in downtown Ithaca to Cayuga Heights, nearer the university and more convenient for my father, but less so for my mother. It was further from the shops. We had no car. Our carlessness was as unAmerican as our intention to return to Scotland. In Cayuga Heights we lived in a smart new apartment block rather than the bottom half of a rather rundown clapboard house. There was plenty of child-friendly space, a playground with swings and a seesaw, paving and tarmac for bike-riding, a large grassy area for football, and across from the apartments an open field sloping up to woods, and in the woods a creek.

Alan and I devised a wonderful ploy and our sharing of it brought us closer than at any other time in our childhood. There was a scattering of houses beside the creek, and in one of them lived a graduate student of my father's and his wife, Slim and Mary. They had a beautiful red setter called Duke. I don't remember how our first visit came about, but we were supplied with glasses of milk and Mary's home-made chocolate brownies. The ploy was this. We told our friends that we had a hiding place in the woods and challenged them to find it. They had to give us a head start. We raced up the hill. If they cheated and set off after us before we reached the top we could see them and change our tactics. Once we'd disappeared into the trees they gave chase. We, of course, headed for Slim and Mary's, and disappeared inside their house. They were in on the game. We played with Duke and scoffed chocolate brownies, sometimes aware of the voices and footsteps of our pursuers. They never twigged.

A fallen tree spanned the creek behind Slim and Mary's house. Alan walked across it; I never managed to. There was a drop of several feet to the water. There were always things that Alan could do and I couldn't, either because he was bigger and stronger, or because he was older and allowed more independence. But it wasn't just the gap that defined my sense of difference. I knew very early on that he was treated differently from me. Alan was given lessons in Latin, Greek and Hebrew by my father. I felt that he had more of my father's time. My father helped me with my piano practice, and he gave me Hebrew lessons, but I did not feel that I was a focus of interest in the same way as Alan was. I don't think I questioned it at the time, but I absorbed the knowledge that girls were different.

Yet, inside my head, I adopted all kinds of male roles. I was a cowboy, an explorer, one of King Arthur's knights, a schoolboy adventurer. My imaginary friend was a boy called Bob. My furry animal toys were all male: my two horses, Jesse (after Jesse James) and Tony, Jimmy the penguin, above all Tim the bear who occupied as important a place in my life as my imaginary friend. Tim had a mind and a personality of his own.

Like most fathers in the 1940s my father is often not a presence. He is away or he is busy. I love the rare occasions when I go with him to the office on a Saturday. He wears, like most academics, grey flannels and a tweed jacket. In its pockets various essential tools are stowed: his diary, pens and pencils, a small pair of scissors in a little case, tobacco, pipe and pipecleaners. He sports a moustache, grown, I suspect, to make him look older as he was so youthful-looking when he started his first job that he was mistaken for a student.

We cross the creek on a swaying suspension bridge. Once Elizabeth looked down at the water far below and announced she saw a fish. What kind of fish? asked my father. A kipper, was the reply. It can't be a kipper, said my father, kippers are smoked fish. But it *is* smoking, said Liz. We didn't eat kippers in New York State. Liz, with glorious logic, was transposing a Cullen summer.

We walk across the campus of Cornell University on a path painted with white footprints which link two statues. I am told the footprints are proof that they change places in the night. We go to my father's office, where he has work to do. I explore the campus on my own, or roam up and down the empty corridors. Sometimes I go into a classroom – no classes on a Saturday – and draw pictures on the blackboard. Or sit in a corner of the office with a supply of paper and crayons. At lunchtime we go to the cafeteria. I always have a hamburger and pumpkin pie.

Food is as defining as language or dress. In America I eat peanut butter and jelly sandwiches, chocolate brownies, potato chips, alphabet soup, hamburgers, fried chicken, spaghetti, Hershey bars. In Scotland there are kippers, boiled eggs, porridge, Fuller's walnut cake, Cadbury's chocolate, fried fish, cinnamon balls, potato crisps, home-made raspberry jam... and the effects of wartime are still felt. In a hotel in London – it's probably 1946 – on our way to

Southampton to board the ship for New York, I ask for scrambled eggs for breakfast. I get dried eggs and I can't eat them.

My ninth birthday is my last American birthday. My mother is, unusually, away. She has taken Liz with her on the train to visit old friends in Toronto. It seems very exciting to me, and I wish I could have gone, but I would have had to miss school. My father and I have Thanksgiving Dinner with friends nearby, and a few days later it snows. It's the first white birthday I can remember. My mother's train is snowed up at Buffalo. Perhaps she'd intended to be back for my birthday. I think that was the year I was given a ranch set, with a bunkhouse and cattle and cowboys.

Roy Rogers was a singing cowboy, but I learned my cowboy songs from records. We belonged to something called the Young People's Record Club, which meant that every month a new record arrived in the post. These were the foundation of my musical education. Until my parents acquired more sophisticated equipment, we played them on a wind-up phonograph. The records were wonderful. There were several on different instruments – the piano, the clarinet, the violin. There were folk songs arranged by topic – sea songs, cowboy songs, pioneer songs. There were spirituals and at least one on the origins of jazz. There were tasters of classical music. My parents had their own record collection of mainly classical music. My mother used to play a stack of 78s while she was doing the ironing. Round about 1950 the first long-playing records became available and I think it must have been then that my father bought a new record player. Among the first LPs he bought were records of the shows he and my mother went to in New York – *Gentlemen Prefer Blondes*, *Kiss Me Kate*, *Pal Joey*. But there were classical recordings too, and I developed a passion for Rachmaninov's 2nd Piano Concerto, which I would often insist was put on when I went to bed, with the doors left open so I could hear it.

We had a piano at home and I had my first piano lessons when I was about eight. My father played the piano and the violin. Sometimes, mainly on special occasions but often I think just when the mood took him, he would sit down at the piano after supper and we'd gather round and sing. He had kept his old student song books, and we had Carl Sandburg's *The American Songbag* and

The Fireside Song Book. We sang 'Huntingtower', 'A Lum Hat Wantin a Croon', 'Swing Low Sweet Chariot', 'Willie the Weeper', 'The Eerie Canal', 'Flow Gently Sweet Afton', 'Casey Jones', 'Henry Martin', 'The Twa Corbies', Christmas carols... It was from this that Liz and I developed the habit of singing over the washing-up, especially after a big family dinner. My own children continued it. Perhaps it explains why I've never wanted a dishwasher.

Our musical evenings were times of intense happiness. I loved to sing, though I was never much good at it and have very little voice. But they were also the source of an odd and disturbing experience. In the midst of confirming the warmth and solidity of my family there would come a moment when I felt suddenly transported outside the circle, when I no longer seemed part of what was going on around me, when a stabbing sense of sadness and exclusion would possess me. As if I knew that I was only a child, an American child, and couldn't share what bound my Scottish parents.

I am rather in awe of the Alan I meet again in the summer of 1951. He seems distant. He has become a British schoolboy. He is wearing unfamiliar clothes and uses words I don't understand. He talks about a wholly different world, peppered with the names of friends and teachers. He has become addicted to cricket.

Later that summer my father joins us. We go to the station to meet him and stand on the single strip of platform, craning our heads to spot the steam that announces the train. It will billow under the bridge, beyond which are the wild raspberries we pick for jam making. Memory creates a picture of myself and Liz wearing navy smocked dresses, but these are the dresses that he brings us, bought in Macy's, New York, and we could not have been wearing them yet. I don't see him stepping off the train, just two illusory pigtailed girls in navy cotton frocks, smocked in red and white.

Usually I'm in shorts, or in an American outfit called a playsuit, shorts with a bibbed front. Little Scottish girls are all in dresses. Many of them have ringlets. I feel stared at, but not enough to want frocks and ringlets. But I like the Macy's dress. It's unusual for myself and Liz to be dressed the same.

The summer, and all the summers we spent in Cullen, stretch out towards the blue Moray Firth, through the blue square of the bedroom window. But there were grey days, days when the wind whipped up the breakers, days when we walked the length of the Big Beach to Portknockie and watched the spray fly over a different pier. Or stayed inside with books and crayons and paper. I always had my precious box of American Crayola crayons in forty-eight different colours. I spent hours drawing, illustrating the stories in my head, experimenting with identities: cowboys, Indians, families with complicated histories. In my drawings I was an intrepid rider of horses, jumping high fences, galloping across the plains, driving cattle across the Red River, riding bareback with the Sioux, winning prizes in gymkhanas. I began riding lessons when I was eight, having first watched enviously as Alan learnt to ride. The university had a stable of retired US cavalry horses and working polo ponies. My first horse, Iroquois, was a huge and placid chestnut. Then I graduated to Ticonderoga, willing and friendly, and then to Hapvare, a speedy polo pony who could not understand the merit of trotting round in a circle when it was so obvious that the quickest way to the other side was straight across. At the end of the lesson we had to groom the horses, which I did standing on a box, and clean the tack. Our next door neighbours took me to a polo match for what must have been my ninth birthday. I think it was my first experience of being almost sick with excitement.

Horses became a key feature of my imaginative worlds, and those worlds defined my childhood as much as any aspect of 'reality'. By this time I am reading Robert Louis Stevenson; my grandmother's flat in Edinburgh is only a few doors along from where he grew up. The first poem I learn by heart is:

I have a little shadow
That goes in and out with me...

Years later I begin to see how Stevenson captures and values the child's imagination. Indeed, Stevenson understands the adult's imagination as being qualitatively no different from the child's. To deny the value of the imagination at any stage of life is drastically sterile. Stevenson never loses the immediacy of the child's world – the excitements, the escapes, the terrors. The longing for involvement, the sense of exclusion from adult life. To the child sent to bed in Stevenson's poem 'North-West Passage' the grown-up world is safe, warm, friendly – 'O pleasant party round the fire'. But the child has to face 'the long black passage up to bed'.

> The shadow of the balusters, the shadow of the lamp,
>   The shadow of the child that goes to bed –
> All the wicked shadows coming, tramp, tramp, tramp,
>   With the black night overhead.

Shadows again. Childhood is perilous. And Jim Hawkins in *Treasure Island* discovers that the adult world is too, thick with dangers created largely by adults themselves, their cruelty, greed and weakness. Part of Stevenson's achievement is his ability to bring a child's power of imagination to bear on the threats and hazards of adult life. Is imagination the resort of the lonely child? Stevenson was certainly often alone. But I suspect that all children are to some extent lonely, in so far as they are powerless in the place of adults and more often than not deemed as alien, especially in Britain, and perhaps northern Europe generally, which has a particularly strong tradition of regarding children as 'other'.

Recently I discovered letters written by my father to his parents when I was about two years old. Apparently I learnt to talk early. He describes his daughter as talking, singing and dancing through each day. I am more extrovert and noisier than my big brother, and, according to my father, less sensitive. I do not recognise that child. What happened to her? The child I remember is some years older, introverted, even shy, and spins stories out of her head that are never told. But it may be that that reticence came with England, when I tried to become something different.

A favourite wet weather walk in Cullen was to Crannoch Woods. Once on a Crannoch Woods walk I was unhappy and wanted my parents to notice my unhappiness. But they paid no attention, so I lagged behind and then took off into the woods on a different route while they continued along the track. I lingered deliberately, while they went on and home. I don't remember now what the problem was but I can recapture the confusion of feelings: I wanted attention, but since I was ignored I would put into action the message they seemed to be transmitting. I removed myself. They might not notice my presence but surely would be aware of my absence. I wanted them to worry. Of course, eventually I went home and had probably not been out of their sight for nearly as long as I thought.

Whatever else is going on in the summer of 1951 the struggle to change my nationality is part of it. Even in my tenth year I know that I am not Scottish in the same way as my parents are. I also know that my father was born in England and that the fact that he is Jewish makes him a different kind of Scottish from my mother. I know that I am an American child, almost, and also Jewish and that 'home' is Scotland, and that soon I will be living in England. I know that the way I look and the way I speak are different from the looks and speech of the Cullen children and the Glasgow and Edinburgh children.

At the end of the summer we go south. It's September, after the 2nd, my father's birthday, which we celebrate in Cullen, traditionally with a picnic. Perhaps we go to Sunnyside, a four-mile cliff and shore walk from Cullen, a beautiful secluded bay with a fine beach and the ruins of Findlater Castle at the far end. We swim and make castles and harbours, perhaps play cricket under Alan's influence – I stoically accept the transition from baseball – have our picnic, and perhaps my father makes a driftwood fire, just for the fun of it. Then the long trail home. Liz is only five (does she complain or get piggy-backed? I don't remember) but I feel then that she receives attention different in kind from what comes my way, and know now that this is the inevitable tipping of the scales towards the youngest child.

We are nearing Edinburgh on the train. I know from earlier visits the stirring approach to Waverley Station. A tunnel, the deep cutting under the towering castle rock, another short patch of darkness, the station. Is there someone there to meet us? We have a great deal of luggage. Or do we, with the aid of a porter, make our way unescorted along the crowded platform, past the ticket barrier, to the line of squat black taxis? I am not wearing blue jeans and baseball cap, but a neat grey coat, probably bought for the return to Scotland, and American saddle shoes with white socks, and I am carrying Tim, already somewhat dilapidated (by this time he has lost an arm), too big to fit in a suitcase.

Perhaps my Uncle Lionel is there on the platform, in pinstriped trousers and black jacket, with his elaborate and alarmingly mannered courtesy. Or maybe he boarded the train at Haymarket, a few minutes from Waverley, and rode the last mile with us. Lionel has an enthusiasm for trains. I regard him with some suspicion – although I encountered him first when I was four, he is not easy to deal with. He is unlike any other adult I have met. Although the father of two sons, Uncle Lionel seems not to have a clue about how to respond to not yet matured personalities. And he, like other of my relatives, mocks my American accent. He calls me Thumper, because I speak like Thumper the rabbit in the film *Bambi*.

I am unlike my relatives, and my relatives are unlike those of other people. Relatives are kin, members of the same clan, your own flesh and blood. Mine are strangers, and strange. From the beginning – that is, 1946, when I met them for the first time – I felt I had nothing in common with them: more than that, I felt I was regarded as something of a freak. My brother and sister seemed to escape this, or so I thought. Liz was small enough to be warmed to as a cute baby, my brother old enough to be included in at least some adult activities. Besides, he was male and the firstborn. And now, in 1951, he has the advantage of a ten-month start in the process of becoming Scottish, and also, of becoming independent.

We proceed to Heriot Row. There were many visits to my grandmother's flat at 10 Heriot Row. The very name and number of the street still have a resonance which owes almost everything to those stays in the 1940s and '50s. A black taxi takes us from Waverley, up the ramp, turning right into Waverley Bridge, across Princes Street, up and then down Hanover Street. The journey is not new to me. I know these streets, the forbidding statue at the splendid intersection with George Street, the small, stubby British cars, the horse-drawn coal carts and milk carts, the trams.

The taxi draws up outside number 10. Heriot Row is broad and in 1951 almost empty of cars. The single terraced row looks across to the trees of Queen Street Gardens. Heriot Row, I still believe, is the most handsome street in Edinburgh's New Town, though as a child I am not impressed by its unrelieved vertical austerity. It was, simply, boring. Years later it was with a flash of recognition that I read Ruskin saying much the same thing, if in considerably more passionate language, in a lecture to an Edinburgh audience:

> Walk around your Edinburgh buildings, and look at the height of your eye, what will you get from them? Nothing but square-cut stone; square-cut stone – a wilderness of square-cut stone for ever and for ever; so that your houses look like prisons.

But the gardens allowed me to forgive the severity of the neo-classical terraces – it was unbroken terracing ('graves of the soul', Ruskin said) that seemed so tedious to me as a child. My grandmother had a key to the locked gates: only residents who paid had the privilege of using the gardens, which were surrounded by high iron railings. Even wartime needs for iron hadn't intruded on these havens of privilege. Robert Louis Stevenson used to play there, I was told.

We bundle out of the taxi. Up the stone steps. The heavy front door is opened. The flagged, pilastered hall echoes. Looking up, I can see far above the elegant cupola, an intriguing feature. From the first floor a voice calls down a greeting. It is my grandmother, leaning over the banister, looking down at us, a family of five with a large assemblage of baggage.

My uncle – I feel sure he is with us – leads the way upstairs. The scene has been enacted every other summer since 1946. People have gathered to meet us. The bustle of arrival. Suitcases and large adult flanks block the routes of escape. Doors open and swing shut, strange faces swim downwards from great heights, with kisses, and 'hasn't she grown' and 'you must be tired' descending like messages wrapped round stones. Who are these people?

We are taken with our belongings into the large back bedroom which mother and daughters will share. There is only one other bedroom. Are my father and Alan staying somewhere else? One time we all stay in a nearby hotel.

In the drawing room, spacious, high-ceilinged, are the people. Gran is there and Uncle Lionel. Is Beryl there, the youngest of my father's siblings, with Uncle Jimmy, her husband, who makes tiny goblets out of discarded silver paper, and little Gordon, my cousin – when was he born? Is Dorothy there, Lionel's wife, a lady of grand dimensions whose voice makes me shrink with alarm? Auntie Sylvia and Uncle David? Sally, another young cousin? Max and Frances? Their daughter Susie, a cousin once removed, with whom for a while I am very friendly? (We play together in Queen Street Gardens.) Abie and Rosie? The names crowd and jostle.

I hesitate in the doorway. Or I find a corner where I hope to be out of sight. Every chair is occupied by an adult. Elizabeth is at my mother's knee. I'm too big for that, too small for anything else. The blinds are half drawn, for the sunlight mustn't be allowed to reach the grand piano. I look up at the photographs on the walls, particularly those of my grandfather, whom I never knew, and great-grandfather. They are strange, exotic, bearded and – a word I discover later – rabbinical. Appropriately. But my grandfather has kind and wise and humorous eyes, which are a source of reassurance.

The table is laid. A white cloth. Silver. Back and forth from the kitchen, at the end of the passage and as far as possible from where we eat, people pass carrying dishes. Salad, white bread, a large platter of, oh joy, gefilte fish, boiled and fried. The agony of deciding which is my favourite. At last I can take refuge at the table, and eat, and be seen by those who wish to see me, and not be expected to talk, for she's hungry and a child must be fed, and indulgence allows that she need not be expected to speak, except when offered another piece of fish, when an almost whispered 'yes please' will do very well.

No, they cannot all have been there. But they congregate in my mind, my father's family, my family, names with an incantatory ring, names repeated through my childhood like prayers. Familiar yet strange. Not a part of my life, yet populating my world. I watch them as if my eyes are inside me, internal. I like doing this. I feel safe, peripheral. I don't know that word yet but I know the feeling. I don't choose to be other, but I accept it. At the same time, in 1951 I have already embarked on my willed transformation into an English schoolgirl.

I cease to be an American child. But I am still a child, and to the observer that is the initial definition: not fully grown, not adult, not mature, concerned with childish things. Children are assumed to have their own language, their own realms of interest, and generally to require restraint and control. A child is often 'it'. A child is anarchic, in some cultures a child is inherently sinful. 'Children are animals,' said the headteacher at my children's primary school when a parent complained about her daughter being punished with the strap. At the same time, a child is – or expected to be – innocent, free of corrupting knowledge and experience, free of the responsibilities that burden and sour the lives of adults.

Vast amounts of nineteenth- and twentieth-century depictions of children in words and pictures underline this 'otherness'. In western society children are excluded from the adult world, yet are expected to conform to adult presumptions about how they should behave. In some traditional societies children from their birth take their place in the life of grown-ups. They are strapped to the backs of their mothers as they work in the fields. They care for younger siblings at an early age. They learn the necessary skills of survival by watching, imitating, participating. They have their place in the group.

The ways in which children have been valued intensify the ironies of childhood and the ambivalence of our attitudes. They have had dynastic value, as pawns in political alliances. They have had – and continue to have in many parts of the world – economic value, for small bodies and small hands can do many tasks more effectively than large ones. Boys are often more valued than girls: boys will be economically productive, girls will require a dowry when they marry. In many societies the inference has been, boys produce, girls consume, boys are an asset, girls are a burden. When my son was born in Kenya, African friends were hugely congratulatory. It was nice enough to have two daughters, but a son was in a different league.

Children can be an economic burden, more mouths to feed. There is a shocking logic in the fate of Jude Fawley's son in Hardy's *Jude the Obscure*. 'I ought not to be born, ought I?' he says, as the family are turned away time after time in their effort to find lodgings. 'Then if children make so much trouble, why do people have 'em?... we don't ask to be born.' And little Jude the next day kills his siblings and then himself. I was probably fifteen or sixteen when I first read this. I read most of Hardy at around that age and was mesmerised by the inexorable annihilation of human potential that permeates his stories.

Whatever place children have on the spectrum of value, they are usually defined – except in some tribal societies – by their exclusion from the sphere of adults. Stevenson catches the emotional impact of that exclusion with great precision, and equally explores ways in which the uninitiated young encounter and attempt to deal with the adult world, and he does it as much on behalf of the grown-up as of the child. Other writers, E Nesbit for example, or Anne Fine in our own time, are advocates more specifically for the child. Between the ages of eight and twelve or so, I read Arthur Ransome over and over again, relishing the way his child characters take responsibility for their own lives. He awards them adult-free zones in which they are not defined by their childishness.

Stories help to ease the reality of exclusion. But to be aware of it is part of childhood. And to have an older sibling underlines it. Why can't I go with my father and brother when they set off on their cycle trip round Scotland? Why can't I go with my parents to the Edinburgh Tattoo? Why do I have to go to bed when the people I want to be with are talking and laughing and having a good time? Why am I not allowed to stay up to meet Dylan Thomas, whose voice I have heard on 'The Pleasure Dome', a wonderful record of poets reading their own work? (He was probably drunk; he is put to bed in my brother's empty room, to sober up before he gives a reading at Cornell University.)

And how can one avoid perpetrating the same exclusion on one's own children?

CHAPTER TWO

Dead or Alive

NARRATIVES ARE PART of the fabric of our lives. As a child I had a continuous commentary running through my head, a blend of fact and fiction, which gave a shape to what I was doing and extrapolated all kinds of imagined possibilities. These narratives emerge, probably for most of us, as pictures, stories, sounds and songs, games and dramatisations. They don't necessarily require language. They certainly don't need to be written down, but they do need to be allowed out. They are who we are. My childhood commentary has grown up, but it is no more possible now to separate it from my consciousness than it was then.

It is not unusual for people to make up their lives, or at least augment them, for the purposes of connecting with or impressing others. I suspect that we all do this sometimes, perhaps a great deal of the time and perhaps unconsciously. There are also parts of the narrative which we suppress, for the same reason. For the purposes of this book I am leaving out a great deal. I have indicated in the Prologue that I am doing this because it is not relevant to my theme. I can argue that I am omitting what is unlikely to be of interest, but I know that other reasons come into play. I am shutting away parts of my experience to protect myself, and to protect others. I am in control, which is a satisfactory feeling, although also dangerous. I might be tempted to believe that in writing about my own life I have a responsibility to no one but myself. Or I might be tempted to believe that I have a responsibility to tell 'the whole truth' regardless of the consequences. In my view neither of these approaches is valid.

I am also conscious of the fact that I am constructing a narrative which I want readers to enjoy and appreciate. So things get left out which don't fit, because they are awkwardly shaped and I can't figure out how to deal with them, or because they strike off in a direction that doesn't interest me. There are things that the structure of my theme and the rhythm of my prose won't accommodate. If 'art' is an attempt to impose some kind of order on the chaos of living it is also a justification for manipulating reality. We cannot avoid this, of course – the words that go on the page or the paint on the canvas cannot be more than representations – but we should be aware of what is going on.

I believe narrative to be organic to human existence. There have always been stories and always will be stories, though these have not always been written down and encased between covers, and possibly this particular way of delivering narrative will not survive. (For reasons of convenience and pragmatism I think it probably will.) But narrative, whether fiction or documentary, poetry or history, presented on the stage or through the camera, can never be more than a version. Narrative is organic because the instinctive interpretation of our lives is part of the human condition. This effort at interpretation is vital to individual and social wellbeing, and there will always be those who strive to get it right. And we have to go on trying, precisely because there will never be a definitive version.

It is now about fifteen years since I began to draft what has become the first chapter of this book, writing longhand in an orange notebook in a London hotel room. I was on a trip connected with my work at the National Museums of Scotland, and these visits were characterised by a mix of intensive activity, dashing across London from one appointment to the next, with pauses over coffee, typically in a museum café, and intervals over meals and in the evenings when it was handy to have a notebook. But is it actually true that this book began then? I still have the notebook, I can confirm it is orange and it does indeed contain my embryonic first chapter. Did I start writing it in London, or was that something else? I'm not sure. Can I recollect what exactly I was doing on that particular trip? No. Does it matter? Not to me, and my guess is probably not to anyone else. Would I remember more clearly if this had been a vital turning point in my life? Perhaps, but we don't always recognise turning points when we see them. And when with hindsight we identify and describe them, we don't necessarily record them as they were.

Here are two turning points, as I remember them. It is September 1982. I have been at a conference in Manchester and return late at night on the train. I get off the train at Dalmeny station and wait in the dark for my husband who is coming to meet me. Headlights rounding the corner signal his approach. When we get home, five miles away, the house is quiet. We sit down at the kitchen table and have a conversation which heralds the end of our marriage. Ten years later I am driving home after spending a few days at Carradale in Kintyre where I have been interviewing Naomi Mitchison. I am writing her biography. I have arranged to stop in Ardrishaig to visit a man who has Carradale connections. He makes coffee which we drink by a window looking out over Loch Fyne. We go for a walk along the Crinan Canal in the July sunshine.

These are snapshots from memory. Even if they are accurate I have cut out the blurred shadows at the edges. They would spoil the pictures, or would make them so dense they would be scarcely comprehensible, or would introduce distractions from the narrative I choose to represent. I haven't made them up, but they are reconstructions. During one of my conversations with Naomi Mitchison she reminisced about World War II and painted a vivid picture of helping Jews to escape from Denmark. I was quite sure she hadn't been in Denmark during the war. Then she stopped suddenly and asked, But am I remembering that, or is it just what my Danish friends told me? This underlined the dangers of depending on memory, especially the memory of a writer of fiction, for whom the imagination was a vital tool. Yet memory is the core of who we are.

I have written two full length biographies, as well as shorter biographical studies. The first, of Robert Louis Stevenson, I started to work on sometime in 1976. An excellent biography of Stevenson already existed, *A Voyage to Windward* (1950) by JC Furnas, whom I knew as a friend of my parents. He and his wife Helen visited sometimes as I was growing up. My father had himself written a critical work on Stevenson as well as *Robert Louis Stevenson and His World* (1973). These seemed very good reasons for me to steer clear of the subject. I certainly had not planned to write a life of Stevenson, or of anyone else. At the time I had wanted to write a book about Victorian adventure stories, which would have included Stevenson, but my publishers were not very keen. We think it's time for a new biography of Stevenson, they suggested. In the end I agreed to undertake this, but my doubts continued. Was there any real need of another telling of Stevenson's story, and was it appropriate that I should be telling it, inevitably in the shadow of both my father and Joe Furnas? I did not anticipate that RLS would continue to absorb me long after the book was finished and that I would still be re-reading his work and writing about him after nearly thirty years.

The second biography I undertook was that of Naomi Mitchison and this also came as a suggestion from someone else. Joan Lingard knew of my interest in Mitchison, and when Naomi told her that she was contemplating authorising a biography Joan phoned me. A few months later I found myself in a small basement flat in Notting Hill drinking very strong coffee made by Naomi in an earthenware jug (one of her few culinary skills) and listening to her talking about her life. I said very little, but it seems to have been enough to win her approval. She was about to give up her London flat to live permanently in Carradale House which had been her part-time residence and focus of her participation in Scottish life for over fifty years. I was instructed to visit her there.

Stevenson died in 1894. The main facts of his life were in the public domain. Any misleading myths had been dispelled by Joe Furnas. I thought it unlikely that anything new would turn up that would radically alter perceptions of the man and he was no longer around to be interrogated. The evidence of his life seemed immutable, contained in printed work, in manuscripts, in museums and above all in letters. The latter in particular are so vivid, so palpable, that they instil an illusion of flesh and blood, of the sound of a voice and the cadence of gestures, but this remains an illusion. Naomi Mitchison saw my story of her life in published form, out in her centenary year, and went on to celebrate her hundredth and her hundred-and-first birthdays. For over four years I was visiting her regularly, taping her recollections and making notes on our conversations. My interpretation of her life was radically informed by my understanding of the woman I got to know. She was a key player in the process. And player is the key word because for her life was theatre and it was her apprehension of this that drove her writing. In a sense my biography was her last shot at a starring role. By the time I was working on it she was no longer writing. It was also her last shot at risk taking, an activity she had relished all her life.

Both my subjects were theatrical. They both used amateur dramatics as a gateway (though not the only one) into a life of writing. Louis Stevenson loved dressing up and posturing and creating multiple persona, and was an enthusiastic participant in theatricals organised by Ann Jenkin, the wife of his professor of engineering. He once said he wished he could live life as an opera. As a teenager Naomi Mitchison wrote, directed and acted in plays, in which her older brother and his friends also performed. Her keen sense of drama informed her life and she, too, liked to dress up and to appear in unexpected guises. In Botswana, invited to a simple meal in a thatched rondavel, she dressed for dinner. Such theatricality makes the biographer's task difficult as there is always the danger of being dazzled by the performance. But it also makes it easier to construct a strong narrative. 'Adventure to the adventurous' was the motto on a jug Naomi purchased at a jumble sale and adopted as her own. 'Life is far better fun than people dream who fall asleep among the chimney stacks and telegraph wires,' wrote Louis from the South Pacific to his friend Sidney Colvin. The individuals whom we like to describe as being 'larger than life' are those who are most successful at projecting themselves.

From time to time I read biographies written in a spirit of antipathy if not of actual antagonism. Sometimes there can be good reason for this: not every life it is instructive or simply interesting to read about inspires liking. But the level of engagement required by a biographer is such that distaste for the subject can be damaging, especially if it masks understanding. There are subjects that clearly challenge a biographer's empathetic skills – I've never read a biography of Hitler – yet living in an intimate relationship with someone whose personality or opinions or actions generate an aversion is likely to distort the outcome. Other biographers have clearly strained for a new angle on a well-rehearsed theme. An example of the latter is Frank McLynn's biography of Stevenson, one of several that came out to mark the RLS centenary in 1994. In my view, it misrepresented in a way that seemed wilful Louis's relationship with his father and demonised without justification Louis's wife Fanny. In the meantime, the Stevenson scholar Roger Swearingen has been working for what must be at least a quarter of a century on a biography that has for some time been billed as 'definitive'. Although I anticipate a first-rate account, and a fuller account than any that has gone before, it will not be definitive, because there is no definitive. You can argue that 'facts are chiels that winna ding', but interpretation is not static. Each generation brings its own baggage and its own perceptions to stories of the past, which is precisely what makes history and biography continually interesting.

And there is an apparently insatiable appetite for stories about real people, dead or alive. We want to know. We *need* to know. We need a means of testing our thoughts and actions against those of others, of validating our own lives and times, and we are voraciously, vicariously and salaciously curious. All biography and autobiography feeds that curiosity; some do so cynically and manipulatively. The process of writing biography involves the same kind of curiosity. All biographers are spies and peeping toms with a capacity for living vicariously. We all hope to discover something new and unexpected about our subject and some of us will go to enormous lengths to find it. Some biographers will like Richard Holmes scrupulously endeavour to follow every footstep of their subject to get a sense of how he or she experienced each place and environment. I did not do this for either of my biographies. I did not reach Samoa, where

Stevenson spent his last years, until nearly two decades after my book was published. I did not attempt to follow every path taken by the much-travelled Naomi Mitchison, which would have taken me to India, Africa, North America, the USSR, France, Italy, Greece, Denmark, Austria, Yugolavia, Israel, Egypt and probably some other countries I've overlooked. But there was one country I believed to be essential to visit. This was Botswana, which commanded Mitchison's attention and influenced her work for a quarter of a century. The village of Mochudi in particular was a place I felt I had to experience myself, to see and smell, to walk about in, to listen to. Most valuable of all was the opportunity to meet the people she had known there, whose lives had been affected by her presence. It didn't seem to me necessary, and indeed would not have been possible, to experience, say, Vienna in the same way.

In writing about a living subject you are engaging with a participant. The nature of the 'bargain' between author and subject may vary, as may the nature of the relationship. I had no formal arrangement with Mitchison, except as regarded permission to quote, which was agreed with her agent. She did not ask to see what I was writing, although I sent her some early chapters and the whole of the final draft. She responded positively to the chapters and made no comment at all on the completed text. The final draft was also sent to members of her family, and at their request I made one small change, not to protect her, but because another individual might have been caused distress. This highlights the potential minefield of writing about living subjects. You not only have to negotiate a relationship with your subject, you have to be aware of all the other characters in the story who may be affected. Naomi's multistranded life brought her into contact with people in many different contexts, and she had a large family. I had to engage with many of them as well as with her. They all had a stake in the narrative I was constructing.

With a live subject you are also writing a story that has not yet ended and which has not attracted the attempts to sum up and define which the conclusion of a distinguished life inevitably generates. Obituaries are interesting because they are obliged to focus on the highlights and précis achievements. They are generally the first step, often the only step, in assessing a life, yet they are written, inevitably, still within the magnetic field of the subject. Although it was clear when I began to visit Naomi regularly that her creative and professional life was over, she was still the custodian of her own past and it will be some time before anyone writing about her will be able to take themselves beyond this guardianship. She had her own views on what was of significance, reflected in the memories she chose to reveal. She had opinions on a wide range of issues. In her nineties and fretting at her immobility she made gestures of independence that seemed to me to be characteristic. When we went for a walk down to the shore she refused to be helped over the stile. One afternoon she vanished for an hour or so, much to the consternation of her 'minder', her live-in help whose presence she clearly resented. She wanted to demonstrate that her movements weren't totally dependent on others. (She had gone to visit a neighbour.)

In the early stages of my research I drew up a list of all the people I thought it might be worth interviewing. It was a very long list. In addition there were many others who had some impression to convey or anecdote to tell. I did not see all the people on my list. Almost all those I did see were generous with their time and their memories. But were they reliable witnesses? To what extent had stories been improved in the telling, or were opinions influenced by hindsight? Could I detect the sound of the grinding of personal axes? I felt it important not only to make clear the nature of my sources, published or private, casual comment or taped interview, direct or indirect, but to draw attention to the uncertainty of the terrain. I felt it necessary to highlight my experience as a biographer of a particular personality at a particular time in a particular place. Naomi Mitchison died a year and five months after my biography was published. The experience of her next biographer – and I hope there will be more – is bound to be different, and so is the outcome.

My biography of Stevenson was published in 1980. I have lost count of the number of biographical studies of him that have appeared since then. There has been a surge of interest in RLS, partly a growing academic discovery of the complexity and modernity of his writing, partly a result of the magnetic attraction of his life and personality. Many more of his books are in print than when I started my research; a scholarly collected edition of his work is currently being published by Edinburgh University Press. Graduate students and university lecturers in several continents are beavering away on RLS topics. There seems to be a particular interest in Stevenson and South Pacific colonialism. *Treasure Island* was one of the BBC's Big Read top one hundred books. Everyone has heard of Dr Jekyll and Mr Hyde even if they don't know the name of their creator. The landscape of Stevenson awareness is very different now from that in 1980.

All of this illustrates the mutability of interpretation, of life as well as work. Even if the facts are static, the ebb and flow of interest and fashion, of cultural and national factors, affect the emphasis they receive. So does context, the scope of which can expand or contract. Perhaps this should not be so. When I undertook my biography of RLS I saw part of my purpose as reintroducing him to readers who had perhaps read *Treasure Island* and *Kidnapped* but kept them in a box labelled 'adventure stories for children'. If I had begun on it ten years later I would have given more space to his work, because I discovered that while my biography fuelled an interest in the life of this attractive, mercurial, courageous personality this did not necessarily take people to his books. Or if it did, it did not move them beyond a very limited reading of them.

So even with a dead subject the business of biography is fluid. New evidence may come to light, but this does not close the space for debate. Many column inches were given to Orwell's list of crypto-communists put together near the end of his life to assist the British intelligence services. (One of those on the list was Naomi Mitchison.) Some, like Scott Lucas in his book *Orwell* (2003), argued that this changed our perception of Orwell. Others, like Bernard Crick whose biography of Orwell came out in 1980, argued that it did not. The two debated the issue at the 2003 Edinburgh International Book Festival in a session which I chaired. The discussion was vigorous, stimulating and instructive, a totally valid, indeed vital, part of the continuing process of reinterpreting and reassessing the narratives of peoples' lives. The dead do not lie quiet in their graves.

Nor is memory sacred, though so radical a part of a life's identity.

And maybe its very mutability is part of that identity, as memory itself is adapted and rearranged. Stevenson's ability to remember his childhood and to recapture the experience of being a child is organic to his writing. We can go to Colinton manse and recognise the garden from his description, but there is no way of testing whether his re-creation of playing there as a small boy is 'true'. My belief that it is genuine (which is not quite the same thing) is an act of faith. I also believe that such acts of faith are implicit in the relationship between biographer and subject. Historiography of any kind which is not informed by faith and imagination is likely to be sterile.

Richard Holmes in his book *Footsteps: Adventures of a Romantic Biographer* (1985) argues that it is not possible to cross what he describes as the bridge into the past. At the same time you have to 'produce the living effect, while remaining true to the dead fact':

> The adult distance – the critical distance, the historic distance – had to be maintained. You stood at the end of the broken bridge and looked across carefully, objectively, into the unat-tainable past on the other side. You brought it alive, brought it back, by other sorts of skills and crafts and sensible magic.

Although this begs some questions, and the whole notion of objectivity is problematic, I think Holmes's 'sensible magic' is what you get when you combine faith and imagination with writing that is empathetic with both its subject and with language itself. There are many prosaic biographies which fail to create that 'living effect'. The material is there but the magic is missing. And this in spite of the fact that every individual's life is in some measure potentially interesting, so the historian of people's lives begins with a huge advantage. There is historical territory which is difficult to populate with individualised human beings but when you are dealing with people there is more likely to be a willingness on the part of the reader to collude in the narration. In writing about childhood experiences in *A Child's Garden of Verses* and elsewhere Stevenson encourages us to want to know about his own childhood and provides memories, stories of himself. As a biographer, I continue the process and add interpretative garments to the memories, which are already separated from the event by 'the broken bridge'.

Memory is a tool we all use to fix ourselves in a particular moment in space or time, but it is an artifice, because we are never stationary. Our lives are continuing and memory itself fuels that continuum. And neither can the biographer fix her subject, for the same reason. A life story may have a beginning, a middle and an end, and the conventions of narrative and readers' expectation impel the biographer to respect chronology. We talk about journeys through life, and following in the footsteps (the title of Holmes's book) of those who have gone before, but in some respects lives are more like strata, layers built up through accretions of time and experience. The more complex the personality and the more multifarious the life, the harder it is to distinguish and identify the layers.

There is a view, implicit at least if not overt, that if an individual emerges unscathed from biographical treatment the author has not done a good job. One or two reviewers of my Mitchison biography were critical because they felt I had been over-generous. They wanted more warts. Hatchet jobs, or the exposure of salacious detail, create a possibly spurious illusion of 'truth'. Realism is understood to be almost synonymous with the nasty, the unpalatable, the gritty. 'Real people' are selfish, violent, greedy. But reality is as likely to be bland, boring and repetitive, even when it moves beyond the pattern of daily life, and real people can have all kinds of minor flaws, including selfishness and greed, and still be decent, even admirable, individuals. It is a misconception to assume that every cupboard contains a skeleton.

The search for warts, however, may have arisen from an awareness of flaws that I had overlooked, which is fairer comment. Did I modulate my narrative to avoid offence to its subject? Was I pulling punches? My interpretation was, of course, the result of my experience, my research, my scrutiny, my assessment of the personality of my subject, my selection and arrangement of material. It was influenced by my generally tolerant view of human behaviour and my respect for my subject. Someone else working in exactly the same circumstances would not have written the same book. That hardly needs to be said.

It was clear to me that Robert Louis Stevenson and Naomi

Mitchison, in writing about their own lives, and in the latter's case speaking about her own life, were no more reliable as witnesses than others. In some respects they were less reliable as the very skills that made them writers of distinction enabled them to bring their own 'sensible magic' to bear on the interpretation of their own lives. Working on them made me acutely aware of the pitfalls of all kinds of biographical writing. Yet I decided to write about aspects of my own life, without any claim to being more reliable than anyone else. My motives are mixed. There are certain things I wish to clarify in my own mind and being a writer by instinct I turn to the written word. Although I love conversation, the very qualities I love about it, its fluidity, its give and take, its hesitations and silences, its voices and the gestures and expressions that go with it, are what make it inadequate. And of course the published word can reach a much larger audience.

Every book I have undertaken I have believed to be dealing with a subject worth writing and reading about. I have never been under pressure to publish for the sake of it, though I have been under pressure to publish to make a living. Neither pressure applies in this case. Naomi Mitchison said she wrote her volumes of memoirs in response to grandchildren who asked questions. I have no grandchildren, but to a certain extent I am addressing my children. I am conscious of wanting to create a record, however partial (in both senses of the word). My own mother wrote down an incomplete genealogy of her family and some fragments of memory, but died before she or anyone else could shape them into something more. I always meant to record my grandmother's reminiscences of growing up in Liverpool and the early years of her marriage. I never did, and now they exist only in the patchy memories of myself and my father, and perhaps of my siblings and cousins. Such memories, however unstable, however tenuous, are our link with our inheritance.

My father dedicated *Two Worlds* (1956), his memoir of growing up in Edinburgh, to his mother, and described it as a portrait of his father. But I read it at the age of fourteen, and read it now, as both a self-portrait and a portrait of a father–son relationship from the perspective of the son. I think there were two prominent motives in his writing of this book. One was to stake out his own territory. The other was to keep faith with his upbringing and his heritage, both of which in some eyes he had abandoned. He hadn't, of course, but even as an adolescent I was aware of his sensitivities. Perhaps the great achievement of *Two Worlds* is that he accomplishes both, although they are implicitly contradictory. The sequel, *A Third World*, was published in 1971 but is much less satisfactory, largely I believe because it is not driven by the same sense of purpose. It is a curiously unrevealing book.

I, too, want to stake out my own territory, perhaps rather late in the day. My father wrote *Two Worlds* in his early forties, 'in a mood of pure self-indulgence' as he puts it in the foreword to the 1987 edition. (This may have been his mood, but, as suggested in the above paragraph, I believe the motives were less serendipitous.) I am twenty years further along the road, and write in the consciousness that I have not in the past been sufficiently assertive in laying claim to either personal or professional space. It is an underlying theme of this book, and arises from issues of identity that come with my origins and have become more insistent with experience. These issues have been troubling, but they have without a doubt spurred creativity and made my life more interesting, if more complicated. Alongside these is a primal urge that strengthens with age. Family, past, present and future, grows in importance, and in that context I want to construct a picture of who and what I am.

Autobiographies are not life stories in any complete sense. As well as what is deliberately omitted and unconsciously suppressed there are influences and aspects that one is simply not aware of. Just as with a poem the reader may find meanings that the writer does not recognise, there are currents in one's own life that can often be detected only by an outsider. The attempt to reconcile the outside view with the inside is part of the biographer's task. The autobiographer is not in the right place to attempt it, although she can open the door, even if inadvertently, to others.

At some stage in our lives we discover that what we see and hear and feel can never exactly correspond to what anyone else sees and hears and feels, or if it does we can never know that it does. Even if it is possible to detect exact correspondences in the brain's activity, how that is translated in terms of felt experience almost certainly cannot be measured. I can try to describe the sound of a Mozart piano concerto heard through an open window on a summer evening, but will never know if anyone else experiences it as I do or understands my description as I intend it. I can identify the autumn colours of the trees around my house as gold and copper, but the gold and copper you see may not be the same. We may agree that the word 'copper' is the right one to use, but will never know what the other's brain registers as copper. My son and I are both synaesthetes; we see letters and words as colours. But we don't both see the same colours and although we understand each other's experience we do not experience it in the same way. But it is almost impossible to describe to those who have no notion at all of what it is to experience one sensation as another. I have tried, and the response is generally total bafflement.

Language is a rough and approximate shorthand. Writers, and poets especially, are constantly trying to refine it and make it work better, which is why writing and reading are such essential and rewarding activities. But the effort to communicate is a Sisyphean task. It seems to me that as good a description as any of the purpose of human life is the effort to reach beyond isolation. Even the hermit who avoids all human contact is striving for some kind of spiritual connection. Most of us, though, see ourselves as part of a human community which involves finding a place in a continuum that connects us with the past and the future as well as the present. Without narrative we cannot do this, yet narrative is a pretty crude tool. It's a tool we have to use, though. We can't replicate reality, but we can tussle with it, play with it, express it, imitate it, evoke it, experiment with metaphors and ways of seeing it. That's what art is all about; it is perhaps, as I've suggested, what life is all about.

So narratives about our own lives and the lives of others will continue and we will continue to recognise and apply the conventions that identify biography and autobiography. We have little choice but to accept these conventions at face value, although we may at the same time examine and cast doubt on them. Such contradictions are also endemic to our response to the efforts to make sense of human life. Raphael Samuel in his book *Theatres of Memory* (1994) talks about the silences and gaps that are inevitable in our attempts to put together historical narratives. This applies to the way we record our own lives as well as our attempts to reconstruct the lives of others. It is an iterative process. As Samuel puts it, 'History is an argument about the past, as well as the record of it, and its terms are forever changing.' He argues that there is a vital role for the imagination. Richard Holmes would agree. No amount of tracing the footsteps of a biographer's subject will replicate the original experience, but it can fuel the imagination to make a connection with a life as it was lived. Artefacts can do the same. To work with the actual letters written by RLS diminishes distance in time and space in a way which no bound volume or facsimile of the same letters can replicate. The snowshoes that once belonged to the Arctic explorer John Rae can trigger at the very least an effort to imagine the realities of Arctic travel. That effort to imagine is the best that historians can do.

Playing devil's advocate, Michael Holroyd, in an essay in his collection *Works on Paper*, describes the biographer as a parasite feeding on the lives of others. He cites many writers who have condemned biography, in some cases stipulated in their wills that their own lives should be exempt from biographical treatment. Most stipulations seem to be ignored – George Orwell and Philip Larkin are just two examples. To deny the biographer is in a sense to place oneself outwith history, and implies an extraordinary arrogance, suggesting as it does that certain lives are so special that they should be beyond the reach of investigation. Biographers, Holroyd argues, are dismissed by 'real' historians for dealing in small-scale fragments – 'it takes ten thousand biographies to make one small history'. The biography deniers flinch from the prospect of voyeuristic tittle-tattle, and in the case of writers from the possibility of their work being subsumed in layers of irrelevant quotidian detail and messy ineptitudes. Laundry lists and love affairs may distract and detract from the art which should be the only testimony to a writer's life. But perhaps writers in particular are nervous because they know only too well what the imagination can do, its transforming power. Novelists, and poets of course, make things up, and they, too, feed on the raw material of human life. What's to prevent biographers doing the same? Holroyd having made the case against biography then puts the other side of the argument. Serious biographers, he says, work on ethical foundations. They don't make things up. They discipline the imagination, although it is a vital tool and without it the creative leap into the past cannot be achieved. The urge to recreate peoples' lives, to sustain narratives, is born of the need 'to keep death in its place'. Without access to other people's lives our own lives would be immeasurably the poorer and harder to understand. Good biography is a way of connecting readers with the larger narratives of history, of plugging us into the past, of confirming the actuality and authority of individual lives.

With luck as much as judgment, writing autobiographically may both contribute to the debate about the past and spark the imagination. It is equally the child of the need 'to keep death in its place'. Those of us who write about our own lives and times are bearing witness, perhaps only to a fragment of human experience and almost certainly with prejudice and imperfections, but nevertheless preserving something. That something may turn out to be more important than we know at the time. Thirty years after writing *Two Worlds* my father recorded that he was 'pleasantly surprised to see it taking its place as a piece of sociocultural Scottish history', and he went on, 'Looking back now, I can see more clearly than when I was writing it that I was documenting a short-lived period of cultural interchange in the life of Edinburgh that has its counterparts in other cultures and other periods.' Looking back is a valuable activity. If the past is another country, its landscapes and borders are constantly changing. We need to know that, but we also need to keep looking.

CHAPTER THREE

Names

WHEN MY FIRST child was born I was disturbed to find new parents whose babies were still nameless when they left the hospital ward. To me it was of enormous importance to give my child a name as soon as she entered the world. It was the first signal of her identity. And the name itself was crucially important. It reflected the way I and her father thought of ourselves and how our child would relate to the families into which she had been born. Names are the most personal things we have and bestow on others.

I didn't question my surname, but even in multi-ethnic America it was odder than many and always had to be spelt. Some people thought it was a Scottish name, and it almost could have been. As a small child I didn't think about its origins, which were made more confusing by the fact that it was pronounced in a variety of ways, most of which my parents tolerated. Later, I enjoyed explaining its Dutch origins and its journey to Scotland by way of Lithuania, Poland, Germany and England. Jews and Scots had no problem with 'ch', but the English did, so when my father went to Oxford he accepted an Anglicised pronunciation (but also tells a story, I suspect apocryphal, of being 'Dai Cheese' in Wales) which travelled with him to Chicago. The surname I grew up with was 'Day-shes'. At school in England I was sometimes 'Daitches', to which I objected. A girl in the class above me used to taunt me – 'Jennifer Daitches drops her aitches'. In Scotland we were, and are, Di-ches with the 'ch' as in 'loch'. The other day my name was pronounced as if it were French. I don't put people right unless they ask, but each variation is another spin on identity. The name I grew up with denotes someone not quite the same as the person who on occasion chooses to be known as Daiches with a Scottish 'ch'. When I married, I was glad to get rid of it, but underestimated the not so subtle change to who I was.

I didn't like my first name, but was pleased and intrigued by my second. It was the sound of Jennifer that I objected to – I thought it ugly. It seemed especially ugly when my father sang the nonsense song he made up: 'Jennifer the Pennifer, the Eenifer, the Onifer...' and so on. It made me scream with fury. But Rachel, my middle name, was different. I knew that Rachel was my grandmother's sister, a gifted violinist who had died young. I was shown a photograph of her, and when I reached adolescence people sometimes commented that I resembled her. (I thought her beautiful and mysterious, so I was pleased at the implication.) I would have liked to have been called Rachel, but my parents pointed out that it did not sound well with Daiches pronounced in the English way. I saved the name to give to my own daughter.

I was usually 'Jen' as a child. Elizabeth became 'Lizbeth', then Liz. Alan was never shortened. His middle name is Harry, after another relative who had died young, this time my mother's older brother who was killed in the First World War. I was told the story of how he had lied about his age so that he could enlist in the Gordon Highlanders. He transferred to the Royal Flying Corps and became an observer, taking photographs behind enemy lines. In 1917 his plane was attacked and he was fatally wounded. My mother told me how on Armistice Day she was on the streets of Aberdeen, with her mother, amidst the cheering crowd. She waved a little union jack and cheered with the rest of them. Her mother was silent, until she said, 'All the cheering in the world won't bring Harry back.' I was very young when my mother told me about Harry but I embraced his death as part of me. It was my earliest sense of a link with a part of family history which was momentous and tragic. Later, I learnt about the Holocaust.

In my aunt's flat in Glasgow there was a photograph of Harry in his uniform, a handsome young man looking older than the nineteen years he'd reached when he died. There was always a red poppy in the corner of the frame. My aunt showed me the box of Harry's letters she had kept, which I now have. They say little about conditions in France. On 17 July 1917 he is asking for his parents to arrange to have a new tunic made – 'khaki whipcord, highland style as usual' – and a pair of Gordon tartan trousers. By the end of that year he was with the RFC; 'I have done about fifteen hours over the line now and we have been credited with our first Hun', he writes on 7 December. Later he tells them that the intense cold when flying at heights of several thousand feet has given him frostbitten fingers. Most of the letters are low-key, but there is a graphic description of a narrow escape when his camera saved his life by coming between him and machine-gun bullets. Next time, he wasn't so lucky.

Growing up with the knowledge of Harry's death, it seemed to me right that Alan should bear his name, just as I felt it appropriate that I should have the name of another Rachel. These names were more than echoes of the past, they were links and signifiers. They were reminders of who we were. And perhaps part of my antipathy to Jennifer was that it seemed to have no significance at all (although my parents pointed out its Celtic origins). Alan was an appropriately Scottish name. Elizabeth was one of the names of our Auntie Ethel. Liz's middle name, Mackay, was my mother's maiden name. They all added up. But Jennifer didn't fit.

I was happy to be 'Jen', which evolved into 'Jenny', I think after we were living in England. I even persuaded some of my teachers to call me Jenny. But then I found myself in a class with three other girls called Jenny. I must have been about fourteen when I decided it was time to rescue my individuality. My parents had a German-American friend called Jenni. I would call myself 'Jenni', and duly inscribed the name on school notebooks, rulers etc and began to sign myself 'Jenni Daiches'. One school friend accused me of being pretentious. But I stuck to it. It was much more than a change of spelling. It was a gesture of independence, of control. I realised that I could have a say in how I identified myself.

But not necessarily the last word. Sometimes, in a doctor's surgery for example, I hear the name 'Jennifer Calder' with the dislocated sense that it must be referring to someone else. Am I less 'Jennifer Calder' than I am 'Jenni Daiches'? Which of all the different mixes of names that have been used to identify me is nearest to who and what I am? Does it matter?

In January 1960 I went to Israel for the first time. I was eighteen years old. I had just left school. I travelled alone on a mission that was all about finding an aspect of myself that seemed elusive. When I signed on for my first class at an ulpan, a language school, it came as something of a shock when I was informed, with all the others, that I had to have a Hebrew name. Of course, I had a Hebrew name. At last I could be called Rachel, but pronounced in the Hebrew not the English way, which transformed it. Some of my fellow pupils had to go rather further afield for another name. The more elderly members of the class didn't find it easy to respond to a new identity. At first I found it disturbing to be Rachel. It was a denial of identity as well as a gain, and it underlined the distance from my familiar world. I was away from home on my own for the first time.

I got used to being Rachel, and valued an experience which was wholly my own. The change of name underlined the sense of adventure, the feeling that I was carving out territory for myself. Perhaps something of the same need was behind my decision to change my name when I married. I wanted to detach myself from Daiches, which at times seemed like a millstone. I married a few months after graduating from the university in which my father had taught the subject of my degree. Although he left at the end of my first year to take up a chair at the newly founded University of Sussex, his reputation remained. Every student of English literature knew of him, and of course I was being taught by his colleagues. I was wary of preconceived expectations, and deeply irritated by the attitude of some of my fellow students, who saw not me but my father's daughter. Or perhaps not even my father's daughter, but simply a name with which they wanted to be associated, for reasons that had nothing to do with me. It bred a distrust of the way people responded to me, which can be particularly intense in the offspring of those in the public eye. Publicity, whether on your own account or through attachment to another, is bound to muddy your perception of who you are.

Daiches is still a mixed blessing. In Edinburgh, most people who know the name link it with my father and uncle and are aware of their distinguished careers. Although I generally continue to use my married name, many people are aware that I am a Daiches. (They are mostly not, of course, aware that I am a Mackay.) The experience I had after giving a lecture in Perth is typical. My subject was some aspect of women's writing. Afterwards an eager middle-aged woman came up to me. She made no comment at all on my lecture, but enthused, 'I am such an admirer of your father, what a wonderful man.' I laughed, and she clearly couldn't understand why, and had no inkling of the irony and extraordinary tactlessness, perhaps even hurtfulness, of what she said. I do find it quite amusing, but also frustrating and rather sad: sad because of the many people, especially women, who struggle for an independent role, and sad for the woman herself who was so unaware. I have had this experience many times.

Traditionally, women exchanged their father's identity for that of their husband. Here is a parallel experience which suggests that in the 1980s the tradition was still alive and well – I am sure it still flourishes, but as I am no longer married I do not encounter it in this particular guise. It was at the launch of a book by my husband, an important book which he had worked on for a decade. A woman, I can't remember who or even if it was someone I knew, said to me in distinctly condescending tones, 'I am sure you were a great support to your husband while he was working on this book,' and went on to talk about the unacknowledged wives who typed their husbands' manuscripts and kept the children out of their hair. I made a rather tart remark about being too busy with my own work to do much of that. At the time my marriage was disintegrating, and a contributing factor, in my view, was my husband's difficulty in living with the realities of my professional life.

But when I married in 1963 I was glad to become 'Mrs Calder'. My mother addressed her letters to me 'Mrs Angus Calder'. I wasn't too happy with that. The convention that 'Mrs Jenni Calder' would signal widowhood reinforced the notion that as long as there was a husband around a married woman could not have her own name. In the early Sixties none of my contemporaries kept their names when they married. The new wave of feminism was only just beginning. Even five years later, I might have taken a different view.

The change of name registered a change of status. As a married woman I had a different sense of myself. I was only twenty-one. My three years at the University of Cambridge had been, if anything, narrow and constraining. The acute artificiality of living in a shrunken world dominated by men – in the early 1960s only ten per cent of the students at Cambridge were women – transmitted no notion at all of how to occupy a larger territory or indeed of what are normally thought of as adult responsibilities. I had not learnt how to be less timid. I had discovered a little of how to outwit authority and I knew I wasn't stupid. I had a firmish grasp of two strands of my inheritance, the Jewish and the Scottish, but I wasn't at all sure how, or if, they added up. I was marrying a man who was also a Scottish transplant, and that seemed to weigh the balance in favour of Scotland as a signifier. We talked of how we would prefer to live in Scotland. But I was ultra-sensitive about my Jewish background (by 1963 I had been twice to Israel) and it was important to me that this should be recognised.

I liked the idea of marriage (although my idea of marriage was idealised) and I was quite sure I wanted children. I saw the future built on a creative partnership, two people supporting each other emotionally and intellectually, sharing responsibilities, bringing their children up together. I did not reflect that the very fact that I took my husband's name could be understood as indicating a partnership that would not be equal. I felt liberated from my family, but was only half aware that my new identity as a married woman was compromising. It took a few years, and another country, to make me understand the risks of taking on a name that had belonged to someone else from birth. It not only belonged to Angus, my husband, but to all of his large family (except of course his mother). Whatever my feelings towards the Calder clan, I was never going to be a member of that family in the same way as I was a member of my own.

The Calder clan, whom I met in the summer of 1963, were warm and welcoming. But, as in my own family, life revolved around husband and father. Peter Ritchie Calder was a journalist, a prolific and influential writer on science and politics, and the author of many books. In 1966 he was made a life peer. Mabel, his wife, was the mother of five children and, like my mother, kept the domestic and social wheels turning. In her teenage years she had wanted to go on the stage. Instead, she married a man whose career involved him at times in considerable drama. Something Angus and I shared was that we were both the offspring of exiled Scots; that heritage was reflected in the names of the younger Calders. Both our mothers grew up with the accepted convention of married women becoming subsumed in their husbands' names: Mrs David Daiches, Mrs Peter Ritchie Calder, later Lady Ritchie Calder. That was the convention I inherited. Imprinted as I was by the conformism of the 1950s, which strove to put the women released by war back into their domestic boxes, I did not act on my discomfort at women's disappearing names.

There is a fine Scottish and Scandinavian tradition of women retaining their original names after marriage. On gravestones you often find a wife commemorated with a name that is not her husband's, although of course it is her father's. If I had known of this in 1963 I might have been less inclined to shed my name. I did know of the American custom of keeping both names, but I felt this would be ponderous – Daiches Calder just sounded silly, although my aunt Sylvia became Daiches Raphael when she married, and her husband did too. I approved of this, but it didn't occur to me to suggest to Angus that we might emulate it. I knew a Clydeside woman, who died a few years ago, who reverted to her original surname after her (rare) divorce in the mid-1930s, and was addressed as 'Miss' for the rest of her life. As 'Miss' by choice she brought up her son.

The names of our three children were debated for hours. Our children's names should reflect their heritage – family, Jewish, Scottish. We did not want to pick names out of thin air which had no reference to who our children were. So our elder daughter became Rachel Elizabeth, Rachel my middle name and Elizabeth a family name on both sides. Number two daughter became Gowan Lindsay, a Scottish word borrowed from Burns – 'We twa hae run about the braes/And pou'd the gowans fine' – and Angus's middle name, and our son became Gideon James, an alliance of the Old Testament and Scotland. To us these names held immense significance, and I still find it strange that there will no doubt be, for example, a generation of Liams and Ewans with no Celtic connections, and are already Esthers and Ruths with no cognisance of the Old Testament.

The giving of names is important for parents, but of course it is the children who have to live with them. Gowan was ambivalent about her name for a long time, partly because people often thought it was a boy's name – Gawaine, perhaps. When she was small we called her 'Goon', which was not inappropriate to her personality but may have reinforced a prejudice against Gowan. She wasn't too keen on Lindsay either. As a teenager Gideon, always Gid to the family, renounced his first name (perhaps because at school he was Skids or Squid) and became James for a time. I found it disconcerting when people phoned and asked for James and on several occasions nearly responded by saying they had the wrong number. Gideon himself often failed to answer to James, and the experiment was abandoned. Somewhere, though, he is down in Labour Party records as James Calder, because that was the name he used when he joined. The metamorphosis of names seems just to happen. How and when Gowan became 'Goon' I don't know. Rachel became 'Rage' – lucky not to be 'Radge' I suppose, but why not the prettier 'Ray' which was what my namesake was called?

Gowan was only a week or two old when we were visited in our rather dingy West Hampstead flat by Angus's elder sister Fiona. She asked about Gowan's middle name, nodded approval, and said, 'Gowan Lindsay Ritchie Calder.' 'No,' I said, 'no Ritchie.' It was only then that I discovered that all the Calder children and grandchildren had Ritchie in their names, after Angus's father. Angus had never mentioned this. Was this a major *faux pas*? No comment was ever made to me by any member of the Calder family, but I remember feeling rather indignant at the whole idea. If there was to be an addition to the weight of names carried by our children, it should surely come from the mother's, not the father's, side. For

Angus, it appeared not to be an issue, although his father was a towering and ambivalent presence in his life.

Family names are an inescapable litany absorbed by children as they half listen to adult talk. They may never meet the aunts, uncles and cousins, but the names are nevertheless part of their distinctive world, with or without their designations. Names wove their way through my childhood: the great aunts and uncles – Dode and Lizzie, Rosie and Abie, Frances and Max; aunts and uncles – Ethel, Lionel and Dorothy, Sylvia and David, Beryl and Jimmy; cousins – Michael and Nicholas, Sally and Anne, Gordon, John and Helen; more distant relatives, in space if not in kinship – Lily and Lena, Isaac and Samuel, Joyce, Maurice, Eleanor, Fred and Millie, Jean, Douglas, another Frances, and many more; my parents' names – David and Billie (Isobel), and their parents – Flora and Salis, Janet and William. And the surnames that were also part of the tapestry – my mother Mackay and her mother Lauder whose sister married a Stephen, somewhere a Macintosh, my grandmother Levin, and so on, back and back, all those names bound into my life, and out and out. There are very few people called Daiches, but are all those Mackays a connection?

On a visit to Australia and New Zealand I looked up Daiches in the telephone directories of the cities I stayed in. There were none (dozens of Mackays, though), and no names that might possibly have metamorphosed from the original. I believe there are one or two in the United States. An internet search found one Daiches, a jeweller in Texas, who, my father tells me, is distantly related. Levin is a more common name, and perhaps there are Levins outside the UK with whom I have some kind of link. But beyond the *frisson* of some kind of shared inheritance the names of total strangers have little resonance. Much more important are the people, related or not, who featured in my childhood. I can hardly remember the faces of many of them, but the names still linger. Slim and Mary of the house in the woods, Russ and Ferne, Marshall and Betty – these were friends of my parents who took an interest in me and whom I liked. They are part of my American childhood. No names occupied quite the same place after we left. But what about friends my own age? Many of their names I have forgotten. There was Jimmy, on

Cayuga Street, who regularly came to the door to ask if I could play. There were the brothers George and Billy, a girl called Sharon, and Maggie, the daughter of English friends. There was my first admirer Tommy, who once took me to the movies. On the way home we fell out and he pulled my pigtails and pushed me into a ditch.

Names of people, names of places and streets. The places I've stayed for significant lengths of time create another personal litany, and it doesn't matter if some I can barely remember. I've never been back to Chicago, the New York and Washington I remember are cities I met as an adult, not those in whose suburbs I lived as a child. Indian Neck, Pleasant Valley, Nairobi, Kampala, Dar es Salaam, Gaborone, Vancouver, San Antonio, San Francisco, Edinburgh, Glasgow, Cullen, Cornhill, Ardrishaig, Carradale, Cambridge, Brighton – this international parade and many more are all triggers of association relating to different stages in my life. And the street names. I can remember Oneida Lane and Chevy Chase Parkway, but not where they are. And how did Chevy Chase transplant itself from northern England to America? Johnson Avenue in Bethesda outside Washington – who was Johnson? I've looked up Johnson Avenue in a Washington street directory and toyed with the notion of revisiting it. Cayuga Street in Ithaca. The eclecticism of American names is always wonderful, Iroquois and Greek brought together. Then Highland Avenue above the lake. I have been back to Highland Avenue, though not to Cayuga Street. On visits to Scotland there were Keir Street in Glasgow, Heriot Row in Edinburgh, and all the other Edinburgh streets where relatives lived or were part of my parents' growing up: Millerfield Place, Crawfurd Road, Morningside Park, Minto Street, Dick Place. There were Frederick Street and Hanover Street – when did I first realise the origin of their names? Victoria Street and Seafield Street in Cullen. In England there was first Bateman Street, and then no street at all when we moved to Hardwick where we were just Chequers Cottage. My three addresses at university in Cambridge were Grange Road, Storey's Way and Silver Street. On to London, with Barnsbury Street, then shabby, now yuppified, and Mill Lane, a rural name which contrasted oddly with the Edwardian mansion block in which we lived.

There was no street name in our Nairobi address. When we came to Edinburgh we stayed first in the flat of my parents-in-law in Randolph Place. I was never happy about Buckingham Terrace as an address, one of a cluster of streets with very English names – Eton, Oxford, Clarendon, Belgrave. It was the first house we owned. But the addresses I've had over the last fifteen years could be anywhere, Springfield Road and now Station Road. I like the simplicity of Station Road. It's a no-nonsense name, anchored in an identifiable moment in South Queensferry's history, and linked with the railway bridge which is one of the world's most impressive structures.

And all the other names, the districts and rivers and mountains and islands. Cayuga Heights, Newington and the New Town, the Forth and the Clyde, the Spey and the Findhorn, the Gog Magog Hills, Big Bin and Little Bin, Ben Vorlich which I climbed with my father when I was fifteen, the Great Rift Valley and the Great Wall, the Sea of Galilee and the North Sea, the Gorbals and the Backs, Loch Ewe and Loch Fyne, An Teallach and Cruachan, Nootka Sound and Gibson's Landing, the Blue Ridge Mountains, the Green Mountains, the White Mountains, Monserrat and Mount Kenya, Isle de Brehat, Ellis Island and Harbour Island, Islay and Jura, Lewis and Harris, the Cam, the Corrievreckan, Sun Valley and Glencoe, the Rest and Be Thankful, the Devil's Elbow and the Devil's Beeftub, Sea Palling and Chesapeake Bay, Lamu, Lake Victoria, Vailima. The magic and resonance of lists, especially lists that are meaningless except to me.

Stevenson commented on the names which echoed through his mind as he made his journey across the United States in 1879:

> None can care for literature in itself who do not take a special pleasure in the sound of names; and there is no part of the world where nomenclature is so rich, poetical, humorous, and picturesque as the United States of America. All times, races, languages have brought their contribution. Pekin is in the same State with Euclid, with Bellefontaine, and with Sandusky. Chelsea, with its London associations of red brick, Sloane Square and the King's Road, is own suburb to stately and primeval Memphis; there they have their seat, translated names

of cities, where the Mississippi runs by Tennessee and Arkansas... Old, red Manhattan lies, like an Indian arrow head under a steam factory, below Anglified New York. The names of the States and Territories themselves form a chorus of sweet and most romantic vocables: Delaware, Ohio, Indiana, Florida, Dakota, Iowa, Wyoming, Minnesota, and the Carolinas; there are few poems with a nobler music for the ear: a songful, tuneful land...

The appeal lies not just in the sounds of American names but in their plurality, in their borrowings from everywhere, and the multiple meanings those borrowings have. Their historical, national and linguistic eclecticism is a reminder of the ingredients America assembled for its mix, and a massive statement, for anyone who reflects on where these names came from, on the inappropriateness of 'melting pot' to represent American experience. These names have not melted.

Edinburgh names have always had a particular resonance for me (and for Stevenson, of course), because they had been a constant in my father's tales of his childhood and in my own experience of visits. My father talked of the Meadows, Blackford Hill, Arthur's Seat, Portobello. On the trams were strange names, Corstorphine, Comely Bank, Liberton, which still have a dual existence for me as both exotic places of my childhood and familiar places of today. And then there were all the names that clustered round Cullen and Cornhill: Portknockie and Portsoy, Banff and Buckie, Elgin, Fochabers, Keith and Huntly.

Ordinary words fill the spaces between names. With their capital letters names are somehow more solid, more real. The changing of names is a big step, and can cause distress for those who feel that names close to them have been changed without consent. The National Museum of Antiquities of Scotland lost its name and then its building, to be subsumed into a new 'brand', with a new building and another name – the Museum of Scotland. It's not surprising that the loss was deeply felt by the staff, and that many members of the public are still confused about the naming of Scotland's national museums. Changing the names of regions and counties also has a personal impact on those who live in those areas. It has more than political and social implications. The identification of where people live affects the way they think about themselves. Businesses and shops change names, but it's often years before the transformation is complete.

There are people who have been born with a name that has never changed and have lived all of their lives in a place with an unaltered name. That is a powerful way of retaining a sense of who you are, especially when the name you are born with is a name that has meaning and continuity within a community. When Scots migrated in their thousands in the eighteenth and nineteenth centuries the meaning of their names had intense significance. They denoted family, kinship and community. And for those who went to North America, possibly because Scots had been among the earliest migrants, their names usually survived intact, unlike those who arrived from the continent of Europe and so often found themselves awarded altered names because the authorities could not spell the names they heard. Others chose to amend their names, to conform with Anglo-Saxon norms. Although the spelling of some Scots names mutated, the names themselves remained, and many were instantly identifiable as Scottish. But Gordon and Ross are also not uncommon Jewish names.

Through marriage I acquired a Scottish name, although outwith Scotland the name is not necessarily recognised as Scottish. Because I do not sound Scottish, the name takes on additional significance. Away from Scotland, when I am asked where I am from, I say 'Scotland'. Within Scotland, my answer to the same question is much less straightforward. When I am asked how long I have lived in Scotland I reply, 'over thirty years' without attempting to explain. Sometimes people assume that I was born here and, like my parents, was educated in Scotland. On the occasions when I find myself thinking that it is all just too complicated to go into for the benefit of others, I remind myself how much more difficult it must be for the Edinburgh born, and Edinburgh sounding, child of Bangladeshis, say, to explain how she relates to the place where she lives and the names of the places her parents have brought with them. For over thirty years I have been living in or near the city whose name resonated through my childhood because it was the city in which both my parents grew up.

Scottish names have travelled well. You find them in every telephone book in the English speaking world and in many where English is not spoken. There are place-names all over the world which owe their origins to Scottish people and places. There are over forty Hamiltons throughout the world. Perth in Australia is probably as well known as Scotland's Perth; there are also Perths in Ontario and New Brunswick. Scottish origins are not always recognised, though. A young woman from Winnipeg I met a few years ago had no idea that her home city's Kildonan was named for the strath in Sutherland from which the area's original Scottish settlers had been evicted.

When my marriage came to an end I remained Calder. I knew a woman who in the space of a couple of years during which she divorced and remarried took on three different surnames in succession. I elected for simplicity. It was easier not to change my name. But I partially resurrected my maiden name by deciding to publish poetry as Jenni Daiches. Although some of my poetry had been published as a student I had written very little since my marriage, so there was a kind of continuity in reverting to Daiches when I began to publish poetry again. It is the name most familiar to some of my literary friends. It has led to a situation where I edited a collection of poems as Jenni Calder in which there appeared a poem by Jenni Daiches.

I find the existence of this alter ego rather satisfactory, especially as it is linked with the regeneration of an activity that I had more or less suppressed during my years of marriage, perhaps because the man I married was himself a poet. It is as if I have recovered a former self, re-established a link with the young woman who so much wanted to write, fiction as well as poetry, but who for many years lost touch with that ambition. I am confident now, as I wasn't in my early twenties, that I can use my maiden name without relinquishing identity to the older generation. I am also making a deliberate distinction between my role as a writer of poetry and fiction, and other roles.

But of course, although names signal distinctions and influence perceptions they don't actually change anything. All the identities that cluster under Calder are the same as those that cluster under Daiches. And in some ways making that distinction goes against the grain of my own beliefs. I have divided this book into chapters with titles that suggest different strands of identity, but these strands are tightly bound together. It is through my poetry that I have been able to express this; poetry is a way of breaking down barriers, a way of not conforming to the conventions of employment and social behaviour, a way of shedding both professional and personal restraints. There are other ways of doing that. But as one whose first and last recourse is to words, writing poetry is the only way I can begin to do justice to everything I am. I believe it is important for all individuals to discover the vehicle for this, and that the lack of it is the cause of much frustration, and possibly despair and self-destruction.

Poetry is itself a way of naming things, articulating feelings and ideas which the conventions of form and rhyme and rhythm render acceptable, if not always comprehensible. And naming is a means of control. The therapeutic value of writing lies not in an outpouring of emotions but in using words, which require hand and brain to put on paper, to represent them. There may be a sense of release, but it is the act of fashioning shape and resonance that is the creative benefit of writing, particularly of writing poetry. But naming of any kind is a form of control. It is what human beings do as a first step towards understanding their world. They give names to things. Botanists and zoologists identify and name species and thus impose order on the apparent chaos of the natural world. Academics identify and name ideas and trends and movements, not always helpfully but again in an effort at control. Curators label objects and specimens. Taxonomies, classifications, arrangements. Where would humanity be without them? The labelling of identity is also a kind of taxonomy. But we do it very crudely. We go for the obvious: skin colour, language, religious belief, nationality. Even the labels we apply to ourselves tend to be external. Our internalised identities respond to the way we think others see us, to the way culture and environment classify us. Some people rename themselves in an effort to overcome this. Sometimes it helps. Titles in front and letters after names have a modifying effect, most people believe for the better. I tend myself not to pay them too much attention.

In naming my chapters as I have, I have also resorted to fairly crude terms, terms that I hope people will recognise and respond to. If you are reading this you probably have a notion of American and Scottish, Jewish and English. You may have experienced marriage and parenthood. Your own sense of yourself is probably bound up with the work you do, whatever kind of work that is. We can't get very far without names and labels, but they are inevitably reductive. I could have chosen ten different titles for my chapters and approached the same themes in different ways, which may or may not have made a difference to the way you, the reader, respond.

In most cultures the naming of a child is a ceremonial event. In some cultures, Plains Indian for example, a different name comes with maturity and reflects the personality or skills of the individual concerned. Sometimes a person's name arrives in a dream: Crazy Horse dreamt his name. Often people forget names, sometimes their own. My father often confused the names of his three children, and indeed on occasion addressed us by the pets' names, but now he never forgets or confuses the names of his six grandchildren.

Some writers choose pseudonyms and metamorphose into their acquired names: who thinks of Eric Blair as the author of *Animal Farm* or ascribes *A Drunk Man Looks at a Thistle* to Chris Grieve? It is not uncommon to write under more than one name, or under a name that is deliberately genderless: JK Rowling, AL Kennedy, even Ali Smith. Not long ago I gave a lecture at the end of which there was a vote of thanks which included the comment that the name 'Jenni Calder' eminently suited me. The speaker did not elaborate on how or why. It is a name I partly chose, but its original elements were not of my choosing. My name and I have grown together, with the name I was born into following me, at first like a shadow but later regaining substance. Whether or not my two names suit me, it suits me to have two names.

CHAPTER FOUR

How to be Jewish

WHEN MY BROTHER went away to school it became more important for me to learn to read Hebrew, for I inherited what had been his role – asking the questions at the Seder, the Passover gathering to commemorate the Exodus from Egypt. My father taught me. Printed Hebrew script has a substantiality, an almost three-dimensional quality, which intrigued me. It seemed not so much an alphabet as a set of building blocks, and I thought of it less as another language (I wasn't taught to speak it) than as a structure that I was learning my way around. The structure of Jewishness, an iconography in itself, inextricably linked with images of pyramids, Moses with his tablets of stone, the Star of David, the menora with the Hanukah candles.

My father did not attempt to replicate his own upbringing. He had grown up in a rabbinical household in a world of faith and tradition which he had not so much rejected as moved away from. But we celebrated Passover, and lit candles for Hanukah, though somewhat irregularly. We also celebrated Christmas, birthdays and anniversaries, departures and arrivals, achievements and distinctions. We were good at celebrations. Most Jewish families are. The first lesson in how to be Jewish is to learn how to celebrate and commemorate. There are certain rituals and traditions: these may be dictated as much by family custom as by religion. I have attended Seders where both my father and my uncle were present. Always they argued over the way their father had conducted things. I began to realise that the argument was itself part of family tradition, and indeed the notion of contention is built into the Haggadah, described by Chaim Raphael as a 'free-wheeling exposition of scripture by the rabbis, in a style which can include ethics, history, folklore or anecdote, hairsplitting logic or mystical rumination, and indeed any kind of speculation, serious or light hearted, which can be spun out of the verses of Holy Writ'.

At the age of nine my contribution to this cornucopia was to ask the Four Questions, beginning with 'Why is this night different from all other nights?' – or, in my father's annual joke, 'Why is this knight different from all other knights?', asked King Arthur about Sir Lancelot. That year we joined the Abrams family for the Seder, and I remember sitting round the big table in their spacious dining room. Our apartment was not big enough for a double family gathering. The Abrams had two daughters, Janey and Judy, both younger than me, Janey I think about the same age as Liz. I remember the giggles when we hunted for the hidden matzos. I don't remember if I was nervous, but I think I acquitted myself reasonably well. I knew that in orthodox households the questions were asked by the youngest male present. I had to show that girls could do it too.

I have always enjoyed Passover. It is, like most Jewish festivals, a powerful fusion of continuity with the past and the coming together of family and friends. It is a challenge to dispersal and fragmentation. It is richly and consciously steeped in tradition and fable, yet hasn't lost its connection with a key episode in Jewish experience, nor has it grown soggy with sentiment.

Christmas was a very different kind of celebration, for we invented our own. Until they came to the United States in 1937 Christmas had featured not at all in my father's life, except as something which concerned others, and only insignificantly in my mother's. They both grew up in a Scotland which barely acknowledged Christmas; my father says there was no holiday from school on Christmas Day when he was a boy. But in their first bitterly cold winter in Chicago there were Christmas trees, lights, Santas, shops full of gifts and decorations... By the time I came to consciousness Christmas had entered the family.

Like most children, I loved decorating the tree, making Christmas cards and paper chains, choosing presents, the secret rustlings of wrapping paper. I ached with anticipation, woke at four in the morning, and still find it hard to describe that moment of incomparable, magical excitement when we went into the living room on Christmas morning to find the tree ablaze with lights and brightly wrapped presents heaped underneath it. My pleasure in what we cheerfully celebrated as a pagan midwinter festival has never diminished. In the early years of our marriage Angus and I, first just ourselves, then with one and later two small daughters, joined my family for Christmas in Sussex. We usually arrived on Christmas Eve and I suspect I have always unconsciously tried to replicate the warm kitchen redolent with good smells, my mother presiding, which greeted our arrival off the train from London.

The afternoon of Christmas Eve my mother and I continued the kitchen busy-ness, making stuffing perhaps, peeling spuds, chopping vegetables for my mother's 'Christmas soup', and always with the radio on for the carol service from King's College Chapel. It is a ritual I maintain – culinary activities on Christmas Eve afternoon and 'Once in Royal David's City'. Royal David. My father, David, claims a family line that leads back to royal David. He shares it, presumably, with millions of others.

But there are new traditions. My children were already grown up when I started to make bagels (years before you could buy them in supermarkets) and now bagels for breakfast are an essential of our family Christmas. We build and rebuild traditions. The first Christmas with my daughter Rachel in Cardiff she produced home-made bagels. I hope the next generation will grow up believing that bagels are as much a part of Christmas as mince pies.

I can never be Jewish in the way my father is, nor indeed in any way that would be recognised by a serious adherent. But I believe that a talent for celebration is one of the explanations for the survival of Judaism, and that the richest, most resonant celebrations incorporate rituals and traditions, which evolve and mutate according to individual circumstances. So the celebration of Christmas helps me to feel, if not to be, Jewish. And every festival in which I have no place is a reminder of what I am. It's a kind of negative identity. I feel uncomfortable at a church service because I have no way of explaining my presence there. It is not just that I am not a Christian, but that all the social expectations surrounding churchgoing are absent. On the rare occasions when I have gone to church I have felt alien. Being Jewish, however vestigially, encompasses alienation; a reminder of being alien is, almost inevitably, a reminder of Jewishness.

In the United States I was aware that Jews were different but not that they were alien. They were part of a patchwork of difference. That changed when we went to England. More precisely, it changed when I went to grammar school in Cambridge in 1952. I began to pick up echoes that disturbed me. In the private preparatory school I went to at first we had a service every morning, sang hymns, and said grace before school lunch. It had all been rather jolly. At the Perse School for Girls the whole school assembled for prayers at the start of the school day, presided over by the headmistress. Miss Scott had a habit of holding her head slightly on one side, her hair scraped back, with an expression of glum piety. I felt I shouldn't be there, but neither did I want to draw attention to myself by getting my parents to request that I was excused prayers. My father, of course, had always been excused prayers at school. My parents' view was that it was up to me. I agonised over this dilemma, lying awake at night trying to figure out a way of making myself feel better. I liked singing the hymns. In the end I continued going to prayers and crossed my fingers whenever there was mention of the New Testament.

In fact, the prayers dilemma was more easily resolved than a much more insidious problem. In each year there were two parallel classes, and there was a Jewish girl in the class parallel to mine. Her name, Shoenberg, identified her immediately, while my name was more ambiguous. It wasn't long before I heard other girls talk about her – she was Jewish, she was different, she was odd. Years later Ann Shoenberg and I would become good friends, but at this stage, we had little contact. From a distance I admired her. She seemed to cope quite straightforwardly with her Jewishness. I, still struggling to be English, did not want to be thought different or odd. Gradually I realised that, whatever I thought I wanted, I did not and could not fit into a conventional, conservative, English environment. I felt my incompatibility must have been obvious.

I never said a word about being Jewish. It was bad enough being laughed at because of lingering American pronunciations of words. I didn't want to add another layer to my differences. As I grew older I became less reticent, but I was remarkably successful in disguising this part of who I was. Immediately on leaving school I went to Israel. A friend reported a conversation with my Classics teacher, who asked what I was doing. When told that I was spending a few months in Israel the response was, 'What on earth for?' The teacher had no idea that I had a Jewish connection.

The subterfuges imposed by school increasingly angered and disturbed me, and this may have contributed to a growing interest in my Jewish inheritance. I think I was eleven when I first learnt about the Holocaust. The revelation took place in the living room of the house we moved into in the summer of 1952, the first house my parents ever owned. I don't remember how the subject came up – perhaps my father felt it was time I knew. He sat in his usual chair, my mother opposite, and told me about the concentration camps and the murder of six million Jews. I knew about Hitler, of course. I vaguely remembered the war. I'd heard the phrase 'concentration camp'. (My daughter Gowan tells me that when she first heard the word she thought it meant a special place where you had to concentrate extra hard.) But I didn't know what it meant. My reaction was of disbelief, that such a thing could have happened, that any human beings could do this to other human beings. At the same time, I couldn't not believe my father. I knew he wasn't making it up. Suddenly, the sense of Jewishness as a burden grew out of all proportion. Not only could it not be denied, I dimly perceived that it would be profoundly wrong to deny it. My father told me of the Danish king who, when the occupying Nazis ordered all Jews to sew a yellow star of David on their clothes, also wore a yellow star. I, too, should wear a yellow star, I thought. I, too, should defy prejudice and ignorance and persecution. But school was too much for me for some years yet, and it was a while before I was able to follow my convictions.

Taking shape on the horizon was Israel. By the time I was sixteen or so I was beginning to pick up a notion of a heroic little country putting socialism into practice at the same time as creating a homeland for displaced Jews. I read Arthur Koestler's *Thieves in the Night* (1946), which profoundly influenced the way I thought about Israel. It seemed to offer me a way of being Jewish, by embracing Israel rather than trying to engage with a complex tradition to which I was not fully attuned. Literature so far had offered me very little help on this front. I decided I would go to Israel. In the late Fifties my father was there, lecturing, and came back with names I could contact. I had no locus in a Jewish community, so didn't go as most youngsters went, as part of an organised trip. I just went.

I took my A level exams in the summer of 1959 and stayed on at school to take the Oxbridge entrance exams. As soon as I learnt that I had been accepted by New Hall, I left school. I sold my pony, and used the money for my fare to Haifa, by train to Marseilles and then boat. I had booked to study Hebrew in an ulpan for two months, but I had a month to myself before that. A contact of my father's was to meet me at Haifa. Beyond that was the unknown.

I set off on 2 January 1960. I was eighteen years old and had never travelled alone before further than to London. I had with me a large Letts desk diary in which I wrote something every day until 30 March. At Calais I only just got the train. 'I threw my cases at a porter,' I wrote, 'who went pounding up the platform looking for my carriage with me racing after him. There were thousands of people in the train which was very badly organised and took a couple of irate guards and lots of lost tempers to sort out. I finally got to my seat in a compartment with an English family – quite pleasant but v. British & Tory – a South African girl, a Russian born British citizen working in Paris, & his English wife. We talked politics mostly.' Politics? I have no memory of this; there can't have been much common ground.

Re-reading the diary now I am struck by how international the experience was. On the boat I met Americans, Australians, South

Africans, Israelis, Dutch, Germans, Spaniards... And in Israel I would meet people whose first languages were Hebrew, English, French, German, Yiddish, Polish, Russian, Romanian, Arabic. It was exciting. It changed my perspectives of Jewishness. And it profoundly affected how I thought of myself, simultaneously reinforcing and undermining my Jewishness.

I was met at Haifa by Dr Wittkowski, a gentle elderly man, in his seventies I think but still teaching. My diary tells me that the sherut, communal taxi, which took us to Tel Aviv drove through floods – a one-and-a-half hour journey took four hours. When we eventually arrived at the small apartment, Mrs Wittkowski, as gentle as her husband, had a meal waiting. The Wittkowskis, and their daughter and son and their families, treated me with a casual but warm friendliness. 'Everyone is anxious to make me feel at home,' I wrote in my diary, 'but not in any oppressive way. I don't feel that they are making a tremendous effort, just that it comes completely naturally.'

The Wittkowski family were wonderful to me. They showed me Tel Aviv and Jaffa, took me to markets and mosques, museums and galleries, introduced me to Arab and East European food, took me twice to the theatre. I also went twice to Dr Wittkowski's school and talked to two of his classes. On one of the mornings there was an air-raid practice, a reminder that Israel lived with an ever-present possibility of attack. We visited Givat Hayim, the kibbutz where Ruth, the Wittkowskis' daughter, taught. I heard about how, when Ruth and her brother were themselves at school, just after the end of the war, they spent many of their nights helping to smuggle illegal immigrants ashore, refugees from the camps who had made their way to Palestine in leaky, blockade-dodging ships. Their teacher turned a blind eye if they dozed off in class the next day. He knew very well what they had been doing. I felt I was on the edge of the world described in *Thieves in the Night*. Dr and Mrs Wittkowski had left Germany in the 1930s and spoke English with a German accent. Jacob, Ruth's husband, had been a prisoner-of-war in Jordan during the War of Liberation. Later, in Jerusalem, I would meet young men who had fought in the Sinai campaign.

My diary tells me that one evening I was taken to a Youth Movement meeting by a student at Tel Aviv University called Dan.

'The atmosphere was a mixture of gaiety and determination, not something you often find in England anyway. They began with singing, then a crazy play of Red Riding Hood, first in English, then Yiddish, then Arabic, then German. It was killingly funny and everyone roared.' Dan invited me to go sailing with him, but I had to decline as the next day I was off to Jerusalem – in spite of the fact that it was the sabbath.

The Wittkowskis were extraordinarily kind, clearly concerned not only that I had a good time but that I learned something about Israel. I was in Tel Aviv for over a week and after a few days I could find my way around and catch the bus back to their apartment block on De Haas Street. I felt I was absorbing a huge amount of information at great speed, too fast to digest or to think about how it might be affecting me. I was excited, dazzled even. Jerusalem would be very different.

I was to stay with friends of my parents. My memory is that the Daleskis had been in Cambridge. They were South African. I arrived at a bad time – they had recently moved house, and had two small children and an elderly mother to look after. They were pleasant to me, but I was aware of strain and felt awkward. I explored the city on my own and tried to stay out as long as possible. Within a couple of days I'm writing in my diary, 'It gets more and more embarrassing. Mrs D yells and screams at Mr and the kids; they're all tired and harrassed about the house and settling in. It's rather hellish for me.' It was probably hellish for them, too. Mrs D made it fairly clear that I was imposing and suggested I moved into a hostel. I readily agreed. 'At last, today I am free,' I wrote in my diary.

I stayed for two-and-a-half weeks in the Anglo-Saxon Hostel in Rassco and got to know some of the odd mixture of mainly English and Americans who were there. There was Aubrey, an excessively talkative engineer, and Steve and Abbie, bohemian Americans whom I clearly took to – I describe them as 'a socialist couple from Harvard'. There was a Cambridge University student called John, a South African called Martin, an Englishman working for Kol Yisrael (the Israeli radio station) called Dave. Ben, a Canadian who also worked for Kol Yisrael, took me to the pictures – we saw *Imitation of Life*. Later Ben took me to Kol Yisrael and showed me round. He bought me lunch, and at some point I informed him that my mother had not been born Jewish, although she had converted after marrying my father. Ben told me that he couldn't possibly have a serious relationship with anyone who wasn't a hundred per cent Jewish. By this time Israel had challenged my notions of being Jewish in many ways but this was the first time my failure to measure up had been put into words.

In fact, challenge was everywhere. I was not prepared for the Israel I encountered. How could I be? I was just eighteen and straight out of a school whose only acknowledgement of Israel was in a geography lesson where it was still 'Palestine'. I was away from home on my own for the first time, and was often homesick although I did not admit it. (There is, however, a revealing page in the diary, dated July when I was in fact long since back home but written on 18 January while I was in Jerusalem. I am clearly missing my family and friends, and equally clearly feel that this is something that is not admissable in the diary's main narrative.) I did not know how to deal with people – neither the Wittkowskis' kindness nor the Daleskis' difficulties. And I wasn't Jewish enough to feel at ease in situations that were designed to accommodate Jews from every nation. The Friday evening dinners at the hostel were a test – I didn't want to betray my ignorance. I knew none of the rituals, none of the prayers, none of the songs. My family had not kept the sabbath, and although I had seen my grandmother light the Friday evening candles, I had scarcely paid attention to the words that accompanied the ritual.

I roam Jerusalem, on my own or sometimes with a companion. I discover No-Man's Land, the territory of rubble and shorn buildings that lies between the two Jerusalems, east and west. Since 1948 the city has been divided. I am warned not to venture into the area, although children play among the debris. I watch the dusty white UN cars moving through the Mandelbaum Gate. Norman, whom I describe as 'a little fellow with a beard' and wearing 'striped trousers, a sheepskin lined suede jacket, and a beret', takes me on the back of his Lambretta to Abu Gosh, an Arab village on a hillside about twelve kilometres from Jerusalem. Abu Gosh had fought for the Jews in the War of Liberation, because they felt they had benefited from their presence. We wander along narrow muddy streets flanked by crumbling, ancient buildings. The sun is setting as we make our way back, and the hills around Jerusalem are red.

On my first full day in Jerusalem I had met a young man called Alik, a telephone engineer who had come from Poland as a child. He spoke excellent English (and several other languages) and introduced me to coffee bars, concerts and some of his friends. They had all been in the army. Alik and his friend Mordecai had fought in the Sinai campaign, and were still reservists, as were all male Israelis up to the age of, I think, forty. They were liable to be called up at a moment's notice, and kept their equipment, including weapons, in their homes.

Alik was good-natured, lively and entertaining, with a fund of jokes. He treated me with affectionate protectiveness, as if he were an elder brother. I enjoyed being with him enormously. I had gone to an all-girls school, my own brother had been away at school from the time I was nearly nine, and I did not know what it was like to be friends with a member of the opposite sex without any ripple of awkwardness or sexual undertones. He invited me to a party at his flat, on the other side of town from the hostel. The 'party' was seven of us, including Mordecai and his twin sister Dina. We drank coffee and cherry brandy, played records and danced. Aubrey was there, with a girl from Mea Shearim, the ultra-orthodox district of Jerusalem, and a boy in the police force called Giddy. At midnight Alik escorted me back to the hostel. We hitch-hiked. Everyone hitch-hiked in Israel, even in the town.

On another evening I went with Alik to see Otto Preminger's *Anatomy of a Murder* – in my diary I describe the ending as 'rather weak'. That was the evening I discovered Alik was reading Zola in French. For the next weekend he promised a special trip. He and Mordecai were going to take me walking up one of the wadis outside Jerusalem, within sight of the Jordanian border. The evening before we went to a party, then back to Alik's flat, where we drank coffee and talked until one in the morning about 'the Arab–Israeli problem'. 'Alik was very reasonable,' I wrote, 'perhaps more than necessarily fair to the Arabs.'

The next morning we set off on our expedition, Alik and Mordecai carrying rifles. This is how I recorded it:

First we walked down the wadi from Jerusalem. It was lovely. There were almond trees in full blossom, little pine woods and groves of olive trees and lots of flowers. It was pretty rough going at times, clambering over rocks & jumping down terraces. When we got to an absolutely deserted place they taught me how to shoot. It's rather a wonderful feeling. I didn't think I would like it at all. It was extraordinary that when we did some serious target shooting I shot just as well as Alik and Mutty [Mordecai]. They were astonished. We walked along the wadi for about 15 km, then climbed a steep but not v. high hill to an old ruined Arab village where there was a lovely mountain spring. We made a fire and had a delicious lunch of hot tinned beef & bread & tinned apricots. After lunch we shot at the empty tin cans for about an hour before setting out for home. This time we walked along the road in the hope of getting a lift but we went for 6 km before we actually got one.

It is a day I have never forgotten, not just the events themselves, but the feel of it: the empty valley, the spring blossom and flowers, the reddish dusty rock, the proximity of the border and the hint of danger, the companionship of the two young men, handling a rifle, the thrill of firing and hitting a target, the ruined village (I don't record this, but almost certainly abandoned at the time of the war, its Arab population fleeing into Jordan for safety). Here was a new experience, another layer of the Jewish inheritance. But it was more than that. I had not before encountered anything like the comradeship which Alik and Mordecai extended to me. It matched an expectation I hardly knew I had, an expectation about personal relationships with a hint of something larger, something about communality and shared endeavour, something about helping to build a new society. I was not unaware of the paradox – drawing from these two veterans of Sinai an extrapolation that fitted my passionate belief in social justice and regeneration. At the same time, during this and my second stay in Israel the following year, I heard no one else talk of the Palestinians, many of whom Jewish Israelis encountered every day, with such good-nature and respect.

I continued to explore Jerusalem: the hills, the Tomb of David, the market, narrow streets, crumbling doorways, families living in the half-destroyed houses that edged No Man's Land, new and soulless blocks of flats to house the quantities of immigrants still pouring in. From time to time a Communist country would ease its restrictions on Jews emigrating, and there would be a fresh wave, from Romania, perhaps, or the Soviet Union. They had to be housed, taught Hebrew, found work. New streets ended suddenly in fields of stones. Old walls were pitted with bullet holes. There were places where you could see the Jordanian sentries just yards away and look down at life in the Old City, people in the streets, markets, shop fronts, traffic, and hear voices. Mr Daleski drove me out to Ramat Rachel, a kibbutz surrounded on three sides by Jordan. Wartime trenches were still there, and tangles of barbed wire. The kibbutz buildings had been badly damaged in the 1948 fighting. From them we looked across a rolling landscape of hills and valleys to the church spires of Bethlehem.

I spent evenings talking with Steve and Abbie and others at the hostel. There was quite a vigorous poker school going, in which I didn't participate. It rather interfered with conversation. I went out with Ben again, in spite of his reservations. We went to the Biblical Zoo and then for dinner. I think he must have paid. I read Faulkner and Kafka, both borrowed from Abbie. Alik had promised to phone but I did not hear from him for several days. When he did phone he explained that he had just got back from three days fighting on the Syrian border, having been called up in the middle of the night. The Syrians, apparently, had been fortifying a village on the Israeli side of the demilitarised zone. I met Alik that evening and we went to a cafe called Peter's, in a quiet street in the German quarter. He talked about his war experiences. The Syrian soldiers, he said, were much tougher and 'more civilised' than the Egyptians, for whom he had little respect.

On 8 February I left Jerusalem on the train, heading for Netanya, a small, scattered town on the coast between Tel Aviv and Haifa. I spent the next two months there, at Ulpan Akiva, a residential language school where I learnt to speak rudimentary Hebrew and met a great many more people who played a part in my Jewish education. It was a strange existence. I shared a room with two others in a recently built, bare block of rooms and bathrooms, with spasmodic hot water and occasional failures of electricity. Every morning except Saturday we had classes from eight to one. The only common language was Hebrew, and the basic teaching principle was that only Hebrew was spoken. (In fact, this rule was often broken, as Ilana, our delightful young teacher, spoke English and there were several English speakers in the class.)

On the first day I became Rachel, a change of name which, as discussed in Chapter Two, jolted self-awareness. I was surrounded by people who were also learning to respond to new names. Some clearly resented it. I had been in Israel long enough to be aware of the clashes that a young country struggling towards nationhood inevitably generated. In Jerusalem the different ethnic groups stuck together: the Germans, the Russians, the Poles, the South Africans. Old country ethnicity was often mocked by the sabras, those born in Palestine. And the sabras themselves had an image very different from the traditionally Jewish. The Vista book on Israel I had with me contrasted photographs of blond, confident young people with dark-haired victims of persecution. And indeed, Mordecai and Dina, sabras, were light-haired and blue-eyed. Alik, Polish-born, was dark and more conventionally Jewish looking.

Trauma and upheaval did not necessarily shake people's social expectations or their preconceptions about class. Deeply ingrained attitudes were easily transplanted. Old countries maintained their identities in the midst of the new, but the whole ethos of the new country was to reshape those identities. A Hebrew name was a start.

There was a strong emphasis on collective activity – a lot of singing, dancing, working in groups. I had begun to meet it in Tel Aviv. Now I found the ulpan reinforcing its language teaching with organised recreation which was designed to encourage the transmutation from Jew into Israeli. Most of the students were new immigrants, of all ages and from all over the world. Some, like me, had come to get a taste of the country and the language. All the younger people who stayed, men and women, had in front of them the most collective of all activities, service in the armed forces. Israel needed to protect its borders; equally, the forces could provide a highly effective means of creating a new, cohesive identity for newcomers.

I enjoyed the language classes and soon discovered a number of other ways of passing the time pleasantly. I had ambivalent feelings about the forced breaking down of inhibitions, but was nevertheless convinced it was good for me. There was never an option to refuse to join in, and in the participation there was a sense of release from Anglo-Saxon inhibitions. You had to speak Hebrew, however badly (I wish I had been taught French in the same way) or dance the hora, however reluctantly. I made new friends, in particular Helga, a Californian journalist in her thirties, divorced, streetwise and cynical. We spent a lot of time together. Though we had no classes in the afternoon we were meant to work. Often, Helga and I, and a few others – there was a rotund rabbi from New Jersey, known as 'Daddy', and his wife who were frequently of the party – would walk into town to the Cafe Antwerpia for coffee and superb cake. I can still recollect the taste of a lozenge-shaped chocolate cake which was my favourite. The food at the ulpan was awful and inadequate, and the temptation to supplement the diet was considerable. Cakes at the Antwerpia, fellafel or a paper of freshly roasted spiced peanuts from a stall, a bottle of yoghurt from the corner shop, all helped. As the weather got warmer we would go to the beach and lie on the sand reading and talking.

Every other weekend was free, two days without classes or activities. With Helga I went to Caesarea and Ashkelon, and to Akko (Acre), where we walked on the medieval fortifications built by the crusaders and treated ourselves to a meal in the Abu Cristo restaurant right by the sea. Akko was a fascinating mix of Christian, Muslim and Jewish, Arab, Turkish and European – different histories and traditions jostling each other. One weekend I set off with Eileen, who had grown up in Egypt, to Ein Gev, an old established kibbutz by the Sea of Galilee and under the Golan Heights. We arrived in Tiberias after the start of the sabbath, so had to negotiate for a taxi to take us the last stage of the journey. At Ein Gev we were casually given a spartan room to sleep in and taken to the communal dining room where we ate chicken and quantities of local produce. Kibbutz food was infinitely better than the ulpan. We fell in with a Belgian called Joe who gave us mint tea. He had served in the French Foreign Legion. Otherwise, apart from Yemenite friends of Joe's the kibbutzniks ignored us. That was a lesson. We were of no interest or importance to them as we had nothing to contribute to their way of life and work.

My diary reminds me that there were frequent parties at the ulpan (no alcohol, but lots of coffee and singing), long talks into the night, exchanges of life histories which ranged from Holocaust victims to privileged youngsters from Brazil, and a session the day before I left sitting outside in the darkness of a balmy spring evening making music on chalilim (recorders) with an American jazz musician called Mel. I got to know an elderly photographer from Czechoslovakia, a boy from Cuba whom we all – of course – called Fidel, an Italian who asked me out and attempted to start the evening with a snogging session, a young woman called Michal whom I clearly liked a great deal but have no recollection of... people who were in Israel for a huge variety of reasons, some from choice, some because they had nowhere else to go, some because their families had insisted. There was peroxide blonde Esther, a redhead from Finland, dark-skinned David. Mel was recovering from a nervous breakdown; for some reason, I ironed his shirts. Most, but not all, were Jewish in some way or other. The ingredients of a melting pot? Out of it all would a single Israeli identity emerge? I didn't think so then, and I certainly don't think so now.

I was back in England in time to participate in that year's Aldermaston march, the annual protest organised by the Campaign for Nuclear Disarmament which culminated in a massive and exhilarating rally in Trafalgar Square. I returned with experiences of my own to help delineate my Jewishness; at the same time, my three months in Israel had underlined what I did not have in common with those I met. I had learnt a lot. I felt equipped to deal with Israel, but that was not the same as feeling equipped to deal with being Jewish in England. What I wanted was to cloak my Jewishness in an Israeli identity, and I played with the idea of emigrating. But I think I always knew I was only playing. If in England I did not feel sufficiently English, in

Israel I did not feel sufficiently Jewish, and although I met others who were equally adrift it didn't help.

My second visit to Israel, a year-and-a-half later, underlined the features that I found hard to reconcile with other influences that were taking hold in my life. I went with Ann Shoenberg. We had both finished our first year at university, she in London, I in Cambridge. She had never been to Israel, where she had relatives; I was eager to return. We travelled by train to Athens, then by boat as deck passengers from Piraeus to Haifa. We fell in with a group of student actors from London, some of whom Ann knew, who were taking a production of *A Midsummer Night's Dream* to Israel. We seemed to meander across the Mediterranean in perfect weather. At night we lay on deck in our sleeping bags, talked, sang, conducted mild flirtations, watched the stars. If we stirred early enough we were able to slip into the first class showers before the bona fide passengers were around. We had bought food in Piraeus – bread, cheese, tomatoes, dates.

Ann and I spent six weeks in Israel, staying first with my ulpan friend Helga in her tiny Tel Aviv flat. She was now a journalist on the *Jerusalem Post*, Israel's English language newspaper. I was upset to find that I was unable to recapture the friendship I had enjoyed so much before, perhaps because I was there with another friend and Helga herself had a boyfriend and we were probably cramping her style. Then on to Jerusalem where we stayed in an empty flat offered to us by other acquaintances who were not yet ready to move in. We slept on the bare floor and lived on sesame crackers and cream cheese. In Tel Aviv and Jerusalem we retraced my earlier explorations, and then went on to a kibbutz near Ashkelon where Ann had relatives. There we worked after a fashion, getting up at five in the morning to hoe tomatoes before it got too hot, then preparing vegetables in the kibbutz kitchen. But in fact we spent a great deal of time in the swimming pool. I felt we were playing at being kibbutzniks; there was something unserious about it all.

We hitchhiked everywhere. Most memorable was the trip to Beersheba, where we stayed with an American anthropologist and his wife and small son. He was working with the Bedouin, and we repaid their hospitality by assisting with his researches, being able to spend some time in the women's tent, out of bounds for an American male. Our first meeting with the Bedu chief was in the back room of a cafe where he was illicitly drinking bottled beer. We then drove out to his camp where we sat on a rug on the ground and were served with thick sweet coffee by one of his sons. Then the chief excused himself, to reappear a little later mounted on a superb black Arab horse with a rifle in his hand and an ammunition belt across his chest. He and the horse showed their paces, galloping, wheeling, circling with grace and precision, the chief controlling the horse with one hand on the reins and the other brandishing the rifle. From Beersheba we went on to the Dead Sea, searingly hot, and the sea itself glutinous with salt.

Some time during my first year at university I met a young refugee from Hungary called Paul. His best friend was in an Israeli jail. He suggested I might write to him. I corresponded with Gyuri for several months, and when Ann and I arranged our trip to Israel I decided that I would visit him. By that time, I knew Gyuri's story.

He and Paul had lived in Budapest and were sixteen when the Soviet troops entered in 1956. With their school friends they had fought on the streets but then had to flee. Paul found his way to England where, when I met him, he was working for his A Levels and hoping to go to university. (He succeeded, and later became a journalist.) Gyuri and his family reached Israel. This was a family which had, miraculously, survived the Holocaust. Gyuri's father, a doctor, had been taken to one concentration camp, his mother with their toddler son and baby daughter, went to another. Gyuri told me of desperate hunger and how he had stolen a piece of chocolate which his mother had been saving for the baby. The guilt was still with him. They all survived, and were reunited after the war, returning to Budapest where Gyuri's father set up in practice again under the Communist regime.

Ten years later they were on the run. After months in transit camps they eventually reached Israel. Gyuri had to go into the army. But he couldn't take it, he couldn't bring himself to see Israel's Arab neighbours as the enemy. One night he crossed the border into Jordan, was picked up by the Jordanians and pressurised into broadcasting messages of peace to Israel. In no time at all the Israelis had him back. He was court-martialled and given a prison sentence.

I didn't keep a diary of my second visit to Israel, but I vividly remember going to see Gyuri in the prison outside Ramla, near Tel Aviv. In the midday heat Ann and I walked from the centre of the town, where the bus deposited us, to the prison. Our instructions were to be there at 1pm. The prison stood isolated in dry scrub land, surrounded by a high wall and barbed wire, with watch-towers at each corner. At the gate a dispirited cluster of people, mainly women and mainly Arab, waited to be admitted. We were made to wait a long time.

Visitors were divided from prisoners by a long bench and wire netting. We sat and waited again. I had no idea what Gyuri looked like. I was not expecting the tall, lean, tanned, handsome man in shorts and polo shirt who was eventually led in. His hair was beginning to recede. I knew he was a little older than me, but he looked older than I expected. We shook hands, we smiled, but it was hard to talk. I felt hopelessly young, hopelessly inadequate, hopelessly trivial. All around us were intense exchanges between mothers and sons, wives and husbands. Gyuri was more at ease than I, and talked in excellent English about life behind bars. He shared a cell with a murderer. His biggest problem was fending off sexual advances. He spent a lot of time reading and writing, and took every opportunity for exercise – and indeed, he looked very fit. He was having regular sessions with a psychiatrist.

We had half an hour, I think. When I was standing up to go he smiled and said, 'You look quite different from what I expected – much more attractive.' Shortly after I got back to Cambridge I received a letter from Gyuri asking me to marry him when he got out of jail, which he expected to do in a year or so. He said he would come to England. He did get out of jail, and he did get married, though not to me, and got a job with an import-export firm. Our correspondence petered out. Since my visit, in the summer of 1961, there has been a lot of fighting on Israel's borders and hundreds of deaths on Israeli streets. I don't know what happened to him.

I have never been back to Israel, partly deterred by right-wing governments, partly reluctant to visit as a tourist a country which I experienced in a rather different guise at an intensely impressionable age. In 1998, my son visited for the first time. Before he was allowed to board the plane at Stansted Airport he was aggressively questioned by Israeli security officials. He was targeted, I am sure, because he was young and male, although I am told that his experience is not at all unusual. The authorities were unimpressed by his letter of invitation to give a philosophy paper at a conference in Haifa and questioned him closely as to what his paper was about. Perhaps the fact that he was born in Kenya suggested that he could have Islamic connections. Departure time approached and they continued to grill him. By the time they let him go, at the eleventh hour, he was deeply shaken.

When Gideon told me of this experience I thought of Gyuri, whose Jewish identity was so assaulted, and thought about the transmutations of identity in the next generation, Gid's generation. Nothing stands still. Like everything else, identity evolves and changes. My family's embracing of new influences and its adjustments to different contexts has inevitably diluted the distinctiveness of both its Jewish and its Presbyterian inheritance. It is understandable why minority groups in particular resist that dilution, and has to be acknowledged that Jewishness has survived because of this resistance. The challenge is to find the right balance between conformity and openness to new environments which are themselves unlikely to be constant.

In the equation somewhere is the need to bear witness, the message of Primo Levi, not just in relation to the Holocaust but in respect of the whole of human activity. For me, now, Primo Levi is a fixed point in my sense of my own grasp on who I am, for he reminds me that I have a responsibility not to deny my Jewishness, however diluted it may have become. His writing is a beacon of humanity, a proof that whatever happens, even if it is beyond imagination, survival and creativity are possible. 'Troubles overcome are good to tell,' is the epigraph to *The Periodic Table*, the book in which Levi chronicles his own experience in terms of twenty-one different chemical elements. In the process he draws parallels between scientific investigation and spiritual and creative processes. There is irony in the epigraph. Much of the quality of his writing lies in the fact that he never 'overcame' his troubles – the writing itself is part of the effort to overcome. The telling of his experiences in Auschwitz is good not because these are emotions recollected in tranquillity, although a measured and courageous calm is a feature of Levi's tone of voice, but because it is an essential process. The troubles must be told. The camps must be remembered.

Telling implies communication. It suggests, too, continuum and community. Narration is important because life goes on. Indeed, narration contributes to that continuum, it is part of the flow and survival of the human race. There is community, because as soon as there is a listener, an audience, there is a relationship. And this relationship between teller and listener, writer and reader, is part – I think an essential part – of the network of human relations, of the warm and mutual support without which humanity, in any meaningful sense, cannot endure.

The relationship links generations and links identities. I think of Levi when I read of massacre in the Middle East, in Northern Ireland, in Kosovo. We need our story tellers, we need the keepers of memory, we need to unravel the narratives that give meaning to our lives, even when they are a tale of horror. 'I had the feeling,' Levi wrote in his preface to *Moments of Reprieve*, 'that I had performed a task, indeed the only task clearly defined for me. At Auschwitz, and on the long road home, I had seen and experienced things that appeared important not only for me, things that imperiously demanded to be told.' I remind myself that, however I represent myself, in Nazi eyes I would have been unequivocally Jewish. I believe it is important to keep faith with that. I shouldn't forget the schoolgirl wish to sew a yellow star to my coat. In the context of current events in Israel, keeping faith with a Jewish past takes on another, painfully challenging dimension. It becomes even more important to acknowledge my place in a shared heritage when I cannot condone the actions of the Israeli government led by Ariel Sharon. Identity is a responsibility, even a burden. All Jews should be able to recognise and understand Islamic experience, and at the same time all thoughtful people should be able to understand the way a passionate identity can become dangerously vulnerable. Amongst both Israelis and Palestinians, the young especially are being manipulated.

My personal need for continuity imposes on me a wish to keep faith with my rabbi grandfather – not keeping his faith but keeping faith with him – and with my grandmother who forfeited her talents as a musician to be a rabbi's wife, and with my father who built his own individual brand of Jewishness. My own children are even more distanced from the Jewish mainspring, but the Holocaust and every episode of human savagery that echoes it inevitably impinge on them, too. The ghastly paradox is that keeping faith with the past can lead to just those monstrous distortions of the self that allowed Germans to dehumanise Jews, gypsies and other 'deviants', and people of different ethnic or religious allegiance to perform the most appalling acts upon each other.

A crucial part of Levi's message is that what he calls the 'scaffolding' of life, the rudiments of the ethical, psychological and emotional support structures, must be confirmed and celebrated. For whatever sources of inner strength humanity might have (and these are vital too) it is the scaffolding, fragile as it often is, that holds us up, and because it holds us up we must, at all costs, preserve it. Faced with a machine designed to reduce the inmates of the camps to beasts Levi reiterated, in *The Drowned and the Saved*, the necessity of refusing to become beasts: 'even in this place one can survive, and therefore one must want to survive, to tell the story, to bear witness; ... to survive we must force ourselves to save at least the skeleton, the scaffolding, the form of civilisation'. Perhaps that's why, overcoming a degree of ambivalence, I liked Roberto Benigni's film *Life is Beautiful* – it is part of the refusal to become beasts. And why Charlotte Saloman's storytelling paintings are so vivid, so necessary, so searingly and painfully affirmative. 'I will live for them all,' she wrote. She died in Auschwitz, but her story and her pictures survive to bear witness, to keep faith.

A sense of personal origins is part of the scaffolding, part of 'the ethical, psychological and emotional support structures', part of the moral imperative that directs ones life. But like all good things it can become rotten and eat away the scaffolding to which it contributes. The result, especially among the fearful and deprived, is the loss and destruction of humanity. Primo Levi reminds us that identity is a responsibility. The fact that it is fluid, at times something that is forced on us, at other times something that we choose, makes that even more important, and often difficult.

CHAPTER FIVE
Learning English

I BEGAN TO learn English in the summer of 1951. We had left the USA in June and in the autumn I would be going to go to an English school. I was preparing myself to read in English, spell in English and add up in pounds, shillings and pence. I was trying to remember to use English words: 'autumn', not 'fall'; 'pavement', not 'sidewalk'. Up to now, I had not taken school seriously; there had been no need. My American schools had been quite enjoyable places to spend the day. I quite liked my teachers – I remember red-haired Miss Tyrrell at Cayuga Heights School. I liked reading. I liked drawing and painting a lot. One of the few school activities I can recall is an elaborate project on prehistory which involved the class painting a mural of cave families and men hunting deer and mammoth. I also remember a man who came to the school to tell us about the local Native Americans. He brought with him moccasins plaited out of some kind of fibre. He told us that if we kept our eyes open we would be able to find arrowheads on the lake shore or in the woods.

I have no memory of learning to read, no memory of ever not being able to read. A highlight at school was an annual book fair, with a feast of books laid out in the basement gym. My parents gave me money to buy my own book, entirely my own choice with no adult guidance. I still have three books, all by Marguerite Henry, which I bought there. One of them, *Misty of Chincoteague*, is about a herd of wild horses on an island off the Carolina coast. Marguerite Henry was an American writer of beautifully illustrated horse stories, but she was also part of my English education. Another of her books, *King of the Wind*, is the story of the Godolphin Arabian, one of the first Arab horses to be introduced to English blood stock. It takes the horse, and its faithful Arab stable boy, from Arabia to England in the eighteenth century, in a tale of mishap and prejudice that ends in triumph. It told me about London and Newmarket and English horse racing and class.

There are other books that shaped my anticipation of England. Two favourites were Noel Streatfield's *Ballet Shoes*, sent by my Aunt Ethel as a birthday or Christmas present, and *A Pony for Jean* by one of the Pulleine Thompsons. Both were about success evolving out of unpromising beginnings. Both were also about class. That was something English children's fiction seemed unable to escape. My aunt was very influential on my reading, because she always sent books as presents and of course they were always British. I never came across Enid Blyton, perhaps I was being steered in other directions. If there was some kind of censorship going on I was unaware of it. My mother read to us, and usually my brother and I got the same story, which generally meant that I was hearing a story pitched at a level rather beyond my age. I remember *Lorna Doone* and *Moonfleet*, *Treasure Island* and *David Copperfield*. My mother also read us *The Iliad*, which I loved, identifying passionately with Hector and the Trojans.

That summer before starting at an English school I had few worries about my ability to read, though I knew that English pronunciation was different and I tried hard to get that right. What worried me were sums and grammar. I don't think we did grammar as such at my American school, so from somewhere I got hold of textbooks (possibly also supplied by Aunt Ethel) and struggled to understand nouns and verbs and prepositions. I convinced myself that not only did I face the challenge of £sd, but that English children would be much in advance of me in their arithmetic. I tried to teach myself how to do fractions.

None of this came as a direct result of pressure from my parents. But I was absorbing an ethos of education that was quite different from the easygoing approach I was used to. I suppose it started with the discussions on where my brother should go to school, and then grew when my own educational future came into focus. Before our move to England became a certainty the understanding was that I, too, would go to a British boarding school. The school mentioned as a possibility was The Mount in York. The prospect both thrilled and alarmed me. When we knew that we were going to Cambridge, talk of The Mount was replaced by the Perse School for Girls. The parental view, absorbed by me, was that this was the best school in Cambridge and that it would be wonderful if I were to get in. This was a new notion. School was no longer somewhere to which you just went: you had to 'get in'. You had to take exams, pass tests. I was in my tenth year and had never taken an exam. But I'd show them. Being an American child was not going to be a handicap; in fact, I would show that I could be just as English, and just as clever, as anyone else.

We spent that summer of 1951 in Cullen as usual, and left, as usual, in September. Alan went back to school. Liz and I stayed with my grandmother in Edinburgh while my parents continued south to organise and settle into a rented flat in Cambridge. It was October before we joined them. My grandmother took us on the train to London, where my father met us. We got on another train and went to the buffet car. I don't remember what Liz and I had, but my father had a bottle of Tolley ale. It was dark when we arrived at the long platform of Cambridge station. We got into a taxi for the short journey to Bateman Street, and stopped outside a tall, semi-detached Victorian villa. The hallway was carpeted in red. I thought it was splendid. We climbed two flights of stairs. There was my mother. There was an excitingly new home. Liz and I were to share an attic bedroom.

Ever since, autumn has reminded me of Cambridge. Sometime in the first few days there we went for a walk down to the Trumpington

Road end of Bateman Street and across into the commons by the river, which are a feature of Cambridge. There were ponies grazing there. My parents thought I would enjoy them, which I did. There was a smell of the river and of dead leaves. The smell of dead leaves is still a sharp reminder of new beginnings – a new home, a new school, the start of each school and university year.

That first English winter was desperately cold. I was accustomed to cold winters, but in America we had lived in a centrally heated apartment and the only times I felt seriously cold were when I played too long in the snow, oblivious of the ice encrusting my mitts and my feet growing leaden inside my boots. I sometimes cried when I came inside to the warm and the blood began to flow. There was no heating in our Cambridge bedroom. Getting dressed on a winter morning was agony. In upstate New York I had a snowsuit and woolly hat and ski mitts. In England children didn't wear snowsuits. I had a winter coat which left my knees bare, and a school beret which left my ears uncovered. For the first time in my life I got chilblains. I was told that the damp, bone-chilling wind came straight from the Ural Mountains; there was nothing between us and the steppes of Russia.

Liz and I were sent to a small private school on the other side of town. There was a state primary school nearby, but my parents weren't happy with it. Again, the insidious tentacles of class were entering my consciousness. Chesterton Preparatory School was a small and rather eccentric establishment, a couple of buildings near the river roofed with corrugated iron. There were three teachers. Miss Hodder was the head, usually accompanied by her golden retriever Dido. Miss Honey taught the infants and played the piano, and a young woman called Bernice generally assisted. She was always known by her first name. As it was a name I'd never come across before I was particularly intrigued. There was a large garden, with climbable trees, and one of the college boat houses between the school and the river.

The infants were in one classroom, the rest of us in another, heated by a single coal stove. In the winter it was freezing, and we were allowed to bring our chairs close to the stove. There were five in my year, all destined to sit the Eleven Plus that spring. Helen was tall and blond; Elizabeth and Suzanne both had curly hair, one fair, one brunette, and John was the only boy and rather quiet. I got on fine with them. Suzanne was the liveliest, the ringleader in all kinds of games and ploys, which included rather daring enactments of mothers and fathers in which simulations of sex, pregnancy and childbirth featured.

The Eleven Plus was to be the gateway to the Perse School, which was only feasible if I got a scholarship. I also had to take an entrance exam. Miss Hodder's teaching was focused, determined and kindly. She was probably the best teacher I ever had, and I am sure I have her to thank for the fact that I sailed through the Eleven Plus, £sd and all, and was accepted by the Perse. She drilled me in sums, eliminated most of the Americanisms in my spelling, and had us practising IQ tests until we could do them backwards. She also tried to correct my loopy American handwriting without much success. She was teaching a classful of kids at different stages, yet I got more individual attention than at any other stage in my school career. I can still feel the cheap exercise book paper and the rough covers, and see the heavily pencilled rows of sums and dictation exercises.

When the weather was fine we worked in the garden. In particular, I remember taking our chairs out and arranging them in a circle for a reading lesson. I loved reading aloud. I had to read aloud for my Perse entrance exam, which ameliorated an otherwise formidable experience. My mother took me for the exam. The school looked grim, standing four-square on the corner of Panton Street and Union Street. We went to the main door, never used by the pupils, as I discovered later, who went in at a side door. I sat in a classroom to do a written exam, did my reading in another room, and was interviewed. Everywhere was that distinctive British school smell of disinfectant and sour milk.

Back at Chesterton Prep we learnt maypole dances in the sunshine and performed for parents. I was now destined for the Perse; the other girls were going to Cambridgeshire High School, the 'County', considered to be a cut below. But my summer term came to an abrupt end. After years of grumbling stomach pains, which endless tests and x-rays had failed to account for, I arrived home from school one day in agony. Acute appendicitis was diagnosed and I was taken by ambulance to hospital in Newmarket, presumably because there was no vacant bed in the Cambridge hospital Addenbrookes. I woke in the night after the operation with a terrible ache and a nurse at my bedside comforting me. Her presence in the greyish light and the softness of her voice in a ward of sleeping children is something I still remember with warmth.

I was two weeks in hospital, and after the first few days was up and about and thoroughly enjoying myself. The surgeon teased me into standing upright against the tug of stitches, the nurses were jolly, the other children intriguing. I was encouraged to help those much more ill than I was, and remember a small, pale boy who had polio and couldn't feed himself, and a girl next to me who wet her bed. Relatives sent me books and my parents supplied me with paper and new pencils and crayons. By this time my father had learnt to drive, and when I was discharged came to collect me in the Standard 8 which was his first car. We headed for home, but not to the Bateman Street flat. My parents had become home owners, and my appendectomy coincided with the flitting to the new house. It must have been a hellish time for the rest of the family.

The house we drove to was in the village of Hardwick, about six miles west of Cambridge. It was part of a row of three cottages. Two had been knocked together. The third, which we also owned, had elderly sitting tenants, Mr and Mrs Longstaff. When they died a few years later, the third cottage was incorporated with the rest of the house. I'd participated in the house hunting, bicycling with my father around Cambridgeshire villages. The house I really wanted was a thatched cottage in Comberton. By this time I'd succumbed to an image of Englishness: I wanted something old and picturesque, and was very disappointed when it was explained to me that the Comberton house was not affordable. But Chequers Cottage, Hardwick, was okay.

When I arrived my mother was at the door. My Aunt Beryl and Uncle Jimmy were staying, back from Sierra Leone where they had been teaching. (Aunt Sylvia and Uncle David were in New Zealand. It didn't occur to me then, but it does now, that for several years three of my grandmother's four children were overseas. My grandfather had died in 1945.) There was tea and chocolate cake, which my mother had bought from a woman who sold home baking from a van.

There wasn't much to Hardwick. It was strung out untidily along a single street, with a triangle of green and a lane going up past the church to the school and schoolhouse. It was said that the Roundheads had camped in the field behind the church and that a helmet had been found there. The biggest local landowner was Chivers, the jam people, and there were acres of apple orchards behind us. They owned handsome grey Percheron horses, which often grazed in the field next to us. There were two other farms. My mother soon became friendly with the Sadlers, from whom she bought eggs. We were invited to watch their television when my father was on the Brains Trust. In the other direction were the Fieldhouses, whose nieces sometimes came to stay from Lancashire. One was my age and later I got to know her. Her uncle bought a pony for her to ride when she was staying. She had a pronounced limp, I think a polio victim.

There were two pubs in the village, the Blue Lion across the road from us (now in the *Good Pub Guide*, but then rather rudimentary), and the Chequers next door, though the Chequers soon closed down. Sometimes my father would go across for a jug of beer to have with dinner. But the nearest shop, up on the main road, was over a mile away. All our groceries came from Cambridge, with a weekly delivery from Matthews in Trinity Street. The van driver lived out our way, and delivered on a Friday evening on his way home. My mother never learnt to drive. The Whippet buses (run by the Lainsons, the family of Diana who became my best friend at school) came down into the village only twice a week; otherwise, it was a three-quarter mile walk or cycle ride for the bus that Liz and I took to school.

In the 1950s six miles out of town was a significant distance. Even as a child it seemed to me that my mother was isolated, although it never occurred to me that this might make her unhappy. On Wednesdays and Saturdays she shopped in Cambridge, going there on the bus on Wednesdays, with my father in the car on Saturdays. I sometimes went too on a Saturday. A ritual evolved which culminated in a lunchtime drink at Miller's on King's Parade. I particularly remember one occasion, at the end of my first year at university. Term was over and I was back at home, but I'd gone into town that morning because my exam results were due to be posted outside the Senate House. There was a crowd of students and peering over their heads I could only see the top inch or two of the list. But my name was there – I'd got a First. That lunchtime in Miller's my brother bought me a glass of champagne. I don't think I was aware before then that you could do such a thing. It seemed gloriously extravagant.

Now it seems to me that the public posting of exam results is unnecessarily cruel. It's wonderful if you do well, but harder to take if the results aren't so good. At the end of my second year my father read the news of my disappointing Upper Second in *The Times* when I was still in bed, and shouted the result up to me. In an effort to cheer me up he suggested we went to the pictures that night. The only film on that I wanted to see was *The Magnificent Seven*. Westerns weren't really his cup of tea, but he endured it, though not without some brusquely critical comment.

Memories of the Perse School are dominated by the unprepossessing yellowish-grey brick of its exterior and a dirty looking pale green inside, although there was a pleasant garden with a large mulberry tree. It was a chilly place: in the winters we hugged the radiators. I began my career there on a September morning, dressed in my brand new school uniform of navy skirt, white blouse and striped tie, grey socks. Everything was stiff and slightly too big, but I felt enormously proud. There had been an approximate uniform of green and grey at Chesterton Prep, but it was loosely interpreted and nothing was enforced. At the Perse, being the same as everyone else was of the essence. I think even then, not yet eleven years old, I recognised my first day at the Perse as a transitional moment. I was not only starting a new school, a senior school with a high reputation, I was completing my transformation into an English schoolgirl.

I was wrong. I soon discovered I had a great deal to learn and that the transformation was far from complete. Indeed, it was never completed. At Chesterton Prep we'd had assembly and I'd learnt the Lord's Prayer and cheerfully sung hymns. It was unproblematic. At the Perse each day began with the whole school assembling for prayers. Each class filed into the hall in due order and with military precision. There were prayers, hymns, and a reading from the Bible by a prefect. It was all strange to me, and I was terrified I would do something wrong. Although I was one of many new girls, I felt doubly disadvantaged, confused by the messages of discipline and authority that this daily ritual conveyed, and dismayed by the implication that I was signing up to Christianity.

But there was excitement as well. New subjects to get to grips with – history, geography, French, art in a proper art room with easels, science, music. New teachers. New spaces. Netball and hockey. Clubs. Homework. Quantities of textbooks were handed out which all had to be covered with brown paper. At home we didn't have enough wrinkle-free brown paper and I wasn't adept at making neat covers. My books looked lumpy and ragged. There were lovely new exercise books on which name and subject had to be written. This was the real thing, I thought. This was authentic English education. No more Chesterton Prep eccentricities.

My class was a mixture of girls who had come from the Perse Junior School, old hands, and new girls like me. They, too, probably felt strange and uncertain, desperately anxious not to draw attention to themselves, equally anxious to make friends. My first friend was Rosemary, small for her age and known as 'Titch'. Perhaps that's why I gravitated towards her. She shared my love of horses and seemed slightly exotic because her mother bred Afghan hounds. Another friend was Wendy. The annual mass x-ray revealed that she had TB and she was whisked away to the TB hospital at Papworth. We wrote letters to each other in an elaborate code of our own devising.

My progress at school wasn't helped by the fact that I was often ill. My grumbling appendix was followed by frequent sore throats and sinusitis. Eventually my tonsils were removed. This was quite a different experience from my earlier stay in hospital. This time I went to Huntingdon, too awkward to get to for my parents to visit. I had a wretched week, told that if I didn't eat the food I was given, which was not easy with a raw throat (I had been promised jelly and ice cream but these did not materialise), I wouldn't be allowed home. I was castigated for reading all the time. Why didn't I play with the other children? On the day I was due to go home I was dressed and ready soon after breakfast. All the others discharged on that day were collected by their parents. I had to wait until the afternoon, and endure another grim hospital meal.

I was overawed by the 'clever' girls, three or four who had all been at the Junior School and seemed effortlessly to score high marks. It was not so much their manner that overawed me as the manner of teachers towards them. Facial expression and body language changed when books were handed back to the clever girls. I wanted to be a clever girl, but it became clear to me very quickly that it would be an uphill struggle. I did well in English and history, but wept and had nightmares over my maths. Most of the teachers were either dull and colourless or tyrannical. An exception was the games mistress, and I did quite well at games, never a star but a reliable team player. Although I had little interest in sport, and as an adult none at all, I played in the school netball and hockey teams. The latter could be purgatorial, hanging around on the left wing in damp cold with the action always somewhere else.

There were other exceptions over the years: a young English teacher who was radical in politics and unconventional in method (it was a revelation when she explained the language of Marvell's 'To his coy mistress'); another English teacher whose vivid personality had me eating out of her hand and whose barbed sarcasm had me boiling with despair; above all, a Classics teacher who seemed to belong to another world and another age, but whose Greek lessons were an absorbing cultural and historical journey. She taught me an enormous amount along the way, though I never really mastered Greek itself. In my Lower Sixth year she was my form mistress, and it was she who took me aside one day to let me know that, although I'd been nominated as a prefect by the staff, there were those who considered that I was not sufficiently dignified for that office. I was deeply hurt and furiously angry.

I shouldn't have been hurt. By that time in my school career I was known as a rebel. I'd stood as a Labour candidate in a mock election. Labour came bottom of the poll. I'd been overheard by a member of staff exclaiming 'bloody hell', and spotted by the deputy head outside the school premises at lunchtime without my beret, a double crime. I and a friend had slipped away for a walk in the botanic gardens, almost certainly deep in intellectual conversation. Our apprehension seemed extraordinarily unfair.

My best friend lived across the road from school and, legitimately, went home for lunch. I'd often go with her, and we'd make cups of instant coffee and play records on a Dansette record player. It seemed enormously daring, and I was never caught. Diana was also branded as a nonconformer, and probably each of us was the victim of guilt by association. Our friendship was cemented by this link, and has remained so.

I couldn't shake off an awareness of being different. My eleventh birthday present was riding lessons, for which I had been agitating ever since leaving the United States. At the stables was a gang of groupies, all girls, who had each adopted one of the ponies. They groomed, cleaned tack and carried out assorted tasks in exchange for an occasional free ride. Although I wanted very much to be part of this, I knew that I would never be able to break into the group. I hovered on the edge. Eventually, my dream of owning my own pony was fulfilled, but it came too late. I was fourteen, and growing out of my passion for horses. I became the owner of a black Irish pony with a rather stubborn nature and no great style, the best my parents could afford. The deal was that he was entirely my responsibility. I had to negotiate for a field to keep him in, pay for feed and blacksmithing, look after him of course, and chase him round the countryside on the several occasions that he broke through the fence. The latter activity was usually heralded by a visit from the local policeman to inform me that the pony was in an irate farmer's wheat field. Sometimes my father and on at least one occasion a local ex-jockey called Perce Stevens helped me track him down. The field he escaped from belonged to a delightful character called George who lived in an old railway carriage. He was a Yorkshireman, and had been a miner. His body was stooped, which he explained by the fact that he had spent most of his working life bent double in three-foot seams. His railway carriage was immaculate. He often made me cups of tea when I returned from a ride and chatted to me about his working days. He spent his time painting flower pictures, one of which he gave me. I do not now remember how he ended up in rural

Cambridgeshire. These days, I suppose, such a relationship between a fourteen-year-old girl and a lone man of over sixty would be highly suspect. To me then I felt it was a door into a different world, a working-class world about which I was eager to learn.

I struggled through my first years of school, not wanting to admit to myself that I did not like it and trying hard to do well. I longed for approbation but was constantly disappointed, and the refrain of my school reports was 'could do better'. Twice a year there were exams, and every time I desperately hoped for my name to appear in red at the head of each results list, red signalling an 'honours' mark of over 75 per cent. Occasionally I managed it; usually I didn't. And such successes as there were, were offset by the disappointments. For my first history essay in the sixth form, on Machiavelli, I got the only 'A', and I felt hugely pleased, but later my English teacher told me I'd be lucky if I got into university. No chance of hubris, then, about which I'd learnt in my Greek classes. No chance of self-confidence, either. Whether by accident or design I'm not sure, but the Perse School sent me into the world believing that I was both intellectually and socially inept.

By the time I was fifteen or so I'd given up pretending. I'd been aware from the beginning that the achievers received all the attention and encouragement, and the non-achievers were written off. I was in the uncomfortable position of having been identified as a potential achiever who didn't try hard enough. The school sent pupils to Oxford and Cambridge every year, and their names were recorded on panels in the assembly hall. Even those who went to 'redbrick' universities were not regarded as bringing credit to the school. This offended me, as did the elocution lessons designed to get us all speaking RP. I wasn't alone in my views, but that didn't mitigate my sense of frustration and vulnerability. In spite of all this I continued to aim high, and I knew my parents had aspirations for me. I applied for several Oxbridge colleges, but my first choice was New Hall, which had only been in existence since 1954. It sounded different, much smaller and less institutionalised than the other women's colleges. And its entrance exam asked only for a three-hour essay: essays I could do. I don't remember what I wrote on, but I was summoned for an interview. I put on my best tweed dress and sat in the common room awaiting my turn with a gang of other girls in their best tweed dresses. A day or two later there came a phone call with the offer of a place. It was with huge satisfaction that I left school immediately.

My political sensibilities were developing. I grew up in a leftwing household; in the 1930s my father had flirted with the Communist Party but I think it was probably from my mother that I absorbed my deeply felt sense of social justice. Wherever it came from, it was, and is, in the bloodstream. Over the Easter weekend of my last full year of school, with A Levels looming, Diana and I went on the CND march from Aldermaston to Trafalgar Square. For the first time in my life I had the experience of sharing in a collective effort for a cause I believed in passionately. For much of the time cold, wet and footsore, we trudged the tarmac miles, dropping in and out of different groups from different places. We shouted slogans with Oxford University, sang 'Blood Red Roses' with Liverpool, smoked Gaulloises, ate the sandwiches and drank the tea supplied by supporting groups along the way, slept on floors in school and church halls, and sampled our first half pints of bitter.

CND, the Aldermaston marches and later the more radical Committee of 100, imprinted themselves deeply onto my life over the next few years. I discovered the tradition of English radicalism and protest and got as close to sharing in an Englishness as I ever did. There was an exhilaration in being part of a movement, all the more intense for CND's lack of success in the early years. The passion and the commitment were real and exciting, and I met people who helped me to articulate my half-shaped ideas about the way the world should be. When I went to university I joined the Labour Club and the Socialist Society and continued to be active in CND. I marched the whole route from Aldermaston to London on three successive years, and part of the route for several following years. I read George Orwell and the *New Left Review*. I canvassed and knocked up for the Labour Party. I took part in campaigns and went on demonstrations. I learnt the meaning of the word 'comradeship'.

In September 1961 I was arrested when sitting down in Trafalgar Square with the Committee of 100. Most of the demonstrators had left by the time dusk closed in but a tight little group of us stayed. It was, I think, around eight o'clock when the police began to drag us away. It was dark and there was a fine rain falling. I remember the lights glistening on the wet pavement, the smell of police uniforms, the roughness of being seized and dragged and shoved into a van. It was frightening, but we were lucky. Years later my daughter was among demonstrators against student loans who were charged by mounted police, and my son and a close friend, taking part in an anti-Fascist rally in Bradford, were also on the receiving end of what certainly appeared to be an over-vigorous police response.

Sitting in the van someone passed me half of a lit cigarette which I smoked with shaking hands. I wasn't hurt, but ever since I've been able to understand those who regard the police as the enemy. It felt brutal. I spent a night in the cells of Rochester Row police station. It was a salutary experience, sharing with two other women a cell meant for one. One of the women had young children whom she was desperate to contact and her distress seeped into all of us. I lay on concrete and failed to sleep. I'd had nothing to eat since breakfast. The next day the world brightened when a cheery constable appeared with mugs of tea and ham sandwiches, and from a few cells along to my huge relief came the unmistakable voice of Diana. We were taken to a magistrate's court in an unfamiliar part of London, I think it may have been Wandsworth, and duly fined and bound over. We handed over our fines like lambs – no defiance.

I came out of the court into the sunlight. I was alone. Diana, and the others I had been with, must have been in a different batch. I wasn't sure where I was or how I was going to get where I needed to go. It took me a while to orientate myself. I remember standing by the side of the road watching the buses go past in an effort to work out which part of London I was in. I eventually got to Victoria Station and phoned my parents, hoping that they weren't worried or angry or both that I had failed to get home, which by then was in Sussex. They sounded neither. In fact, it occurred to me that they were perhaps quite proud of me.

It was a kind of initiation. I had won my spurs in a movement in which I believed. Those of us who had stuck it out and allowed ourselves to be arrested felt like heroes. We had put passive resistance into practice. But as the political climate hotted up and people began to use the streets more and more to express their views, their frustrations and, inevitably, to threaten the establishment, non-violent demonstrations faded into an almost innocent past. Within a few years much uglier confrontations were common. My rite of passage appeared quite tame.

It remained, however, an important experience. It knitted me more strongly into the radical tradition I admired, and was all the more important as there were other aspects of leftwing activity which made me very uneasy. I found certain conventions of the left alienating. The rituals of meetings, the self-important language of fraternity, the cliques and counter-cliques, the plotting, the boozing and the inflation of egos all made me uncomfortable. I went along with it, but didn't feel a part of it. It took me a while to work out why. Leftwing student politics, particularly at Cambridge University which I had entered in 1960, were dominated by men. The rituals were male rituals, the way meetings were structured and committees operated reflected male competitiveness. If you were female, you had no choice but to join in or opt out.

In my final year at Cambridge I opted out. For two years I had been on committees, attended meetings, for a while edited the Labour Club magazine, taken part in endless debates and discussions and plans in pubs and college rooms. My official explanation for opting out was that I wanted to concentrate on my exams. In fact, I didn't like it very much. But having opted out I missed the companionship and the solidarity. Both had gelled beautifully in the Easter vacation of my second year when, my parents away, half a dozen of us had spent a week in our Sussex house preparing for exams. We worked hard, knocking off at the end of the afternoon to take the dog for a walk, stop off in a pub, and get back in time to cook a late dinner. One of those participating was Angus Calder, whom I had known since my first days at Cambridge, but it was only in the following term that we began to spend time together independently of the 'gang'.

In this world so dominated by men I had few relationships. At the age of seventeen, a few months before taking my A levels, I had fallen for a young man who was in his final year at university. But the relationship was from the start tentative and fragile, based on a handful of meetings and secrecy. The university year came to an end, and I never saw him again. When I went to university myself I hoped I would meet someone who would obliterate that early disappointment. It didn't happen. Over the following couple of years there were two or three relationships which, for different reasons, all proved unsatisfactory. I was no longer seventeen, and my expectations of men were simultaneously too high and undermined by uncertainty. This, I am sure, was partly, perhaps largely, the result of going to a girls' school. My own children all went to a co-educational school and have good friends of both sexes and various sexual identities. In Israel I had discovered the possibility of men as friends, but, with one or two exceptions, that was unusual in the rarefied atmosphere of Cambridge.

I and my friends discussed sex at length, of course. There were widely divergent views – this is the early 1960s – of what was acceptable. One friend stated that she wouldn't even go out with a man unless she was prepared to sleep with him. Others were determined to save themselves for marriage. Diana and I agreed that if we met the 'right' man we wouldn't hesitate, and when the time came, we didn't. There was a degree of samizdat information about contraception other than condoms. Family planning clinics required a wedding date (one could lie); the alternative was to go private.

In the meantime, before the real thing, there were the inevitable false starts which, for me, ranged from the mildly enjoyable to the tedious. I had absorbed, mainly from my reading, an expectation that sex would be a generous and transforming experience. Such sex education as my generation received was confined to mechanics and morality. I had a couple of unpleasant encounters, both on trains, both involving older men, one arrogant and importunate, the other sad and apologetic. Most women have to deal with the consequences of what many men see as conflicting messages: women, and men too of course, want to attract but reserve the right to reject. It is actually quite simple and also totally reasonable. Denying that right denies the right to discriminate and select; in other words, it denies authority over ones own actions.

Sex education, like any other kind of education, involves teaching how to think and to feel. In most formal educational environments this is virtually impossible. Our education system demands the learning of 'facts' and assembling them in a way that will enable exams to be passed. This is not an encouragement to think, to ask questions, to learn how to relate chaotic feelings to the demands of ordinary life, to relate individual desires to collective survival. Arguably, all teachers should be engaged in sex education. It should not be divorced from history, literature, social studies, geography, art, music, biology, chemistry.

I did not discuss my feelings or my sexual activities with my parents. In my parents' home the bedroom door was literally and metaphorically closed. We did not, of a Sunday morning, pile into the marital bed as my own children did. But the closed door excluded us not just from what was, I believe, a deeply loving relationship between my parents but also from understanding the nature of such a relationship. Very often, children are only aware of their parents' relationship when it doesn't work. My belief was that my parents would disapprove of some of the things I did. Even in the weeks immediately before I got married my father grilled me about where I was spending the night and I felt constrained to lie. I was twenty-one. This was no major rebellion; I avoided confrontation by a certain economy with the truth. Some years later I did the same when my sister moved in with her boyfriend and my parents questioned me about what was going on.

At Cambridge, with women in such a minority, one was always conscious of being a potential target, and at the same time of being a second class citizen. This was manifested in all sorts of ways. The culture of Cambridge was overwhelmingly male. Almost all the lecturers were men, and very few senior academics were women. Although at a women's college, I was taught as much by men as by women. All the charismatic figures were men – FR Leavis, my own father, George Steiner. This mixture of being relegated intellectually and elevated sexually was uncomfortable. Most of my fellow students had also gone to single sex schools. Many of the men I met I found arrogant and abrasive. There were social snobs and intellectual snobs, and many were both. I remember meeting a man at a Friday night Jazz Club session – I can still visualise his rather loud tweed jacket though I don't recall his name – who as soon as he discovered that my father was a well known academic invited me to what he described as an exclusive party. He reeled off the names of various illustrious student figures who would be there (the only name I now remember was David Frost). I accepted the invitation but didn't go.

The symbol of the unequal status of women was the Cambridge Union. There had been earlier efforts to persuade the Union to admit women, but these had all failed. The ethos was that of a traditional men's club, and that was the way the men wanted to keep it. This was briefly punctured when I and five other women gatecrashed the debating chamber. In many ways it was a triumph. Women could attend debates as guests of members, but could sit only in the gallery. The plan devised by several leftwing Union members was simple, but relied on their participation. Six of us were invited to attend a Union debate. Shortly before proceedings were due to start we repaired to the Ladies, which was situated up the stair just outside the main entrance to the chamber. At a prearranged signal we slipped down the stairs, and with the help of strategically placed male co-conspirators were infiltrated into the chamber, whereupon six others vacated their seats and we slid into them. It all happened in moments, timed for just before the prestigious guest speakers took their places – one of them was Richard Crossman, who afterwards was said to have been furious at the disruption. There was a ripple of astonishment, but then Gill Boulind, who had a heart condition, fainted. Brian Pollitt, a Communist and prominent Union member (not privy to the plot), leapt to her rescue and carried her out of the chamber. The rest of us remained in our seats for a few minutes longer before making a dignified exit. We had made our point.

However, the next vote on the motion to admit women as Union members was defeated. It continued to be run as a men's club, excluding ten per cent of the university community, until after I had left Cambridge. There were some small advances, though. The newly opened Churchill College allowed undergraduates to invite women guests to eat in hall, and King's was the first of the older colleges to do the same. (At New Hall we could invite male guests to Sunday lunch.) Now, with most colleges mixed, it all seems unbelievably archaic, but that weight of male prejudice was a part of my generation's Oxbridge education. And feminism was not high on anyone's agenda. The men who supported the gatecrash acted less in a spirit of female solidarity than to make a political point. It was a way of needling the rightwing establishment, and of attracting attention. It did both, with some success. The nature of that establishment can be partly understood when I remind myself that among prominent Conservatives on the Union committee during my time at Cambridge were John Gummer, Norman Lamont, Kenneth Clarke and Michael Howard.

Male student company often made me feel diminished. Men talked confidently and, it seemed to me, cleverly. I felt unable to hold my own. Whatever the individual origins of those I met, the ethos was overwhelmingly English public school, privileged, pretentious and alienating. Perhaps that was why, for a few months in my second year, I was drawn to a boy who was none of these things. He was working class, goodnatured, good fun, and our relationship was easygoing, supportive, but free from emotional intensity. It began and ended without difficulty or reproach. I never managed anything else in the same freewheeling way, before or since.

My three years at Cambridge did not help me complete my English lessons. Although I learnt a lot about English traditions which appealed to me, overall Cambridge obstructed movement towards adopting an English identity. By the time I completed my degree my parents had themselves moved from Cambridge to Sussex, and I was aware that this was a liberation for my father. I don't think he was happy at Cambridge, although he and my mother had good friends there. I think he encountered prejudice of a complex kind and that rubbed off on me. One vacation I returned to my parents' new home near Burgess Hill (Buggers' Hill, as some of my friends cheerfully called it) when my Aunt Ethel was staying. She quizzed me about university, and everyone, including myself, was very taken aback when my response to her questioning was to burst into tears and say I hated it.

In the middle of my final year I had a minor nervous breakdown. It took the form of paralysis. I could hardly move, literally found it difficult to put one foot in front of the other. I couldn't sleep, but could hardly get myself out of bed in the morning. I couldn't concentrate. Reading a book or writing an essay was beyond me. Although I saw a doctor and a psychologist, it was my tutor at New Hall, Robin Hammond, who rescued me. Don't attempt to work, she said. Make a list of things that you'd like to do, as if you were on holiday and had no responsibilities at all. Then go and do them. I followed her advice. I was prescribed anti-depressants, but it was the fact that I had been officially 'allowed' not to work that made it possible for me to get better.

I spent time in the Fitzwilliam Museum. I went to Ely Cathedral. I listened to music – all through my university years I went back over and over again to Miles Davis and Mozart. I still do. I went to see Diana in London. She and Angus were the only people, other than my parents, whom I told of what I was going through. I couldn't bear to admit to other friends that I hadn't been able to cope; it seemed a terrible admission of defeat. For two months I made no attempt to work. In April I gradually began to get back to my books, in gentle stages. Part II of the Tripos began in mid-May. In the middle of all this Angus and I, who had been going out together seriously since the previous October, had a period of hiatus. He didn't know how to deal with this crisis and backed away from it. I found this hurtful, but we got back on track, and within a couple of months had decided to get married.

It was the winter of early 1963 that shaped our relationship. That year began with snow and temperatures stayed below freezing for weeks. The gas pressure dropped and we crouched over gas fires barely alight with a thin blue flame. The Cam froze. I had a room in the New Hall building in Silver Street, where the garden sloped down to the river, and Angus was in King's College. We could walk on the river between the two buildings, which made nonsense of the locked gates whose purpose was to keep students in or out of their respective premises. I could leave King's in the small hours and walk on the river back to New Hall, having arranged for an accomplice to unlock the back door.

My experience of Englishness was skewed by Cambridge. Perhaps if I had gone elsewhere, to a provincial redbrick university, or even to a Scottish university (which I never seriously thought of doing), I would have been happier and felt less isolated. But part of the problem was my own reluctance to admit to isolation. I had close women friends, particularly Penny, also reading English, with whom I spent long and happy hours talking about literature, boyfriends, and most aspects of student life. New Hall itself was still in its early years, small and relatively uninstitutionalised, and it seemed to me much more congenial than Girton or Newnham which reminded me of school. But even so I couldn't shake off the feeling that there was something I wasn't quite able to tap into, something that evaded me. And I was never able to put it into words.

It was books that made the difference. Although I strained against the limitations of the English tripos and longed to get to grips with the twentieth century, for which there were only limited opportunities, reading and writing were my favourite activities. My English education continued with Chaucer, Shakespeare, the Jacobean dramatists, Milton, the Metaphysical and the Romantic poets, the great nineteenth-century novelists, all mainstream stuff. I wanted to look beyond the texts, to explore the social and historical implications, to read philosophy and politics, and American literature, and was constantly pulled back by the requirements of examinations. Nevertheless, most of the work I did I enjoyed, and I enjoyed working hard.

There were moments of great challenge and satisfaction, although many of the lectures were dry and tedious. Penny and I had supervisions with Brian Jackson in which, among other things, we unravelled the sonnets and *Othello*. These sessions were rigorously demanding and wonderfully stimulating. I read George Eliot with passion. I went back to the Greek tragedians, grateful for my introduction to them at school. I read Donne, Herbert and Vaughan with wonder. Almost all the literary voices that rang in my head were English, or had become, like the Greeks, part of an English tradition. I wanted to broaden my horizons.

When the time came to think about what I was going to do next I looked for an opportunity to pursue ideas that had been taking an increasingly strong hold on my thinking. I wasn't particularly interested in another qualification, but doing another degree gave me the chance to explore the books and events that interested me. Shortly before my interview for New Hall I'd been reading Koestler's

Darkness at Noon (1941), in a paperback edition with a rather lurid cover. It had raised questions in my mind which three years at Cambridge had given little opportunity to think about, although we bandied talk of revolution and called each other 'comrade'. I'd also been reading Orwell sporadically. Here was something I wanted to look at, the relationship between political events and literature. By choosing Koestler and Orwell as focal points I could explore the 1930s as a political and cultural phenomenon on a European stage. It would involve issues of class and communication, ethnicity and nationality.

I was cheerful and relaxed when I tackled my final exams, which probably helped me achieve the first class degree I so much wanted. Angus, relying on his considerable innate abilities to make up for lack of work, got an upper second. We could not pretend that this didn't matter. That summer, with six others including Diana, we set off in an elderly Land Rover on a six week trip to Spain and Portugal. Franco and Salazar were still incumbent. Stowed in the Land Rover were socialist leaflets and we were intent on making contact with the Iberian socialist underground. We also planned to have a good time. With eight of us, the Land Rover was crammed. Ralph, who masterminded the whole adventure, organised the purchase of supplies and equipment, and allocated space. Most of the time we were hideously uncomfortable and largely unwashed. We only occasionally used campsites and the amenities of sanitation and showers. We made rudimentary meals and drank quantities of rough wine and rougher brandy. We zigzagged south, Pamplona, Burgos, Madrid, Toledo, Cordoba, Seville where Diana and I refused to join the others when they attended a bullfight, Malaga, Gibraltar, where we made a beeline for the pub and English beer. Then we headed west into Portugal. We camped outside Oporto, where we met up with Portuguese socialists and had a jolly supper of grilled sardines in an Oporto restaurant. We continued north. Near Bilbao there was a meeting in a small room somewhere, with a bottle of brandy. The boys taught local children how to play cricket.

It was a strange, memorable and in retrospect foolhardy adventure. On a switchback mountain road we nearly went over the edge. Angus became quite ill from too much sun. There were quarrels. I had recently come off anti-depressants and for much of the time was rather withdrawn. But I was about to immerse myself in two writers who in the 1930s had been embroiled in the Spanish Civil War and wrote about their experiences in the conflict against Fascism, Koestler in *Spanish Testament* (1937) and Orwell in *Homage to Catalonia* (1938). Spain felt like the right place to be.

That October, 1963, brought me to Birkbeck College, University of London – or, more accurately, the British Museum reading room (it wasn't then known as the British Library) and the library of the London School of Economics, to research literature and politics in the 1930s. It was also the month of my marriage to Angus. We moved into a rented flat in Islington, and lived in London, with one nine month interval, until the summer of 1968. I find that London now makes me literally ill. After a couple of days there I have a sore throat and a headache and am desperate to get out. But I enjoyed it then, even when living latterly in a cramped West Hampstead flat with two small children. I liked its diversity and its anonymity, the Cypriot shops in Upper Street, the exotic bookshops around the British Museum, the ethnic restaurants, although we couldn't often afford to eat at them. It was an antidote to the oppressiveness of Cambridge. I never felt part of London University, huge and sprawling, or even of Birkbeck College. I rarely saw my supervisor and the only students I knew were people I had known before. But it hardly bothered me. I got on with my work and my marriage.

In many ways the most English period of these years was the nine months we spent in the small Sussex village of North Chailey. We rented a house from friends who went to the United States for a year. After a small London flat, it was a treat to have a house and garden, with fields over the hedge, Chailey Common, birds and blackberries. Once I looked out of the window to see the grass covered with snow buntings. They must have been breaking their migratory journey. At Chailey our first child was born and I completed my thesis. It was a peaceful and productive time. Without a car we were quite remote, but my parents were not far away, Diana and her husband Nicky lived in Lewes which we could get to by train, and friends often came for weekends. It was Virginia Woolf country. One Sunday when Rachel was just a month or two old we went to

Lewes to have lunch with Diana and her husband Nicky and in the afternoon went for a walk on the Downs. It was before the days of baby slings and carriers, so we tucked Rachel into a shopping basket which Angus carried over his shoulder. There were appalled gasps from passers-by when they realised that we had a baby in a shopping basket. She slept the whole time.

In 1968 we left England and never lived there again. With my English education incomplete I spent the next three years in Kenya, an experience which defined an Englishness which I did not wish to be part of but which also opened new perspectives on identity. For the first time the colour of my skin was the most conspicuous clue to who I was.

CHAPTER SIX

Outward Bound

FIRST IMPRESSIONS of East Africa were red earth and brown skins. Both were apparent before the plane landed. Both were insistent signifiers of what I was not. The label 'dark continent' had been applied to countries of light and vivid colour by men from industrial Britain. My favourite photograph from three years in Kenya shows three smiling young men in orange, yellow, bright blue shirts, walking hand in hand in a sunlit Lamu street. How different from the London we had left; how even more different from the London described by Dickens or the Glasgow described by Edwin Muir.

My first lighting out had been to Israel. The constraints of school were part of what pushed me, an indefinable restlessness, a feeling that real life was out there somewhere and I wanted to track it down. The pull factor was the hope that Israel would help me to sort out how to be Jewish. What took me to Africa was even less specific. I came in the role of wife to a man who had been appointed to a lectureship at what was then the University College of Nairobi but which would shortly become, with the break up of the University of East Africa, an independent institution. For months we had discussed the next step in our careers, and working abroad was high on the list. Our thoughts flitted from India to Africa to South America. A lectureship came up in Kenya, Angus successfully applied. Would Mrs Calder be interested in doing some teaching also? She would. It seemed ideal.

It was less that we'd had enough of England, more that we wanted to spread our wings. We arrived in Nairobi in August 1968, with Rachel, just three, and Gowan, fifteen months. Shortly before we left the Russians had invaded Czeckoslovakia and brought the Prague Spring to an abrupt end. With a certain irony Angus was on a cricket tour when the news came through, playing the most English of games on village greens around Tewkesbury and Ludlow. He would play cricket in Nairobi, too. I had found it hard to come to terms with his passion for a game that he wasn't very good at and in which I had little interest. It seemed to me to occupy a space in our lives out of all proportion, as well as contributing to defining me as a wife. Cricketing wives were not expected to take an interest in the game, which was just as well, but they were expected to remove grass stains from white flannels and make the sandwiches for cricket teas. To refuse was a breach of solidarity with the other wives, and it was also to invite criticism – or so I thought. In the early 1960s the suggestion that a married man might be responsible for cleaning his own trousers was revolutionary.

So cricket was an issue, but I felt that it would be childish to admit to it being an issue. A few days after Gowan was born, when I was just home from hospital, Angus went off for a day's cricket. When Gideon was born he missed a hospital visit to play cricket. I was, of course, not happy, but I felt trapped. It seemed both a trivial cause for resentment and a disturbing disjunction of priorities.

We were met at Nairobi airport by Jim Stewart, Head of the English Department. Without Jim, his wife Joan, and their five children, we would have floundered desperately in those first weeks. As it was, they sorted out the convoluted bureaucracy of finding somewhere to live, invited us to their home, lent us blankets, utensils and all kinds of bits and pieces while we awaited the arrival of our things from England, and gave us invaluable advice. Jim and Joan were South Africans of Scots descent, but they had lived in England and the USA as well as moving around Africa. Leftwing and deeply committed to the struggle against apartheid, they had had to leave South Africa, and had taught in Lesotho for a while before coming to Nairobi. In the mid-1970s they went to Swaziland, where they died in a car crash in 1984.

The urge to define oneself provides motives both for travel and for staying at home. A sense of place is a reassurance of identity: your place, your people. A different environment sharpens recognition of the essentials of how we describe ourselves – personally, socially, nationally – and can also blur boundaries. This is part of the appeal of travel writing. It's not just the pleasure to be had in reading about exotic places but the challenge, vicarious on the reader's part, to assumptions about attitudes and behaviour.

The Nairobi that we came to was a curious mixture. Un-reconstructed colonialism was deeply ingrained, but in a nation that brandished its independence. After three years I remained uncomfortable with having a house servant, yet was very fond of Martha, who worked for us all that time, and admired her warmth and her skills. She handled a relationship that was the product of generations of white domination much better than I did. I did not like being a white employer of a black servant who lived in a small concrete box, the servant quarters attached to the university apartment block where we had a pleasant first floor flat. Martha cleaned the entire flat every day except Sunday, washed and ironed every day, and looked after the children when they were not at nursery. She babysat if we were out in the evening. When I was pregnant with Gideon she took on extra duties without a word and without being asked.

In return she expected from us, as well as a meagre wage and minimal accommodation, a kind of benevolent paternalism. She asked for money to buy cotton fabric to make into dresses. She asked for help with her children's education – money and advice. When she had to go into hospital for an operation she expected us to pay. It was all part of the deal, part of the relationship, and I had to learn as I went along. Meanwhile, on another part of the black/white spectrum, colonial ladies in beautiful suburban homes complained about their servants and shuddered at the encroachment of African neighbours as the Kenyan middle class began to buy the houses next door. When in our first weeks in Nairobi we went to view the apartment we were to move into, the incumbent tenants' dogs, confined to the balcony, began to bark loudly. 'Don't worry,' said Mrs Fuller, 'they only bark at Africans.'

Most of the university staff were expatriate, European, American and Asian, but there was pressure to employ Africans whenever possible. In the English Department there was one Kenyan, James Ngugi, later known as Ngugi wa Thiongo and forced into exile, whose novels we had read before we left England. The rest, apart from the Stewarts, were British. But the wider university environment was pleasantly cosmopolitan. We had Kenyan, Ugandan, Indian, Danish, English, Scottish, American and Canadian neighbours and friends. The girls went to an Israeli nursery. There were visitors from many other African countries, Francophone as well as Anglophone.

The students themselves were a mix of Asian and African, highly motivated, mostly older than university students in the UK, many married with families and adult responsibilities. They were a joy to teach; no other students I have taught have matched them in their commitment and alertness. And teaching in Kenya was hugely educational. Reading Jane Austen or Thomas Hardy through the eyes of Africans was a revelation. The students grasped with ease and delight the nuances and aspirations of polite early nineteenth-century English society, and equally responded to the elemental contests of rural Wessex. But I also remember teaching Tennyson's 'In Memoriam', highlighting the analogy of grief and rain, and becoming aware of puzzlement. Rain, in a country with long dry seasons, is a cause for celebration.

And all the time there was a sense of dislocation. Why were these young men and women studying the traditional canon of English literature? How was this going to help and inform them in the lives they were hoping to lead? Although I have always argued for the benefits to be gained from reading and understanding a good book, our teaching appeared to be reinforcing a dependence on a culture that, however relevant, was not indigenous.

The English Department, very much aware of this, was in the process of restructuring the curriculum to allow the introduction of new courses – more African literature, a course of European literature in translation, and American literature. The last was my concern. I was aware that I was being exploited by the university. I was employed, and paid, by the term. Much of the vacation was spent preparing for my classes and devising a new course in American literature, but I was not paid for this. I had no office of my own, and sharing an office with Angus meant that, inevitably, I was seen as an adjunct to his role. It wasn't a satisfactory arrangement. It lasted for a year. A new professor was appointed and additional teaching was no longer required. But who was going to teach the American literature course? A Kenyan was returning to Nairobi from the United States, to take up a senior administrative post in the university. A job was required for his American wife... she came to me for advice. Again, it seemed churlish to complain. Besides, I had a book to write and was looking forward to getting on with it, but at the same time I felt undermined. This was almost my first professional venture in academia (I had done some extra-mural and summer school teaching in London). I felt I had not got off to a good start, however much I had enjoyed the teaching and liked my students.

My professional identity would take more knocks over the years, until I gave up the struggle for the university career I had always assumed I would have. Later, I would apply unsuccessfully three times for a lectureship at the University of Edinburgh and once, in 1975, for a research fellowship. I was interviewed for the latter, by four men, three professors and the Head of Department. The first question I was asked was what arrangements would I make for the care of my children if I were given the fellowship. I was stunned, and completely thrown off my stride. I still sometimes wake up in the middle of the night furiously running through my head the answer I should have given.

When I was turned down I was told it was because the board believed I would do the research anyway (I was a married woman, and therefore did not need a salary), and was asked to do some part-time teaching (I was a married woman and therefore grateful to be employed for pin money). It was implied that if I agreed to work part-time I would be a frontrunner for the next permanent post. As it happened, I never carried out my research project, being obliged instead to write the book my publishers wanted to publish, a biography of RL Stevenson. I have no regrets about this, but it wasn't what I had planned. When the next permanent post came up I wasn't shortlisted and received no communication at all from the department in which I had worked for three years.

We went to Nairobi initially for two years. We were part of a university based expatriate community that was itself part of a larger and older expatriate presence. We liked to think that our lives in Kenya were very different from those of the white colonials, but we could not escape the fact that the first thing that identified us was the colour of our skins: before all else we were *wazungu*. There were large numbers of Europeans in Nairobi, tourists as well as residents, and there were parts of the city that could almost be Europe. Nairobi was at the time often described as the most 'westernised' of African cities. But first impressions highlighted all that was exotic, the smells, the dust, the beggars in the street, the contrast of splendid hotels and ragged small boys who found you a car parking space in return for pennies.

For the first few months we had no car. I walked everywhere, down the hill to the campus, to and from the shops, to the park with the children. On Saturday mornings I went to the market, which overflowed with fruit and vegetables, meat, and fish from the Indian Ocean and Lake Victoria. Many expatriates complained about high prices. Imported goods were expensive, and if you couldn't survive without Heinz baked beans and Kellogg's cornflakes your food bills were high. But Kenyan fruit and vegetables, dairy products and beef were all excellent, and for us, after years of living on student grants and fragmentary earnings from writing and part-time teaching, a new lifestyle opened up. We adjusted to expectations of plenty embedded in an environment of want. Welcome to the third world.

Most of our colleagues at the university were men. Most of the expat lecturers had wives who, in contrast to the old colonials, either found jobs when they arrived or did voluntary work. Many were as well qualified as their husbands and taught in schools. The imbalance was no different from what we were used to, and by and large accepted. In professional terms, the men came first. This was even more so in the African context. I was appalled by attitudes to women.

We sometimes found that when we invited a Kenyan couple for a meal, only the husband would come, with no explanation. At social occasions when wives accompanied their husbands the women would congregate at one end of the room, the men at another. Any woman who mixed with the men was fair game, and Kenyan middle class men were breathtakingly arrogant in their assumptions. They did not expect to get turned down. Among professional men adultery was commonplace, and aside from an occasional scandal involving a student it was not much commented on.

I found this blatant inequality disturbing and difficult to handle. I liked many of our male friends and colleagues but hated the way some of them behaved. There was a lot of radical talk, but where were the women? Socialism, I thought then and have thought many times since, begins at home. Kenya was beautiful, vivid, stimulating, challenging. I loved my time there, but there were nagging doubts. There were some alarming contradictions. Traditional tribal values were disappearing; politically they were seen as inhibiting progress, but at the same time tribal loyalties were exploited for political ends. Old structures were breaking down, including those imposed by colonialism. New structures were exclusive, vulnerable, manipulated. Kenyatta orchestrated an image of stability dependent on his own role, a smiling, bearded, paternal figure with his fly whisk. But if you chanced to be on the street when the presidential cavalcade processed from parliament to State House you were liable to be beaten up by the thugs who cleared the way for Kenyatta's Mercedes.

We were away from Nairobi, visiting Arnold Kettle in Dar-es-Salaam, when Tom Mboya, leader of the opposition, was shot in a chemist's shop in Government Road, and missed the riots that swirled along the bottom of our road. But we had been very much present when, a few months earlier, government response to student unrest closed the university. We continued to teach our final year students in our flat. Our comfortable middle-class existence was scarcely affected by this, although we knew many of the more radical students and staff, and it did not feel risky. But people were hurt. In later student disturbances, people were killed.

Angus threw himself into the heated talk, which involved long hours drinking beer. I was sometimes worried. The night the police moved in to get the students off the campus he vanished for hours. I did not like to admit my concern, but when Jim Stewart phoned I confessed I didn't know where Angus was. Jim came round to reassure me. Angus reappeared late that night. It would not have occurred to the company he was with that there was any need to inform wives of where they were or what they were doing.

After the first year my involvement with the university became vicarious. It was easy to keep in touch with students and colleagues, but much of the continuing contact was through Angus, who got more and more drawn in to a whole range of political and cultural issues. He was addicted to teaching, needed his students as much as they needed him. Sometimes this could be intrusive. Students (almost always women) often phoned him at home, something which it was clear to me he encouraged. On one occasion, I had cooked a special meal to celebrate our wedding anniversary and one of his Asian students phoned in a state of great distress. It wasn't the first time she had done this, but now she was threatening suicide. Angus went to see her. I would have done the same, but nevertheless I was angry.

I was working on my book, in libraries or writing at home. It became clear that I needed to spend time with better resources than were available in Nairobi, so planned to return to Britain in May. Our two years were nearly over but Angus had negotiated an extension of his contract for an additional year, which allowed us a period of leave in the summer of 1970. While he remained in Nairobi until the end of the summer term, I went to Edinburgh with the girls. I stayed in his parents' flat in Randolph Place, enrolled Rachel and Gowan in South Bridge nursery, and immersed myself in the National Library of Scotland researching the American West.

Mabel and Peter were in London most of the time so my stay in Edinburgh was quite solitary, except for the company of my two small daughters. It was the first time since our marriage that Angus and I had been apart for any significant period. I have the letters that he wrote from Nairobi, which indicate that in my absence he led a rather dislocated life. I don't know if I read between the lines then; doing so now, with hindsight, suggests his need for people and for involvement. Passionate as he was about his work, any chance of a slice of action was eagerly embraced. In Edinburgh I settled into a quiet routine, working in the National Library, picking the children up from nursery and if the weather was fine walking home through Princes Street Gardens. In the evenings when the girls were in bed I continued with my work. It was a pleasant and peaceful couple of months. In July, I went south to my parents in Sussex, and Angus flew to England to join us there.

By the time we returned to Nairobi in September I was pregnant. I did not enjoy pregnancy. I was not one of those who breeze through nine months of radiant happiness. I hated being slowed down and constantly tired. My third pregnancy brought all kinds of side effects, none of them serious in themselves but cumulatively demoralising and debilitating. I had backache and cramps and swollen ankles, and felt continually exhausted. I think living 8,000 feet above sea level was a contributory factor. I finished my book, *There Must Be a Lone Ranger*, in January and sent it off to Weidenfeld and Nicolson, just before the 1971 postal strike closed down communications. I was looking forward to having a relaxed couple of months before the baby was due, and decided to spend it re-reading Dickens. But after two or three weeks I was restless.

Although writing had kept me busy, even before finishing the book I was increasingly unhappy at what seemed to me an absence of relevant occupation. Angus was more and more absorbed by the university and all kinds of tangential schemes. More and more often he came home late after drinking sessions with the lads, while I was increasingly rooted by the need to finish the book and by pregnancy. Many of the students I had taught had completed their degrees; I was less and less in touch. With the book finished, I was waiting for the birth of the baby. When the baby was born, I was waiting to return to the UK and start the next phase of my life.

We made plans for our return. We had always talked about living in Scotland and now it seemed feasible to contemplate a life as freelance writers. Angus's *The People's War* had been published to great acclaim. My book on Orwell and Koestler had received a respectful response and my second book was under way. Somewhere within striking distance of Edinburgh would give us a first-class library and an intellectual focus. We thought of the Borders. We had ideas for future books and hoped there would be a chance of doing some teaching. We were both excited at the prospect of the Open University, which Peter Ritchie Calder had contributed to establishing and where our friend Arnold Kettle was going to be professor of English. I reckoned teaching part-time for the OU would fit in fine with childcare.

In June 1971 the flights were booked and the flat half packed up, tea chests filling the living room, when Angus came home one evening to announce that Andy Gurr, his professor, had asked him to stay on for another year. Angus was enthusiastic, already planning what he would do. I told him that he could stay if he chose, but that I was returning to Britain. There didn't seem to be a role for me in Kenya. It was the first time I made an unequivocal choice without any discussion, and I made it instantly. Angus was taken aback; he had not seriously considered that I would have other ideas. I already knew that he found it difficult to understand my needs when they diverged from his own agenda, or to acknowledge the strain I had been under. He had convinced himself that something he wanted badly would suit me too. It was the price I paid for reticence.

It is not possible to separate a specifically African influence from personal and professional developments which were at least partly coincidental. Three years in Kenya focused and intensified currents that were a crucial part of the experience of marriage, parenthood and work. When I returned to Africa twenty-three years later I was at a very different stage of my life and my perspectives had changed. I went alone for a specific purpose, and I had only myself and my professional needs to think of. It was a very different kind of experience, although it confirmed some of the lessons of Kenya.

I stepped off the plane at Gaborone with a sense of elation. The red earth and brown faces, the feel of the African sun on my skin, the smell of heat and dust, the timbre of African voices, flooded me with recognition. Africans hold themselves and move quite differently from Europeans, their gestures both more contained and more eloquent. I had come to Botswana to research my biography of Naomi Mitchison and was to be met by Chief Linchwe, to whom she had for so many years been friend and mentor. He was nowhere to be seen. But I noted a weatherbeaten middle-aged white man who was looking at me questioningly. It was Sandy Grant, with whom I had been in correspondence, who, knowing Linchwe well, had taken the precaution of coming to the airport himself. I had read enough of Naomi's experiences in Botswana to know that the odds were against Linchwe being there on time, if at all.

Sandy took charge of me, and without him my stay in Botswana could well have proved hugely problematic. He had lived in Botswana for many years, and had got to know Naomi in the mid 1960s. He took me first to his home in Odi, a few miles from Gaborone, where he lived with his Zimbabwean wife Elinah, their two-year-old son, and Elinah's older son. As a journalist and photographer he knew everyone and, even more usefully, knew where to find them. He knew when they were likely to be at home, at work or in a favourite bar. In a place where telephones were for the privileged his contacts were invaluable. With his help I managed to see many of those who had known and worked with Naomi over the years.

News of my presence and my 'mission' travelled fast, and within a day or two of arriving I was being stopped in the street. Was I the lady writing a book about Naomi Mitchison? And then a story about her would follow. On one occasion, in Mochudi, the village where Naomi had spent most of her time, a beery young woman greeted me with rapture: 'Lady Mitchison! Lady Mitchison!' I'm not sure if she thought that I was 'Lady Mitchison' or whether this was some kind of acknowledgement of what I was there for. But I certainly found that something of Naomi Mitchison's legacy rubbed off on me.

I recorded interviews with a number of people, and the high spot was undoubtedly the session with Kathy, Linchwe's wife, whose vivid and often hilarious account of experiences with Naomi I taped in the rather dismal government flat I was staying in. On the tape there are voices of children playing outside. In contrast Linchwe himself was guarded, answering my questions politely but without any elaborations. He volunteered very little. He bought me lunch at an expensive hotel and took me in his expensive four-wheel drive on a tour round some of the Bakgatla tribal lands, but conversation was a struggle. He was elegantly dressed, good looking, courteous, intelligent, but wary. He was a man of status and influence in

Botswana public life, and he knew Naomi knew him too well for comfort. Their relationship had been difficult and erratic. Naomi projected onto him her own passionate belief that Botswana could blend the best of tribal values with a progressive social agenda, and had identified him as the instrument of this. He had proved a disappointment to her but she had never given up on him. The impression I was forming of him was not very favourable. I wasn't sure what to expect, but Sandy expressed surprise that I wasn't invited to Linchwe's house. I had heard stories of his heavy drinking and his habit of picking up teenage schoolgirls who were flattered at his attentions and in any case felt unable to refuse their chief. It was no secret that Kathy was not happy.

There was a cool arrogance about Linchwe that I did not care for, and that contrasted sharply with the warmth and helpfulness of other old friends of Naomi's I met. By 1994, when I went to Botswana, my tolerance level for male arrogance was nil. I had had too much experience of it in its many different forms to have any inclination to forgive or excuse it. I had seen too many men parade their egos and demand attention, been patronised and required to thole the self-important too often, to have any remaining tolerance for men (or women) with an inflated sense of themselves.

I was relieved that Linchwe did not play the host as Sandy clearly felt he should have done, though aware that Sandy himself was irritated by Linchwe's expectations that he would supply the deficiency. I got the impression that he had been doing this for many years. But this did not impinge on Sandy's helpfulness to me, and was a personal sideshow in an experience of Botswana that suggested a country, with all its problems of a shaky democracy and the ghastly onslaught of AIDS, that in comparison with so many other African states has a great deal going for it. It was lucky to have been largely overlooked by rapacious colonialists who saw little potential in a land of which so large a part is desert or swamp. It was already independent when diamonds were discovered. Naomi Mitchison characterised the Bakgatla as good-natured and easygoing but unreliable. I was perhaps lucky to encounter more of the first two qualities than the third, but also aware that experience is shaped by expectation. In terms of research I came away with more than I could have hoped for, but it was also an extremely valuable personal experience.

Travelling alone inevitably brings encounters that bypass you if you have a travelling companion, and you inevitably respond differently if you are thrown on your own resources. There is a lot to be gained from the chance to reflect in and on an unfamiliar environment. I spent a few days in the Mochudi motel. I had some people to interview, but I also wanted to take time getting the feel of the place. The village is large and sprawling, and the only way to explore was to walk, so I wandered the dirt roads, checking off the places I knew from Naomi's writings: the library which she helped to found, the community centre, the kgotla, the school, the museum. The latter was up a hill from which there were wonderful views – red earth, outcrops of rock, the sluggish river, scrubby trees, scattered houses, cattle kraals. There were some traditional rondavels with beautifully decorated walls (Sandy and Elinah wrote a book about traditional house decoration strikingly illustrated with Sandy's photographs), but increasing numbers of corrugated iron structures. On the roads the ubiquitous pick-ups threw up clouds of dust, people walked in the slow, measured fashion dictated by hot countries, donkey carts passed, dogs scratched around. I felt simultaneously conspicuous and invisible. People knew who I was, but in the greater life of Mochudi I was of no significance whatsoever.

Naomi Mitchison believed she could get under the skin of Africans. I don't believe it is possible, even with the talent for empathy which Naomi undoubtedly possessed, to get under the skin of anyone other than oneself, and even to understand one's own feelings and actions can be difficult. No one with a light skin can understand what it is to be dark. Brunettes cannot think like blondes, or small people behave as if they were tall. All of these features bring with them their own advantages and disadvantages, and curiosity about how they affect personality and the way the world is viewed is a crucial part of creativity. Three weeks in Botswana reawakened a dormant love for the continent, but I had no illusion that I could trespass on an African identity. On the contrary. Like every other experience of another place, it made me more aware of what I was not, and therefore a little clearer about what I was.

I left Gaborone to travel by kombi to Johannesburg. Naomi had been proud of her status as prohibited immigrant to South Africa. Now things had changed; there had been a few months of a black majority government. I had planned to make the journey by train, but there were only two trains a week and neither fitted in with my needs. When I announced my intention to go by bus people shook their heads. Not a good idea. Then a proposal was made by Kathy that I should travel by kombi in the company of Esther, a friend of hers who was returning to Johannesburg from a visit to Mochudi.

Esther took me under her ample wing. I was the only white in the kombi and everyone insisted I occupied the front seat. At the border we had to get out of the vehicle and walk across the no man's land between the border posts. The paperwork took some time. Esther told me that it was much easier now than in the old days, when there was considerable traffic in illegal immigration and the authorities were on the lookout for false papers. We stopped again for refreshments, a sandwich and a coffee bought from a dusty deli, and had another unscheduled stop when a tyre burst. I had heard tales of the taxi wars, of rival drivers shooting each other and passengers getting caught in the crossfire, but there were no incidents. We headed south-east to Johannesburg through rolling country, partly wooded, increasingly green as we got more distant from the Kalahari, a few small towns, a scattering of farms.

In Johannesburg I was going to stay with Rachel Stewart, the eldest daughter of Jim and Joan. The bus station was teeming. I called Rachel to tell her I had arrived and waited for her to come and pick me up. Esther had left instructions with the man who ran the phone booth to look out for me. She assured me I would be okay so long as I stayed put.

Rachel lived in a jacaranda-lined street in a pleasant suburb of the city. There was a spacious park at the bottom of the street. But as we drove there she told me of a neighbour whose car had been hijacked by armed men. She had had to plead with them to let her recover her baby from the back before they drove off. While I was staying Rachel's son Benjamin was mugged on his way home from school. He shrugged and said that all they'd got was his maths homework. There was a locked iron gate at the entrance to the drive and the front door was always kept double locked.

Rachel's sister Clare had the previous year been murdered in Kwazulu Natal where she had lived and worked for many years. She had been closely involved with the ANC. Rachel was looking after Clare's two young children, in addition to her own Benjamin. All three children had African fathers. In many ways this Johannesburg household was more outside my experience than anything else I had encountered in southern Africa. It was an emblem of past, present and future Africa. The Stewart children lived their lives in the tradition established by their fundamentally decent, committed parents who lost neither their political nor their religious faith. The accident that killed them may not have been an accident. The death of their daughter was a political murder.

Also staying with Rachel was the youngest of the sisters, Alice, a New York lawyer, and her three small sons. We sat in the kitchen that evening and ate spaghetti in an atmosphere of cheerful chaos. In planning how I would spend my time the next day I was warned not to walk down certain streets and to avoid using taxis. A couple of days later Rachel, Alice and I spent a wonderful day walking in the hills south of Johannesburg. It was beautiful, calm and quiet, and we saw only a handful of people and distant herds of antelope. On our way back to Jo'burg we passed sprawling shanty towns. Everyone was expecting so much of the new South Africa. That evening Pete, Rachel's brother, came round for dinner, and the siblings discussed plans for a memorial to Clare.

This was family life. Sitting at the kitchen table, drinking wine, eating pastries which I'd bought in a classy bakery in Hillbrow, talking about the future but heavily aware of the past. A family of Scottish descent in a city founded on gold in a country savagely wrested from black Africans by the Boers who had first crossed the Vaal in 1836. The first of the Boer republics had a short life: founded in 1852 it was annexed by the British in 1877. The Boers fought back and in 1884 the Transvaal became again an independent republic. But two years later gold was discovered, and British imperialist ambitions were reawakened. The Boer Wars were Britain's last imperialist wars and saw some of the worst imperialist blunders. They were also a bloody rehearsal for the bigger and bloodier wars that were to come, and which intensified a national awareness to the point of grotesquerie.

Greed, and its handmaiden inequality, has dominated the history of the Transvaal and left a legacy which the new South Africa cannot escape. Part of that legacy are the layers of identity on which the whole political edifice shakily sits. Tribal and religious identities, ethnic and cultural identities. Identities that are crudely and confusingly obvious – black, white – and inextricably mixed – Rachel's and Clare's children, and the millions whom officialdom for generations identified primarily in terms of being neither white nor black. The Stewarts' commitment to South Africa is part of their inheritance, a much more important part than their Scottish roots, whatever the extent of their interest in their more distant origins. Their children, whatever their colour, are part of that commitment, just as they themselves are emblems of the commitment of their dead parents. They could have escaped this inheritance, but have chosen not to.

I was chastened by my few days in Jo'burg. I flew back to Scotland reflecting on how extraordinarily stable and unthreatened my life there was. How unusual, in global terms, and how lucky, to be living in a country where violence was rare, food and water plentiful, education and health care readily available. A country where, whatever the deprivations of the loss of employment, of drugs, of desperately awful housing, the vast majority of people have access to a decent life. That decent life, and the deprivations that parallel it, owe a great deal to Scotland's willing partnership in exploiting the less lucky two thirds of the world.

However much I hate spending time in airports, I love the sense of being on the move, the expectation, the uncertainty, the mingled anticipation and uneasiness about what I will find when I arrive. In the autumn of 2001 I travelled to a conference in San Marino. Northern Europe was blanketed in heavy fog and I missed my connecting flight, so it was very late when I arrived at Bologna and I assumed I had missed the last train to Rimini. I made my way to the airport information desk. There were no staff there, just two travellers who had the same expression, I suspect, of mingled anxiety and dismay as was on my face. It transpired that they were both going to Rimini and that one of them, a Norwegian, was heading for the same conference in San Marino as myself. The other, who was Japanese, had the train times: there was a midnight train to Rimini. A shared problem, a shared solution. Hans and I eventually got to San Marino at two in the morning, the streets eerily empty and silent. A little adventure, a modest traveller's tale... but one of the reasons for travelling, to be jolted out of easy assumptions of comfort and security.

The biggest jolt to these assumptions came when I spent three weeks in China in 1986. Nothing prepared me for China, although I had a theoretic knowledge of some aspects of Chinese history and culture. It was the most different, the most alien, place I had ever encountered. I met westerners who simply could not deal with China. The scale, the sheer numbers of people, the elemental disjunctions between east and west were overwhelming. I had wanted to go to China for a long time, and when my old friend Diana was seconded from her university job in Toronto to the post of Canada's cultural attaché in Beijing it provided the perfect opportunity. I had the benefit of her knowledge of the country and the language, and her contacts with people I would never have met as a tourist. I spent about half the time in Beijing and the rest travelling. Diana took me to the highlight destinations. At the Ming tombs, surreal avenues of mounds and sculpted animals, we picnicked on bread and cheese and Chianti and then walked round the ramparts. I noted in the diary I kept: 'every feasible space cultivated, even around the trees in orchards. Single-bladed ploughs used, pulled by small horses, donkeys'. I walked the Great Wall, which is quite stunning and extraordinary in the way it seems simultaneously to defy and imitate the natural contours of the hills. But Diana also introduced me to out of the way places I would never have otherwise discovered. We wandered through the hutongs in the dark, the narrow alleyways of crammed houses with barely room for a bicycle to pass. She took me to the Tanzhesi temple, a thirty-mile drive from Beijing, a thousand years old, sheltered by hills and trees, beautiful and profoundly peaceful. We went to first-rate and amazingly inexpensive restaurants, and with Diana I ventured onto a bike and launched myself into the terrifying torrent of cyclists that advanced through the streets like a cavalry charge. I explored on my own, too, hours in the Forbidden City, the dusty, seedy but magical Confucian temple, Beihai Park, and just generally wandering, watching, reflecting. Families shopping, boys playing football in the street, bands of well disciplined children on a school outing. I got lost and found myself in the hutongs again:

> Lots of open shops & carts selling food: fresh fruit & veg., beancurd from a cycle cart; also minced meat of some kind in great pale pink slabs. People carrying home their purchases in the palms of their hands as clearly no bags are provided... so I saw a woman passing with a chunk of bean curd in her hand, & another with mince in a scrap of paper. Bikes pass with a bundle of radishes or spring onions attached to the back. Cafes selling beer & bottled drinks. Around the station (& around the Palace) food sellers. People squatting eating bowls of soup or noodles, or rice out of polystyrene boxes.

I often found myself carried along by a dense mass of slowly moving people, buried, inconspicuous.

The dislocation of China was partly the result of a profound contradiction. Never had I felt so close to humanity and so much of humanity, but never had I felt so powerfully a deep-rooted and intrinsic difference in the experience of life. The whole framework, physical, mental and emotional, within which life was lived was strange to me. At the same time, you could not remove yourself from certain realities, and most of all you could not remove yourself from people. I took the train to Xian, a nearly twenty-four hour journey sharing a compartment with three men with whom I was not able to communicate. When I got off the train I found myself wedged in a compacted surge of humanity and their bundles and belongings. Beijing is a vast, sprawling, dusty city, and although stunning old buildings survive, much was destroyed during the Cultural Revolution. Xian, though also a large urban sprawl, was on a different scale. In Xian I walked everywhere, and everywhere life was lived on the street. People cooked, ate, washed themselves and their clothes, played cards and dice, bought and sold, argued and courted, on the street. The notion of private space seemed quite alien. Many westerners find this threatening. I found it intriguing, but I knew that I would be appalled to have to live like that. Having space and time to myself is, I feel, so integral a part of who I am that any prospect of being deprived of this is profoundly disturbing.

In China it is impossible not to feel intruded on by humanity. But although I had a few encounters with people who could speak English, and indeed, was sought out by some who wanted the opportunity to practise their English, most of the time I was unable to communicate, except in a very primitive way, with the people whose lives I observed. Most of all, though, it is the difference that I was aware of. In anglophone Kenya and Botswana my skin colour marked me out as belonging to a minority, a minority with a negative history. But in China there were many occasions when I was the only westerner among thousands of Chinese. In Beijing I was lost in the crowd, and anyway Beijing people were used to seeing European and American faces. In Xian and Luoyang, and perhaps especially in Chengde, where such tourists as there were seemed to be either from Japan or Hong Kong and over a long weekend, I hardly saw a white face or exchanged a word with anyone, I was stared at. I felt I was on another planet. Everything conspired to draw attention to my alien status. It was a salutary experience that made me intensely aware of myself.

I returned from China challenged and exhilarated. I have never been back. A great deal has happened there since 1986, and there is much to be found, in the cities at least, that is recognisably western. I imagine that these years of change, already in train when I was there, would mean that I would not now have so intense an experience as I had then. Those three weeks have stayed with me, vivid and absorbing.

The notion of travelling in order to discover who you are has a long history. In a sense it's the easy way. You define yourself by identifying what you are not. Yet both Scotland and Judaism have connections with China. Kaifeng in Henan province (which I didn't manage to visit) still has a population of Jews, who may have originally made their way there along the Silk Road. Scotland's nineteenth-century involvement in China's opium trade is well known, while Eric Liddell, of *Chariots of Fire* fame, is just one example of the Scottish missionary presence in the east. A friend of forty years is the daughter of Scottish missionaries in China and as I write has returned, post-retirement, to teach there. Some of us are more connected than we realise with distant and different places.

This is often the result of the fact that over the centuries travellers with disparate goals and motives have moved beyond their own boundaries in order to experience places that were then much less known that they are now. Today many forms of modern travel do not allow this crossing of boundaries, and indeed are designed to make them unnecessary. Knowing where our frontiers are is valuable, and their obliteration can contribute to our fear of the alien. We have access now to vast amounts of information about countries and cultures all over the world; paradoxically, it does not seem to help us to connect. In some respects we are less able to accept 'difference' than our nineteenth-century forebears. In the wrong hands it remains cultural and political dynamite, as events in so many parts of the world agonisingly demonstrate, and never more so than when it is used to distinguish groups that are in fact very close.

So do I travel in search of who I am? Not consciously. In fact, I sometimes find it has the opposite effect, confusing rather than clarifying the issue. A recent ten-day visit to New England just before Halloween vividly and almost painfully brought back my American childhood, yet underlined that it was lost forever. That is the consequence of time, of course; but it is not just that decades have passed since I was nine years old and trick-or-treating in Ithaca, New York, but that Ithaca, New York is not my place any more. This particular visit, more than any other to the United States, made me realise how much I don't want to let go. Nor is it reasonable to let go. I cannot consign that American child to oblivion, and no one should be asked to do that. It is perhaps something that the British, more than most, need to learn. To ask anyone to relinquish the place where their journey began is a profound and unacceptable invasion of the self. If 'multicultural' means anything at all, it means retaining a connection with origins, and having that connection recognised and respected by others with different connections.

I came back from that visit to the USA no clearer about identity than I have ever been, but very glad that I had felt that acute revival of my younger self, even though it brought with it an equally acute sense of loss. None of us can recapture the senses and sensations of our earlier selves, but it is important to reach for them from time to time. A reminder of what we once were is akin to respect for the ancestors. We all have a right to respect our ancestors, and part of that right is the retaining of connections.

I have made many small journeys and frequently cross borders, but I don't have to go 'abroad' to be reminded that home is now, and has been in fact for over thirty years and in imagination all my life, in Scotland. But feeling 'at home' is something else, and millions do not feel at home in the country where they have made their homes, sometimes out of choice but often out of necessity. And millions feel that they have more than one home, an ancestral home, or a spiritual or cultural home that is elsewhere. As this becomes so for increasing numbers, it becomes increasingly important to acknowledge the legitimacy and the value of multiple homes and multiple allegiances. There is nothing final about crossing a border: we do it all the time. Most of us lead lives full of departures and returns. They ought to make us more aware of the choices and imperatives that affect us.

There are dividing lines within Scotland also, the Firth of Forth which lies on my South Queensferry doorstep, the Highland Line, the Minch, the Pentland Firth. Scotland is famously a country of divisions and fierce local loyalties. Through the centuries these divisions have often been cruel and destructive, but they seem also to have shaped an overarching identity which, if it doesn't actually reconcile antagonisms, is less hostile in distant territories to what is not Scottish. Overseas Scots certainly have a reputation for being clannish, which is often cited as an explanation of their success. At the same time they have a reputation for openness to new cultures and experiences, which is also offered as a reason for the marked impact they have made in so many parts of the world.

The adoption of tartan as national dress is sometimes mocked by purists who remind us of its mainly Highland provenance and point out that the clans themselves are a Highland phenomenon. It might equally be seen as an icon that unites a historically divided nation, spurious perhaps, as most icons are, but nonetheless powerful, and recognised throughout the world.

Dunedin, in the South Island of New Zealand, is an uncanny echo of Edinburgh, which is explicitly acknowledged in its names. Founded in 1848 by a group of Presbyterian Scots in search of a new life, its architecture and its street names are Edinburgh transplants. Even its topography has similarities: Dunedin's Water of Leith is curiously similar to Edinburgh's. Dunedin, like other parts of New Zealand and many parts of Canada, reflects Scotland back to the Scots. When I walked in the city's George Street and Moray Place I didn't find it easy to accept this reflected Scotland. Edinburgh, surely, was the first, the original, the more authentic. But Dunedin, perhaps more so than Edinburgh, was made by Scots, like Pictou, Nova Scotia, or the Red River Settlement that became Winnipeg. You could argue that there is nothing more authentically Scottish than a community built by emigrant Scots.

Dunedin was once quite a different place. For around five hundred years Europeans colonised the world's other continents and obliterated or irrevocably damaged, often by design, sometimes by accident, many existing ways of life. We live with the consequences. One of the consequences, I believe, is the moral obligation to be aware of history, to remind ourselves of why we now have an inescapable relationship with so many of the world's migrant peoples. Recognising this obligation is a mark of a civilised nation.

CHAPTER SEVEN
Scott-ish

IN THE SUMMER of 1951, when we were in Cullen, a friend of my Aunt Ethel's, Sarah Cockburn, gave me a secondhand copy of *The Flight of the Heron* (1925) by DK Broster. I still have the book, though it's in bad shape, with the binding barely hanging together. I knew about Bonnie Prince Charlie, for I had immersed myself in HE Marshall's *Scotland's Story*. The penultimate chapter is headed 'the story of how Prince Charlie came home'. Not for long. The final chapter tells of the visit of George IV to Edinburgh in 1822, which is as far as Marshall takes her tale: 'And here I think I must end, for Scotland has no more a story of her own – her story is Britain's story.' I did not then ponder the significance of those words, although I had been brought up always to differentiate Scotland from England. Nor had Prince Charlie particularly captured my imagination, although there is a splendid illustration of him on a black horse in front of a cheering tartan army, captioned: *'Gentlemen,' he cried, drawing his sword, 'I have thrown away the scabbard.'*

The two other books in Broster's trilogy, *The Gleam in the North* (1927) and *The Dark Mile* (1929), were given to me by Ethel as my next birthday and Christmas presents. I devoured all three, over and over again. I became a passionate Jacobite. I fell in love with Broster's hero, Ewen Cameron, with the landscape that she described, with the cause, with the culture. Scotland took on dimensions that went far beyond my own limited experience and what I had absorbed from my parents. The sound of the bagpipes, especially when caught unexpectedly, made me cry. Later, I discovered the poignancy of Jacobite songs and laments, which I still find moving. Scotland does loss very well.

It must have been the summer of 1952, the first year we had a car, when I persuaded my father to drive from Cullen to Culloden, not a great distance but in our little Standard 8 a major expedition. We found a bleak stretch of moor, a few weather-worn stones commemorating the clans, and, if I remember correctly, no other visitors. It was the saddest place I had ever been. Culloden is not like that now. Now it is a heritage centre with car parks and information and hundreds of visitors moving over the signposted battlefield. It is a packaged past. I cannot help feeling that my experience as a ten-year-old of the empty moor under a grey sky was more valuable and perhaps more educational. I cannot bring myself to go again to Culloden.

It was the discovery of DK Broster that led me to Scott, although the first Scott novel I read was, curiously, *The Talisman*. By the time I was twelve or thirteen I was happily reading my way through *Waverley*, *The Heart of Midlothian*, *Old Mortality*, *Redgauntlet*, *Guy Mannering*, *Ivanhoe* and the rest. At some point I resolved to read every Scott novel; I was in my twenties before I achieved this. I developed the habit of reading in bed on Sunday mornings (as well as furtively at night, after lights out) and remember setting myself a target – fifty pages before breakfast – which suggests that I didn't necessarily find reading Scott a breeze. But I enjoyed him immensely, and still do: he was my gateway into Scottish history, as he was for his own generation. I read Stevenson also, but liked Scott better. I was an adult before I appreciated the subtlety and precision of Stevenson's prose.

At school in England history stopped at the Border. We studied the Stewarts, but the fact that they were Scottish kings hardly impinged on our understanding. James VI was always James I. We studied the Civil War but the fact that Cromwell's army had defeated General Leslie at Dunbar and gone on to occupy key positions as far north as Aberdeen did not feature. If I had not read *Old Mortality* I would have known nothing of the Covenanters. I don't think the Union of Parliaments got more than a passing mention, and Scotland's role in securing and administering the empire was overlooked. So my Scottish history was self-taught, largely through fiction and picking up bits and pieces from overheard conversations and from places we visited.

It's not a bad way to absorb the past, but it is necessarily fragmented. Scottish history came to me as stories and scraps, which then had to be pieced together. I still have difficulty, even after ten years or so involved in developing the Museum of Scotland's historical displays, in sorting out the sequence of events in the Covenanting wars, or remembering which James was blown up by his own cannon and which was murdered after the battle of Sauchieburn. But as I was growing up the detail didn't matter; what was important was the resonance and the way I responded.

I got to know some of the ballads through our family sing-songs (one of my mother's favourites was 'The Twa Corbies') and later through the wonderful voice of Jeannie Robertson whose raw and lyrical renderings of Scottish folksongs were a revelation. She came to sing at the Cambridge branch of the Saltire Society at the invitation of Helena Shire, an exiled Aberdonian. A few years later she came again. By this time I was a student at the university and had at least one of her records. Word went out that Helena Shire had invited students to her house to hear Jeannie Robertson sing. It was a lovely summer morning, and those of us who cycled out Madingley Road to the Shires' house had the unforgettable experience of hearing Jeannie, in her modest, no-nonsense way with her hands folded on her lap, singing unaccompanied in the garden. Among the songs she sang, I remember particularly 'The Galloway Hills' with its rich, yearning vulnerability.

It was with a real sense of excitement that I began to discover the treasure trove of Scottish folksong. The folk revival was making more and more material available. I heard Ewan MacColl and Peggy Seeger sing in Cambridge, Pete Seeger too; I was also hungry for

American folksong, and an avid fan of his and of Joan Baez. I bought
the early records of Robin Hall and Jimmie Macgregor and later of
the Corries. I wished very much that I could sing; my children can,
which is a source of enormous pleasure.

My exposure to Scottish poetry was much more limited. My
mother certainly read some to me, including memorably William
Dunbar's 'Makar's Lament', and I was aware of the names of
contemporary poets Hugh MacDiarmid above all. But I didn't have
any particular curiosity to read them until much later, and when I
did come to read twentieth-century Scottish fiction and poetry, in
my twenties, the absence of women struck me forcibly. I read Lewis
Grassic Gibbon, George Blake, Edwin Muir, MacDiarmid, MacCaig,
Robert Garioch, Sidney Goodsir Smith and others, by happenstance
more than systematically. But in a period rich with English women
writers, where were the Scottish women? I read Naomi Mitchison's
early historical fiction as a teenager, but only discovered much later
that she was a Scottish writer with books such as *The Bull Calves*
(1947) and *The Alban Goes Out* (1939) to her name. I had never
heard of Catherine Carswell, Nan Shepherd or Violet Jacob until I
was living in Scotland.

The notion that Scottish literary culture was predominantly male
was reinforced in all kinds of ways. It wasn't just that the writers
themselves were male, there was an overwhelming sense that women
were relegated to the background. Sandy Moffat's splendid painting
'Poet's Pub' is emblematic. He brings together the towering figures
of Scotland's post-war literary scene – Hugh MacDiarmid, Sorley
Maclean, George Mackay Brown and others – and paints them
drinking in Edinburgh's Milne's Bar. The single shadowy woman
could be a muse, or equally a tart. And was there any difference?
When my father entered that world, which he did from time to time,
it was clear that it was a man's world, a world of alcohol-fuelled
disputation, where debate was characterised by a willed contention.
I caught the flavour of this on occasion – the tradition dies hard –
and found the competitive environment deeply unappealing. But it
was more than that. It was hostile to women writers. As many have
pointed out – Joy Hendry, Janet Paisley and others – Scotland has
been particularly resistant to allowing space for women artists and

the legacy of that resistance is still with us, although the situation is improving. I look forward to the time when it is no longer necessary to highlight the literary achievement of women by producing volumes of ghettoised women's writing.

The university departments which teach Scottish literature and history are predominantly male. The senior management of Scotland's cultural institutions is predominantly male. It's not just that there are few role models for aspiring women, but that the insistent underlying message is that it's a man's world. Academia and the cultural scene are too often arenas where men perform in order to attract attention, often fuelled by breathtaking intellectual arrogance. The male role models encourage this: look no further than MacDiarmid. As men and women in Scotland unite in acknowledging his pre-eminence, not just in Scotland but on a world stage, his negative influence is reinforced. One of the functions of the hero is to legitimise unacceptable behaviour. Scotland has produced writers who are world players; almost all those recognised as world players are men; Scottish women have no wish to denigrate those men; their heroic status is further legitimised; where are the women?

I, of course, fell under the spell of the Scottish hero when I read DK Broster's books and accepted without question that all the significant action was undertaken by men (in novels written by a woman, although her use of initials suggests a reluctance to advertise the fact). Like, I suspect, thousands of small girls, my instinctive reaction to this was to fantasise about being a boy, rather than to dream of more active roles for girls. Scotland's best known heroic woman had her head chopped off. Things are changing, but sometimes I am amazed at how slow this process is. There is still an overwhelming sense that women are required to meet men on their own territory, that the smoke-filled pub is intrinsically more creative than the child-filled kitchen, that women intellectually and artistically are less serious and less substantial than men. I am still patronised by men, whether professors, building contractors or call centre operators. So are my daughters.

The most conspicuous ways of defining oneself as Scottish have also been appropriated by men. The enthusiasm for sport channels a powerful expression of identity, all the more so, it seems to me, because this is predominantly, though not of course exclusively, male territory. Male friends and colleagues, fathers and sons, bond over football and rugby. Historically in Scotland football developed as a means of getting lads off the streets and into healthy and cohesive team games. Because cohesion depended on division it also promoted rivalries, bracing maybe when focused on football, dangerous when they became ends in themselves. So local and national (male) identities become entwined with competition. Inevitably women join in, to reclaim this area of identity because it seems the most conspicuous.

Another overt badge of Scottish identity is tartan. Go to the Scottish National Portrait Gallery and what impression do you get of the wearing of tartan? That it is almost exclusively male. And when it is worn by women, it becomes less an identifier, more a fashion accessory. Queen Victoria may have adopted tartan because she fell in love with the Highlands, but most of the women who followed her lead had little or nothing to do with the traditions of the Gael. The impact of tartan lies in portraits such as Michael Wright's *Lord Mungo Murray* and Raeburn's *Macdonnell of Glengarry*, or in massed, mainly male, pipe bands.

I longed for a kilt when I entered my Jacobite phase, and was given one in the Ancient Mackay tartan. I took great pride in explaining to the uneducated that Mackay was my mother's clan, and that the old, vegetable-dyed weave was more authentic than the modern, much darker version. The Mackay tartan is subtle greens and blues, but I was also rather taken with the dark red shades of my hero Ewen Cameron's tartan, although I would never have allowed myself to wear it. There were Macintoshes, Robertsons and Munros in my ancestry, but no Camerons that I could find. But I also wanted to sport a sporran. No, I was told firmly, only men wear sporrans. It took me a little while to figure out the significance – but where were women meant to keep their loose change and hankies?

The gender division is not simple, of course. Growing up Scottish has been a dilemma for generations, as the signifiers of nationhood have been chipped away. There has been an element of confusion in Scottish culture ever since James VI rode south, to make only one return visit to the Scotland where he was raised. Perhaps the biggest cultural irony of all is that at the time when Scotland was seen as the intellectual centre of Europe David Hume and others were insistent that the Scots language had to go. He could say, 'This is the historical age and we are the historical people', but abandon the language that was the inheritance of a large part of the Scottish people. At the same time there was a rediscovery of Gaelic, but it expressed itself through translated traditions, and did not help the survival of the language itself. But if Scottish identity has been problematic for 400 years, it has been doubly so for women.

As it happens, I was writing the above on the 2001 anniversary of the birth of Robert Burns, and the radio that morning told me that around 20,000 celebrations of the bard were taking place all over the world. Burns is a figurehead of Scottish identity, and he is celebrated in a tradition shaped by men getting together to eat and drink, orate and recite. The tradition is part of the pleasure, but traditions can and do evolve. These days it's not uncommon for women to propose 'The Immortal Memory', rather than be confined to the 'Reply to the Lassies' slot – I have done it myself. But there are other ways in which we can remember one of the world's greatest poets. On 25 January 2001 my daughter phoned to tell me that she had invited friends to her Cardiff home for Burns night. They would eat haggis and neeps, drink Highland Park and Glenmorangie, read aloud favourite poems (not just Burns) and sing Welsh, English, Scottish and American songs. Rachel, born in England, growing up in Scotland, had lived in Wales for almost half her life.

All over the world there are St Andrews Societies which do not admit women members. Perhaps there are other ways of sustaining an awareness of Scotland and Scottish cultural influence. Two of the foremost interpreters of Burns's songs are Jean Redpath and Sheena Wellington. That it was Sheena Wellington who sang 'A Man's a Man for A' That' so movingly at the opening of the re-instated Scottish parliament made it possible to hear 'woman' as well as man.

As a child my Scottish environment was defined by Edinburgh, Glasgow to a much lesser extent, and the counties bordering on the Moray Firth. Places entered my bloodstream in a way that no other places have before or since. It is above all a sense of place that makes me feel Scottish. Edinburgh Castle and Arthur's Seat, the Firth of Forth and its mighty bridge, Cullen harbour and the Big and Little Bins, the ruins of Elgin cathedral and Findlater Castle: it is a feeling of kinship with landscape and landmarks which has little to do with belonging and everything to do with early experience. These places are part of me because I knew them as a child and responded to them with uncomplicated directness. I climbed them and crossed them and absorbed them.

Later my attention turned to the Highlands and the west coast. In 1957 there was a family holiday near Lochearnhead, staying in the same cottage that my mother had shared with friends decades before. So there was a nice sense of continuity in being there. The cottage looked directly out across the loch. There was no running water. We went to a spring that bubbled down a few yards along the road, and took our toothbrushes along to brush our teeth by the roadside. We bathed and washed our hair in the loch. It was that year that my father and I climbed Ben Vorlich, scrambling up in sandshoes. We had no boots or fancy jackets. We explored the stretch of country between Crieff, Killin and Crianlarich, and went to Balquhidder, with all its Rob Roy associations. I took a photograph, which I still have, of my father fishing in the loch on a very still evening, and the camera caught the clear edge of the ripples radiating out from where his line had dropped into the water.

The first Scottish holiday after Angus and I were married was in 1966, when Rachel was just a year old. We rented a cottage in Portmahomack, Easter Ross, with Diana and her husband Nicky. We swam in the icy sea, walked and bird watched, manoeuvring Rachel's buggy along rocky cliff paths. There was an expedition to the lighthouse and Tarbat Ness. We bought delicious bread and scones from the tiny village bakery; in fact, we ate very well as we were all keen cooks and Nicky was super-keen. From somewhere we acquired live crabs and before they were despatched they were crawling on the kitchen floor, much to the delighted fascination of Rachel. Angus wrote a poem about it. But we learnt a salutary lesson from Portmahomack. Rachel was still in nappies, and the nappies had to be washed every day. Without a thought I hung them out on the line on Sunday. Long afterwards my sister-in-law, Jean, who comes from Tain and through whom we had arranged to rent the cottage, relayed back the local comments: Portmahomack was not amused by washing on the line on the sabbath.

After we made our home in Edinburgh we had a series of Scottish holidays with the children, and gradually expanded a knowledge of the country. The first was in Galloway, in a farm cottage near Castle Douglas, the greenest place I have ever been. With the children we went to Threave and Caerlaverock and Glen Trool, and picnicked on sandy Solway beaches. The following year we went to Skye, and my parents joined us for part of the time. Gideon didn't like Skye. When we arrived, we unloaded the car and generally sorted ourselves out, only to find that while we were busy Gid had disappeared. We discovered him a mile or so down the road, back the way we had come. He had decided (he was two years old) that Skye wasn't for him and had set off back home. Skye has a particularly intense concentration of some of the most striking features of Highland landscape. Empty moorland, the jagged Cuillin, the ominous dark seas around Loch Scavaig, the fact that so much of the island is accessible only on foot, and every feature that much more dramatic for the chasing currents of sunlight and cloud which constantly play over the landscape. I hadn't then read the poetry of Sorley Maclean who grew up on neighbouring Raasay. I have now, and think I understand enough of the Gaelic tradition to recognise that the intensity of place in his poetry is profoundly a part of it. It is that intensity that gives Maclean's multi-national breadth such authority and emotional resonance. And I am quite sure that, historically, the particular nature of Highland sensibility towards place has strongly coloured the culture of the Scottish diaspora.

The year after Skye we went to Orkney. We spent two weeks in a cottage near Melsetter in Hoy, and we all still remember it as the best holiday of the children's growing up. The cottage had gas lighting and an ancient cooking range. Down the road was a little beach with a memorable piece of graffiti on a nearby wall. 'Vote for Jo', it said. This was Jo Grimond, Orkney's Liberal MP from 1950 to 1983. The beach immediately became 'Vote for Jo' beach. On the shore there were seals and sea birds, and a van came every day with Orkney butter and cheese, kippers and oatcakes, and fudge. We had Orkney crabs too. Our friend Tom Lowenstein came to stay bringing a rucksack of crabs he had purchased in Stromness, but these crabs were dead.

We went several times to Rackwick Bay which was usually empty. Three or four crofts were being worked at Rackwick, but their activity didn't take the crofters down to the beach. We knew that Peter Maxwell Davis stayed there sometimes, and that Rackwick inspired his music. It was easy to understand why. The cliffs that frame the bay are sensational, all the more so for the empty sands and the tumbled walls of abandoned homes. Just around the corner from the bay is the Old Man of Hoy. We made an expedition there, and lay on the cliff edge looking across to the extraordinary stack of rock and watching the puffins play beneath us. The children's fearlessness terrified me.

We quickly realised that Orkney is very different from mainland Scotland. I have been there twice since, and that difference was confirmed. The people of Orkney are Orcadian; they are as likely to look towards Scandinavia as mainland Scotland. Everywhere there are reminders of their northern orientation. It's part of the attraction, I am sure, for the artists and other incomers who have made their homes there. It is different. It is sufficiently far from mainland Scotland, and sufficiently big, to maintain this distinctive character and to convey self-sufficiency. The landscape and light are different, the wind is more insistent, but most of all the past is different.

I returned from a second visit to Orkney with Arthur, my companion since 1992. The chief engineer on the ferry turned out to be an acquaintance of his and we were invited up to the forecastle. As the vessel steered southwards we looked out on a vista of grey sea. Suddenly a black rim broke from the water and blew a fountain into the air. The whale sank again, no doubt to continue on its way across the bows of the ferry. That momentary intrusion seemed to reinforce a sense of reversal. As we approached the edge of Scotland's northern mainland I had a vivid impression of Scotland upside down, of the north as the bottom of the map and the south as the top, of the north as where it all starts and the south as the Ultima Thule. Turn the map of Scotland the other way round and it changes radically not only the picture but our sense of where we belong in it.

In July 1981 we had a holiday in the little village of Embo, on the coast north of Dornoch, and stayed in a cottage a few yards from a vast expanse of beach. Embo had been created to house those displaced by clearances inland, part of the plan to turn crofters into fishers. Gowan was on a school trip to France, so there were the four of us and the dog. I was keeping a diary at this time, which I have done sporadically over the years since 1977, and it records the way we spent our time. We walked and played cricket on the beach, read, played Careers and backgammon, did a jigsaw. I remember it as a very peaceful week and I also remember the fact, not recorded in the diary, that Angus was not drinking. It was our last holiday together. The week stands out as a brief interlude of calm before the next phase of deterioration set in.

While we were in Embo we drove across Sutherland to the west coast, and back through empty Assynt. We also visited Dunrobin Castle and Kildonan. We passed through glens and straths where the emptiness was palpable. I wondered whether some of my own Mackay ancestors were amongst those displaced, and if so, where they had gone. My great grandfather William Mackay was from Auchmore, near Beauly in Easter Ross, probably born around 1830. The Sutherland clearances had got seriously underway about twenty years earlier. One year I had given my mother a copy of John Prebble's *The Highland Clearances* for her birthday. I was astonished when she told me the book had distressed her so much she had at one point hurled it across the room; not astonished that she was upset, but that my gentle, mild-mannered mother had been so provoked.

Since that visit to Sutherland I have become more familiar with the particular kind of emptiness that inhabits a place formerly occupied: the emptiness of roofless cottages and steadings, as often alongside major thoroughfares as hidden in glens which once contained thriving communities; the emptiness of abandoned shipyards and sheds, of harbours with only pleasure craft moored at the pier, of town centres at night where there are only office blocks and, ironically, building societies. Last Christmas Eve, in the middle of the morning, I walked along the High Street in South Queensferry. There were two other people in the street. Up the Loan the supermarket was heaving. Here, there was not a single shop remaining that provided for the needs of the last minute Christmas shoppers. No baker or butcher, no fishmonger – the Youngs in Gote Lane had recently retired – no grocer or greengrocer. Ten years ago there were all of these. Now there are eating places and gift shops, and the High Street is empty except when tourists arrive. Like so many communities in Scotland, you would almost think it doesn't exist unless people from elsewhere put it on the map. And a barrier of petrol stations, motels and fast-food outlets on the nearby main roads deflect entry to the place itself.

Emptiness, nineteenth, twentieth and twenty-first century, is part of my inheritance, and it connects with other parts of my past. The Scottish experience of displacement goes hand in hand with Jewish displacement. There are so many places my antecedents have left, places I have never heard of. My grandfather left Vilnius for Germany and then England; where were my rabbinical ancestors before that? What places fill in the gaps between Amsterdam where the original Daicha lived, and Vilnius? How many times were the communities of which my family were a part moved on, or otherwise obliterated? What happened to the spaces they left behind?

This correspondence between Scottish and Jewish experience helps to strengthen a kind of dual citizenship. But it doesn't supply an uncomplicated answer to the question, where do you come from? For Arthur, who shares my life, it's not so tangled. He was born and grew up in a place which he still knows well. Like so many Clydesiders, his origins are Highland, his mother's family from Carradale in Kintyre, his father from Lewis. He has part-way returned to the place of his forebears, as he has for over thirty years lived in Argyll, on the shores of Loch Fyne. It seems to me that he can identify himself with some precision: first of all, as a Scot, which anyone with half an ear can tell as soon as he speaks; second, as a west coast Scot; third as a displaced Highlander. And as an engineer he has an identity that is known and recognised around the world. The Scottish engineer, as celebrated in Kipling's 'Macandrew's Hymn', is as iconic a figure as the Scottish soldier.

Arthur tells of his chief engineer, in dark suit and bowler hat, on the streets of Singapore, greeted by cries of 'Mr Chief, Mr Chief'.

My first stay in Argyll was in October 1979, another family holiday. We stayed in Kilmichael Glassary. We explored the area around Lochgilphead and Crinan, drove to Campbeltown with the children singing 'Mull of Kintyre' (in spite of the fact that they had all picked up a stomach bug; Rachel was sick by Campbeltown harbour) and up to Oban. We returned from Campbeltown on the east Kintyre road, which took us past Carradale. We knew that Naomi Mitchison's home was there; it never occurred to me, in spite of my interest, that I would later get to know it well. Another expedition took us to Islay, getting up at five in the morning to make the ferry at Kennacraig. We took in four of the distilleries – Bowmore, Bruichladdich, Laphraoig and Lagavulin – and the museum at Port Charlotte. From Port Askaig we looked across at Jura and thought about George Orwell, ill and trying to finish *Nineteen Eighty-Four*, deliberately choosing to stay in the remotest part of a sparsely populated island. Since then I have seen the house from the water, out in Arthur's *Lintie* from Crinan harbour, a little white square on a slope. And I've picnicked on the north shore on a perfect summer afternoon, with not a human soul apart from the two of us, and deer, wild goats, seals and eagles not far away. We returned that evening in the *Lintie*, a chill creeping up from the water as the sun left it. We skirted the Corrievreckan. I noticed Arthur concentrating hard, but in my innocence of currents and weather I felt no alarm. It was only later, safe on land, that Arthur said, 'There was a moment there when I thought we might not make it.' Not, he added later, that he was worried about the Corrievreckan, just that if the tide had been against us we might have spent an uncomfortable night.

The most memorable episode of the Kilmichael holiday was when Rachel and I took the dog on what we expected to be a three-mile walk. We set off up Kilmichael Glen and turned right on a track that led alongside the River Add. We were soon in the forestry and crossed the river, thinking to make a circle back to the road. But the track led us at a tangent and we ended up emerging on the main road near Cairnbaan. We had been walking for miles on a muddy forestry track when we had a curious encounter. The dog was trotting in front when we saw approaching us a figure in a dark suit. As he got nearer we realised he was a clergyman, in dog collar, hat and shiny black shoes. The dog, only six months old at this time, generally bounded up to anyone in sight, but we noticed that he paid no attention to the clergyman, who walked towards us and raised his hat and greeted us without pausing. Rachel and I remarked on the fact that his shoes were spotless although the track was so muddy. Then we realised that there were no footprints. I think it may have been the only time I have ever encountered a ghost. It was dusk by the time we got onto the road, and dark when we got home, to find Angus and the others quite worried.

In 1992 I began to work on my biography of Naomi Mitchison, and I met Arthur. I began to get to know Mid-Argyll rather better. It is thick with the past. Dun Add, the centre of the kingdom of Dalriada, is just north of Cairnbaan, but the whole area is crowded with duns and standing stones. Human history here is about as old as it gets in Scotland. The hills are not high by Highland standards, but from prominences near the west coast you can see on a clear day, as well as Islay, Jura, Scarba, Mull and a host of smaller islands and skerries, the Antrim coast. Scotland's west coast, from Lewis to the Solway, is closer geographically and culturally to Ireland than to Edinburgh.

Near the head of Loch Fyne, Inveraray, the centre of power of the Dukes of Argyll, was for centuries a strategic focal point and much fought over. The whole area is criss-crossed with the routes of armies and traders, churchmen and chapmen spreading their wares, black cattle making their way from the islands to the trysts at Crieff and Falkirk. Improvements on the land increased productivity of sheep but destroyed communities of human beings. Traditional lairds were unable to resist the thrusting expansionism of the progressives, who were often newcomers. The Malcolm family, who made their fortune from West Indian sugar, established themselves at Duntrune and bought up land from local lairds. They built Poltalloch House, an impressive pile with views to the south and west, a few miles from the old Duntrune Castle. The house is a ghostly shell now, inhabited by trees.

In the nineteenth century the steamers brought tourists and speeded up trade. Gillespie, in John Macdougal Hay's eponymous novel of 1912, built his success on Loch Fyne herring and easy access to Glasgow markets. The handsome Victorian houses in Tarbert and Ardrishaig are evidence of nineteenth-century boom times. With the opening of the Crinan Canal in 1801 the route from Glasgow to the west coast was significantly shortened. The trippers, including Queen Victoria, came in their thousands. The process of change was inexorable, yet the layers of the past are all there and are all important for those who feel some connection with the places of Argyll, whether rooted or, like me, vicarious.

When Naomi Mitchison bought a house in Carradale in 1937 there was still Gaelic spoken in what was a traditional crofting and fishing community. Her origins were Scottish, of course, but she had grown up in Oxford and since her marriage in 1916 had lived in London. With the purchase of Carradale House she set about reinventing herself as a Scot. She had an enormous talent for empathising with the many different groups and communities that she lived amongst in her long life. She made sure that she had a role in the Carradale community. But she encountered difficulties in ensuring that the identities she valued, as writer, socialist, feminist, enlightened laird, were recognised. The Scottish literary and political scenes were dominated by men. She felt that they did not take her seriously; I think she was right.

Nevertheless Naomi Mitchison is an inspiration in the way she demonstrates the importance of multiple identities. There were certainly tensions, and sometimes conflict, but this does not detract from the value of her aspirations. I found no conflict between my strengthening Scottish and Jewish identities. My mother nurtured the former and my father nurtured both, and was himself an example of how the two could co-exist. But how I thought of myself inside my own head was one thing; how I actually related to the Jewish and Scottish parts of my family was another. To a child the grown-up world is alien. For me that alienation was magnified; I felt a stranger to both my Jewish and my Scottish inheritance. I loved visiting my great aunt and uncle at Nethermills, but it was in effect a foreign country. I loved the farm, the freedom to explore, the animals, the big kitchen, Auntie Lizzie smiling on the doorstep, Uncle Dode stomping in the yard in his big boots. I loved going to the local Highland games (though not the Keith show where a drunk man embraced and slobbered over me) and watching the pony races, the parading Clydesdales and the Highland dancing. At the Cornhill show my mother's cousin Eleanor won second prize for her meringues – there were only two entries. It was a family joke for years. I loved to hear my mother talk about her childhood visits to the farm. I embraced it all as part of who I was, yet at the same time I didn't quite feel that I was part of it.

A few years ago, drawn by a 'For Sale' notice on the road, Arthur and I ventured down the track to Nethermills, just as badly rutted as I remembered it decades ago, and had a look. It was all much neater and cleaner than it had been, clearly no longer the heart of a working farm. As we rounded the corner of the byre we came face to face with the current owners, trying to clear a blocked drain. They turned out to be American. It was three o'clock in the afternoon and they were ineffectually poking at the drain in a cloud of alcohol. I explained why we were there, and they invited us in and produced the whisky bottle. They were not entirely coherent, but explained that they were returning to Texas. It was an oddly surreal experience, sitting in the room where I had spent so many hours as a child, which in many ways had not changed greatly, listening to an American couple who had no clue at all as to the history of the place, and clearly failed to understand my connection with it.

One of the things that drew Angus and me together was his Scottish background. He was born in Surrey, and grew up there, but his father was from Forfar and his mother from Glasgow, and they seemed to me when I met them to be more conspicuously Scottish than my own parents. I had spent much more time in Scotland than Angus had, but he was keen to remedy that. A defining moment in the early stages of our relationship was when he came to Edinburgh for a few days in the summer of 1962 when I was there with my family. When we married we talked often of making our home in Scotland at some point, and that plan took shape when we left Nairobi in 1971. We neither of us had a job to go to. We were embarking on a freelance career which needed good libraries and space to write. Somewhere within striking distance of Edinburgh seemed ideal. In August we parked ourselves in Peter and Mabel's Edinburgh flat and started house hunting. We were poised to buy Innerleithen railway station when we discovered a problem that had been glossed over by the sellers, and pulled out. We decided against an isolated house in Ettrickdale – it was just too remote – and failed in our bid for a handsome farmhouse near Eddleston. So we ended up staying in Edinburgh.

Perhaps Edinburgh made it more difficult to become Scottish. Perhaps it was always going to be impossible. Short of wearing a kilt, what is the first identifier of a Scot? The voice. I had taught myself to speak English but there is still an American tinge in my accent which sometimes people recognise. Although a taxi driver in Salt Lake City once said to me, 'I love your accent, it sounds so intelligent,' no one has identified me as a Scot from my voice. In my job as museum education officer there was an occasion when I had to cancel a planned trip to the Livingstone Centre at Blantyre. I was reprimanded over the phone by a member of the public who felt I was part of an English plot to undermine the reputation of one of Scotland's heroes. It was no good saying, 'but I'm not English'. But that incident aside, in over thirty years of living in Scotland I have not encountered chauvinism directed against me, at least not overtly.

I chose to live in Scotland and have chosen to remain. Only once have I considered leaving, when I applied for a job in Newcastle. I didn't get the job, so escaped the need to make a difficult decision. I know I couldn't now live in the south of England. It feels like a foreign country when I go there, and London I can barely tolerate. Occasionally I have rediscovered a sense of the London I once lived in. Once I walked from a friend's flat in Holloway to Islington, and found an Upper Street full of wine bars and elegant shops and restaurants, and Barnsbury Street where Angus and I had our first flat almost unrecognisable. The Rex cinema, our local fleapit where we saw *Spartacus* and other delights at 2s 8d a time, had long since become the Screen on the Green.

Scotland feels like home, but I don't feel I can describe myself as Scottish, only Scott-ish. Although there are many parts of the world where I would like to spend some time, I have no wish to leave

Scotland, and I have a particular affection for West Lothian, where I have lived for more than twenty-five years: though officially now part of Edinburgh, South Queensferry is historically West Lothian or Linlithgowshire. And West Lothian contains a great deal of Scotland's history. Climb to the top of Cockleroy and you can see prehistoric settlements and burial sites, the Firth of Forth, for centuries a major artery of trade and conduit of war, the parallel links of road, canal and railway, a roofless palace which was once a centre of power, the sites of numerous battles, coal fields, shale mines and iron works now abandoned, petrochemical works still smoking and flaming, the bridges across the Forth, and on a clear day Ben Lomond, Ben Ledi, Ben Vorlich, the Merrick and the mountains of Arran. I am always moved by this concentration of the past, and by the green dips and slopes that characterise the West Lothian countryside.

Due west of Queensferry is Ardrishaig on Loch Fyne. Although on the same latitude, this is the Highlands. The sky and the air are different. Loch Fyne has become the other pole of my existence, and the symmetry, a great firth on one side of the country and a long sea loch on the other, is satisfying. I travel west from Queensferry along the Forth valley, through Stirling with its castle, as strikingly prominent as Edinburgh's. Ben Lomond comes into view and soon I'm heading up Lochlomondside, and if it's a summer weekend there's a stream of traffic heading for the hills. The car takes the long haul over the Rest and Be Thankful with ease, but it's not hard to imagine what it must have been like for those who built the first road through the pass, the mountains shouldering close to the narrow glen. I sometimes stop at the top and have a scramble on the slope of Ben an Lochan. Once I climbed Ben Ime on the other side of the road. I came on a doe and a fawn in a little scooped out hollow in the hillside. However else I am able to define my attachment to Scotland, the fact that I value its physical character as an essential part of its culture is a key element.

CHAPTER EIGHT
Shall I Be Mother?

I HAVE A photograph of my mother as a black-haired young woman. She gazes directly at the camera with dark, compelling eyes, a straight mouth echoed by a straight hairline, a clear brow and heavy eyebrows. She looks alert and determined.

As a child I was aware of none of that. I have no memory of her before her hair was grey – my own hair was beginning to go grey by the time I was thirty. On one of our voyages back to the USA we shared a cabin with a French woman who frantically coloured her hair, claiming that her husband would divorce her if he knew of her grey hairs. My mother found this amusing. I don't think it ever occurred to her to do the same.

I only really discovered my mother when I was more or less adult, and became aware of the affection and regard that many people, including my own friends, had for her. In my American childhood she was an essential part of my everyday world, taken for granted, but not particularly linked, as my father was, with special occasions, holidays, occasional weekends when I accompanied him to the university. My images of my mother are almost entirely domestic and generalised. I locate her vaguely in the kitchen, or returning from a shopping trip laden with brown paper bags. As we had no car she shopped by bus, or sometimes got a lift with a friend. She wore jeans, but never shorts, even in the hottest of American summers. I asked her once why she didn't wear shorts like the other mothers. She showed me her varicose veins; I've inherited those too.

I have another generalised picture of her. It is early evening, in any of the houses or flats we occupied during my first ten years. My father mixes a martini. My mother sits in an armchair, relaxed. Dinner is on the stove, and she will get up from time to time to attend to it, but this is the sacred half hour, when my parents talk about their day and the children are expected not to intrude. A sense of exclusion is a part of many childhoods. Robert Louis Stevenson conveys it strikingly in some of his *Child's Garden of Verses* poems and when he writes about his parents. I was ten or eleven when I began to think about death and lay in bed afraid to go to sleep in case I never woke up. I could hear the voices of my parents, and called for them. I was told firmly to go to sleep.

Here and there my mother comes into sharper focus. It was she who encouraged the two main activities of my childhood, reading and drawing. She read to us, and had herself a real talent for drawing. She kept me supplied with paper, crayons and paints. A new box of Crayola crayons was always a joy, and was one of the things I missed the most when we left the United States. You couldn't get them in the UK at that time. It was always with my mother that I made visits to the library or to bookshops. When I was older and prowled among the bookshelves at home for something to read my father made suggestions, but in my pre-teen years it was invariably my mother who guided my immersion in books.

I know there were times when my mother lost her temper with my brother and me, but I don't have any real memory of this. Alan and I quarrelled often – he teased me mercilessly. There was less tension between Liz and myself, perhaps because of the larger gap between us. There was an occasion when my mother was so furious with Alan that she attempted to spank him with a hairbrush, but the hairbrush broke. I don't remember this, but she used to tell the story against herself. I have no idea what it was Alan had done. My father was often impatient and I hated it when he raised his voice; in fact I would go to inordinate lengths, including telling lies, to avoid his ire. But although I was often aware that my mother was weary, sometimes irritable and occasionally cross, I do not remember her angry. My adult eyes saw her as quiet, firm, of unshakeable principles, in many contexts a background figure but nevertheless influential.

In the months before we left America for good, in 1951, there was tension in the house. I was excited about leaving – going 'home' had been talked about so much – but I think it must have been a difficult time for my mother. My parents had been thirteen years in the United States when they left, and the upheaval can't have been easy for either of them, but I suspect it was particularly difficult for my mother. She had many friends in the US, and inevitably she bore the brunt of transplanting her children as well as herself. My father had a new job and new colleagues, and although he faced many problems my mother's new start was more radical. My memories of her after we left America become firmer and clearer. This reflects my growing up more than anything else. I began to wonder about her life. I was adolescent I suppose before I began to think about the fact she was a qualified librarian who had never worked since her marriage. It never occurred to me for a moment that I wouldn't have a career. Much later I learnt that she had been offered a college librarianship job at Cambridge which she had turned down.

By the time we moved to Hardwick Alan was at boarding school and Liz and I were both at school in Cambridge. We had domestic help. Mrs Kester came twice a week. I always had to have my room tidy on a Monday morning so she could clean it. I was now more aware of the pattern of my mother's life. Her mornings were domestic, but her afternoons were her own and she generally retired to her bedroom with a book. She was also writing, although I am not sure when she started. She wrote, by hand in exercise books, several detective stories and at least one children's story, which I have. I don't think any of them was ever seen by a publisher. I have no idea whether that was an issue for her.

She would sometimes meet a friend for lunch in Cambridge and would occasionally go to the pictures. My father often took me to the theatre but my mother was rarely with us, presumably at home looking after Liz. This was when I discovered Shakespeare in a big way, going to lively student productions of *Julius Caesar*, *Troilus and Cressida*, *As You Like It*, *The Tempest*, *Richard II* and, most magical of all, an unforgettable *Twelfth Night* performed outdoors on a balmy June evening. Once we went for a weekend to Stratford and saw *Romeo and Juliet*. On school trips I saw *Much Ado about Nothing* at Stratford and *Othello* with Paul Robeson and Sam Wanamaker in London.

Of course my parents went to the theatre and concerts on their own, and participated in the Cambridge University social scene. They were often out to dinner or giving dinner parties. For these my mother spent hours deciding on the menu and preparing food, and although I didn't share the meal, I became increasingly interested in what was being cooked. A favourite recipe book was called *Meals for Guests*, and out of that I copied some of the first recipes that I tried out for entertaining friends. One was paprika chicken; another was a delicious concoction of dates and walnuts called 'food for the gods'. My mother was a good cook. In the early Fifties, when Britain was still climbing out of austerity, producing interesting meals wasn't easy. She had the advantage of America's more cosmopolitan eating habits (spaghetti bolognese was standard in our home but in the 1950s was considered exotic by my friends) but must have been frustrated at the limitations of the British larder. There was also the Jewish tradition to draw on, especially my grandmother's recipe for gefilte fish which was a family favourite. Elizabeth David's books were eagerly received birthday and Christmas presents. I remember particularly *French Country Cooking* and *Summer Cooking* on my mother's shelves, but she probably had them all.

Gradually the frontiers of food extended. Our everyday meals were fairly conventional – mince, lamb chops, stews, sausages, a roast at weekends, fish and chips from a van on Fridays, steak or salmon (or sea trout, even better) for special occasions. There were American standards – tuna and noodle casserole, hamburgers, brownies, good salad dressing. A treat was apple pie with loads of cinnamon, or better still lemon meringue pie. One of the first things I learnt to cook myself was a frankfurter casserole, with onions, tomatoes and carrots. By the time I left school I could manage a convincing spaghetti and a reasonable stew. I had been married a couple of years before I learnt how to make pastry. By the early Sixties my mother's cooking was becoming increasingly adventurous, which reflected both the easier availability of many ingredients and the fact that my parents had more money to spend. My mother's dinner party standbys of the Fifties gave way to paella, moussaka and other Mediterranean dishes.

I grew up assuming that the provision of food was an essential part of being mother. My father had little interest in cooking, although he gave my mother breakfast in bed every Sunday and could put a simple meal together. Later, probably dating from the time when my mother spent a lengthy time in hospital and then convalescent, he began to enjoy cooking. He must have been one of Delia Smith's earliest converts. But my mother's days seemed to be shaped by the making of meals. When I married I assumed that mantle myself. I quickly discovered that the real challenge was deciding what to have and acquiring the ingredients. The cooking was relatively easy. There were mistakes and failures, of course, but they were part of the learning curve. Angus couldn't cook at all, and although I felt this should be remedied (I still remember as a milestone the first meal he cooked, a goulash) it never occurred to me to shed the overall responsibility for meals, or to Angus to take it upon himself.

I have always enjoyed planning and cooking meals. There are some aspects of housework I enjoy some of the time. When I married I assumed that Angus and I would share the housework. I am not sure if we ever discussed it explicitly: if we didn't we should have done. I never entertained the possibility that I would be a 'captive' wife and mother. I was going to have a career. However, from day one of my marriage the implicit responsibility for all things domestic was mine. Hindsight tells me that on day one, if not before, I should have done something about it. But I didn't and the pattern was set. It wasn't that Angus never helped with the housework, it was more a question of mindset. His housework was helping me with my tasks. It didn't occupy a space in his thoughts, his plans, his allocation of time. He didn't think, when he invited someone to stay, I'll need to dust the spare room and make sure the bath is clean.

Intellectually, Angus had no problem with 'equality', and he proclaimed himself a feminist. But practically and emotionally he didn't know how to handle it, like many other men of his generation. He had grown up in a household where his father was king, of a most benign and accommodating kind, but nevertheless the focal point of the family. His mother and her responsibilities, it seemed to me, were never taken seriously. Yet it was clear to me that it was women, Mabel and the family housekeeper Betty, who made the Calder family's world go round. Peter knew and valued that, but their children were perhaps too dazzled by their father's achievements and personality to recognise their mother's role. Angus's expectations were inevitably shaped by these circumstances. The males in his family dominated, and were encouraged to dominate.

It was important to me to prove my domestic capability. I was sensitive about being branded a bluestocking, with the implication that this meant practical inadequacy. My mother laughingly quoted a friend of hers who had said that you could always tell a bluestocking by the state of the kitchen sink. The comment stung – *my* kitchen sink would be above reproach. (This didn't last long.) I am not by nature either very organised or very tidy, but I like things to *be* tidy so make sporadic efforts to achieve this. Angus was much tidier in some respects, especially with his work, but there were some kinds of mess and most kinds of dirt to which he was oblivious. He simply didn't care if his clothes were in a heap or the kitchen floor was dirty, so it was a struggle to motivate him to do something about it.

All this I discovered gradually. When I married, I thought that Angus's theoretical views on equality would translate themselves into reality, that he would automatically share in all that was involved in living together. I was naive, of course. The issue was intensified by the arrival of children – there was so much more to do. By and large we missed out on the companionability of shared tasks, housework, cooking, gardening, DIY. We slid into a system of dividing rather than sharing labour.

I can't remember a time when I did not assume that I would have children. Although branded a tomboy, and imagining myself a boy in most of my games, I also played with dolls and replicated domestic family scenes in which I was mother. When I grew up I was going to be an artist or a writer but I was also going to be a wife and mother. As I grew older the notion of an ideal loving husband took shape, but it went in parallel with continuing adventurous dreams, in which I was now more often a courageous girl than a boy. I knew the dreams were fantasy – my real life scenario hardly incorporated being a heroine of the Wild West – and they co-existed quite comfortably with other projections, which saw me as a famed author and respected intellect.

I suppose most of us hold in our minds parallel but incompatible universes in which we simultaneously enact all our desires. I was passionate about love, giving and receiving. My passion was fed by the books I read rather than real life. I never doubted that my parents loved me, but it was never a sufficient kind of love. Long before I understood their relationship, not until after my mother died, I knew that it was qualitatively very different from my relationship with them. I wanted a slice of quality passion. I wanted someone to think I was the most wonderful person in the world, whom I thought was equally wonderful. When I was thirteen I knew a girl two years older who had a boyfriend. (Her name I have forgotten, but his name was David; I never met him.) I longed to be fifteen so that I too could fall in love. But when I reached fifteen the only boys I met were awkward unattractive youths with whom any kind of relationship seemed highly improbable. At sixteen I met a boy at a dance with whom I had a few assignations, but I had no real interest in him whatsoever. I just liked the idea of meeting him. Another boy walked me to the bus stop a few times after United Nations Association meetings (which I remember most for the fact that it was there that Diana's older sister taught me how to dance the Charleston). He was a couple of years older than me and I quite admired him. When I was seventeen I fell in love, and was deeply unhappy at the outcome.

I had plenty of time to nourish my dreams. Much of my adolescence was solitary. Because we lived out of town I missed out on the more casual and spontaneous social life that some of my friends enjoyed. Everything I did had to be planned with an eye to buses or a lift home. On rare occasions I was given money for a taxi. My weekends were usually spent reading, studying and walking the dog. And when there was a social event it was often disappointing. School dances were grim. One event I do remember enjoying a lot was a barn dance – I was probably about fifteen. I did a certain amount of hanging out in coffee bars with friends, always with huge and vague expectations that something interesting might happen, but it never did. In our sixth form summers Diana and I used to wander the streets of Cambridge in tight jeans and bare feet, feeling daringly bohemian and talking endlessly. We'd end up at her house, play records and drink coffee, until I had to drag myself away to catch the bus home.

Middle-class adolescence was, still is, almost by definition, a waiting game. Waiting for school to finish, for grown-up life to start, for the means to bridge the huge gulf between dream and adult reality. For those who left school early and immediately entered the world of work the passage to adult life was more precipitate and possibly easier. Education prolonged the waiting. When I was around fifteen and sixteen I felt desperately caged, frustrated at school, challenged by hormones I didn't understand (nobody talked about hormones then), straining at the leash intellectually and emotionally but with nowhere to go. But I held on to the idea that school wouldn't last for ever, that university would open doors onto a new world.

I wouldn't ever want to repeat that painful combination of longing and contravention, and most of all the anguish of only being able to talk about any of it to friends in thrall to the same frustrations. But even worse, I suspect, is the deprivation of hope and eagerness to get a grip on life which many young people now experience. There were times when I made an idiot of myself, but most importantly I learnt a lot of resourcefulness which has come to my aid over and over again. Of course there were times when my parents, I am sure unwittingly, contributed to my teenage disquiet. My father sometimes criticised my appearance. I think both my parents felt that praise should be rationed, and my father's criticisms in particular had the effect of totally undermining my confidence. I resolved to do everything I could to encourage my own children to feel positive about themselves. The problem is that it's always the things you are not aware of, the casual remarks, the unconscious gestures, that cause the most damage.

I stored in my mind what I would and would not do as a mother. But when my first child was born instinct took over. I read books and listened to what other people told me, but in many ways raising children was like riding a bicycle. Once I got the hang of it, we flew along in fine style, only there were punctures and skids and sometimes the chain came off or the brakes didn't work. And I had my own agenda.

At some point before Rachel was born I sat at the kitchen table in my parents' Sussex home talking to my mother. It was really only after I left home that I began to have real conversations with her on an equal basis, and that deepened and strengthened after I was married. On this particular occasion I was talking confidently about how I would deal with parenthood without compromising my career. My mother said very little. I suspect she was thinking, she'll find out soon enough about the realities of bringing up children. Early in 1965 I became pregnant.

Although the first few months of my pregnancy were difficult (and included a false alarm of twins) everything settled down. We left Islington about two months before Rachel was born, and our time in almost rural Sussex was perhaps the most contented period of our marriage. Angus was doing his D Phil at the University of Sussex, and already spent two days a week there. I was now writing my thesis, so it was less important for me to be in London. North Chailey was about four miles from Haywards Heath, on the London to Brighton line, and about ten miles from my parents in Burgess Hill.

Angus took over the existing study, while I made a working area for myself in the dining room, which indicated the priorities. We inherited domestic help, but I, as before, did most of the shopping and cooking. We worked hard during the day, sometimes taking a break for a walk, and spent companionable evenings listening to the house collection of Scottish folk songs on the gramophone, which included Ewan MacColl and Jeannie Robertson. We played chess, which Angus always won, and Scrabble, which I was better at. But Angus so much liked to win it was almost not worth defeating him.

Life was simple and focused. Friends often came to stay at weekends, and we walked and talked and cooked and ate and drank modest quantities of wine. We couldn't afford excess as we were living on student grants plus a little extra earned from part-time teaching and literary journalism. I was writing for *Tribune* at the time, which paid a pittance. In the early morning of 21 August I went into Cuckfield Cottage Hospital, and Rachel was born later that day. It was a long, exhausting stop-start labour, and Angus sat by my bed reading *Ulysses*. When I woke the morning after I felt indescribably wonderful. I had produced a healthy daughter. I was overwhelmed with a sense of achievement and love which has only been matched by the birth of my other two children.

It took a few weeks for things to settle. In the early days of parenthood emotions chased each other in a mad stampede – panic, love, exhaustion, anxiety. But in fact it didn't take long to accommodate Rachel into our harmonious routine. This was the life I wanted: my husband, my baby, my work, congenial friends from time to time. For those few months I felt things were held in balance. I gradually gained confidence in my new role. I finished and submitted my thesis, and Angus seemed to be working happily although he was easily diverted from a straight course, and immersed himself in Scottish literature when he should have been concentrating on the Second World War. Of course there were stresses, nights when the baby wouldn't sleep, visits from relations who had to be looked after, worries about work and money and where we would go when we left Barn Meadow, but memory tells me they didn't take over. With the start of a new term Angus was teaching both in London and at Sussex University which I am sure made it easier for him to accept rural life. The country was not his natural habitat.

We agreed that we would have to return to London. The spring of 1966 found us moving into a two-bedroom flat in West Hampstead, shabby, cramped, with an erratic coke-burning stove for hot water, but convenient. For the next two years we made our lives there. Angus finished his thesis and wrote *The People's War*, about the World War Two home front, commissioned by Jonathan Cape. I rewrote my thesis on Orwell and Koestler as *Chronicles of Conscience* and was delighted when Secker and Warburg agreed to publish it. I was taken to lunch by Frederick Warburg at *L'Escargot*, an experience which I found rather intimidating. At the end of lunch, which was completed with *marrons glacés* which I had never tasted before, he commented on the messiness of my typescript and recommended that I acquire an electric typewriter. 'They cost only about £100,' he said. I was stunned. To us £100 was a fortune; Mr Warburg obviously didn't have a clue how we lived.

In May 1967 our second daughter was born. This was the year I discovered Doris Lessing, reading enthusiastically her Martha Quest novels, but most of all impressed, inspired and discouraged by *The Golden Notebook*. Here was a novel that opened the door onto a contemporary world where women struggled to make headway through simultaneous independence and constriction. It was probably around this time also that I read a piece by Margaret Drabble in which she expressed her view that of the three roles that women like herself wanted, marriage, motherhood and career, only two were realistically possible at the same time. It never occurred to me that my marriage might be under strain. Gowan was a sunny, good-natured baby, but inevitably two children were more demanding than one. I had a desk in the corner of the bedroom with a view out onto a scruffy back yard. It was there I wrote *Chronicles of Conscience* and other pieces that brought in a little money, often with the children playing literally at my feet. Angus worked in the living room which looked out onto the street. He held the fort when I was teaching, summer school and evening classes, and a reciprocal childcare arrangement with friends allowed me a day a week in the British Museum, but I continued to be the main parent. When it came to job hunting it was Angus who did the applying although most of the jobs that interested him were equally appropriate for me.

My career had now firmly taken second place in the scheme of things. In fact, I think it did so long before I became a mother. Angus's need to succeed was much stronger than mine, and I hated any idea of competing with him. My capitulation is perhaps summed up by the following episode. I had worked for three years on George Orwell. In 1968 his collected essays and journalism were published and I was looking forward to reviewing them for *Tribune*. Angus said to me that he desperately wanted to review them, they were very relevant to work he was doing, and would I mind if he asked *Tribune* if he could review them instead. I agreed. Even as I agreed I knew I shouldn't; I was sidestepping an issue that would intensify.

My ideal of partnership was eroding. Of course I had totally underestimated the impact of children, but I suspect that ideal was never a possibility. I wanted to make a success of parenthood, for my sake as well as for the children's, and although Angus participated more than many fathers of his generation, our circumstances made it difficult for him to share, especially when he had no strong inclination to do so. When I took the children out he stayed at home to work without interruption, and vice versa. In the first part of 1968 Angus was working flat out to finish *The People's War* and any pretence of our work having equal status went out the window. We went to Edinburgh and stayed in his absent parents' flat while he finished the book. At first I was taking one day a week in the National Library of Scotland. But after a few weeks Angus said he couldn't cope with this arrangement and asked me to give up the library. The project I was beginning to research, on radical American fiction, had to be put on hold: I never went back to it.

There were two reasons for going to Edinburgh. One was to get Angus away from distractions, the other was that we had run out of money. By Christmas 1967 our bank accounts were empty. A Christmas present of money from my father bought our train tickets to Edinburgh. My sister moved into the West Hampstead flat and paid the rent and our only expenses in Edinburgh were for food. I am not sure if either of our families realised our predicament, but without their support, direct and indirect, we would have been struggling.

My life was increasingly circumscribed. When I couldn't work I became depressed and difficult to live with. I never blamed the children; inevitably I felt that, if it wasn't actually Angus's fault his lack of sympathetic understanding made it all harder to deal with. Later, that feeling intensified, and I realised that he simply did not know how to relate to my experience. I was rescued from the doldrums by an idea for a new book, on Westerns and the American West, which came to me after a rare night out to the pictures in Edinburgh. Angus shared my love for Westerns, and even if at first I could do little more than explore the idea with him it was something I could begin to get an intellectual grip on without, at this stage, spending hours in a library. Weidenfeld and Nicolson signed me up for a book, and I felt I had recovered my equilibrium as writer. In the event, this book did not have an easy passage, and Weidenfeld rejected it. It was finally published by Hamish Hamilton.

I was twenty-three when my first child was born and in the first two or three years knew few people with young children. The one or two I did know I saw rarely, except for the friends whose baby I looked after once a week in return for them taking Rachel. Later, when I lived among contemporaries with children, I realised what I had missed. We didn't go out often, and when we did we looked to family to babysit – Liz, or Angus's brother Allan and his wife Anni who were living in Hampstead. But my mother and Mabel were both comfortingly present in the background. Mabel was a grandmother many times over when Rachel was born, and had perfected the role. Rachel was my mother's first grandchild. She had said long before Rachel was on the way that she wasn't going to be lumbered with looking after grandchildren. In fact, her rapport with children was such that she became a kind of adoptive grandmother to the children of several friends, and from the beginning her bond with her own grandchildren was exceptionally close. Watching her with Rachel was a huge reassurance, not only because I felt my child was in good hands but because it seemed to echo something of my own babyhood.

There is a photograph of my mother hugging my brother's son Davey, who is probably about three years old. Their smiles express a totality of warmth and delight. That's how I want to remember my mother, in what was in some ways her starring role, as grandmother. It wasn't just that she had such an enviable relationship with her grandchildren, but that that relationship seemed to sum up her personality, and also represented a closer bond with me. After she died I continued for years to reach for the telephone to tell her what the children were up to, and my deepest regret is that she didn't see them grow up. Perhaps I learnt more from my mother as grandmother than as mother.

Did I ever really learn how to be mother? If parenthood is about unconditional love, then I think I managed that. You can't bargain with children about love, whatever your hopes for them. I've been lucky. I like and respect my children a great deal; you can't count on that, but it's a wonderful bonus if it's there. Marriage, however, isn't about unconditional love. It has to be negotiated in order to be successful, unless one partner is prepared to play a secondary role. Women are now less willing to do so. My mother played that role, from choice, like most of her generation. Although intellectually I resisted a secondary role, in practice it was another story.

In my early thirties, with three young children, I was exhausted most of the time. I had some part-time childcare, and an informal reciprocal arrangement with other mothers in the area to share children. One day a week Angus took over, tackling the housework as well as looking after the kids. By this time he was a good if erratic cook, but was often not at home when meals had to be provided. There were days when by five or six in the evening I was shaking with exhaustion, an alarming sensation which I have only experienced very occasionally since. Most nights I found myself longing to go to bed at about nine o'clock and forcing myself to keep going. Until he started primary school Gideon was usually out of his bed at six in the morning. His first port of call was always our bedroom, so there was never a chance to sleep in at weekends.

My working routine had to be ferociously disciplined. I couldn't afford not to use every minute of child-free time and, particularly when I was teaching, often had to work in the evenings. I set myself targets: so many hours in the library, so many thousand words written. I prided myself on not missing deadlines. It was a hard school, but it taught me disciplined working habits which I have never lost and which have been an enormous asset. There were periods when work had to take a back seat, particularly in the summer holidays. Angus was often away teaching summer school, and keeping my own work going was a struggle. But there was a kind of liberation, too, and I enjoyed expeditions with the kids – a walk down to Inverleith Park or the Botanic Garden, a trip to the seaside at Gullane or Aberdour, a visit to Cramond, or just a stroll through Princes Street Gardens.

There were pressures on middle-class mothers, of course, from signing the kids up for endless extra-curricular activities to volunteering to help at the school jumble sale or making a costume for a show or a fancy-dress party. It was here that I felt I didn't measure up on the mum stakes. I didn't want to let the children down, yet work commitments meant I couldn't afford to be seen primarily as a mother. This was the more difficult as most of my work was done at home, which inevitably made me more available. There were times when I longed for a job that would take me out of the house from nine to five and offer a release from what seemed to me an anomaly, and other times when I was tempted to take on an alias and call myself an accountant, say, or a physiotherapist, to avoid explaining my equivocal professional life.

When we returned from Kenya in 1971 we bought a double flat in Buckingham Terrace near Edinburgh's Dean Bridge, after five months unsuccessfully hunting for somewhere in the Borders. By this time the girls had settled into Stockbridge Primary School and we had all made friends in the area. It made sense not to move away. The flat in Buckingham Terrace was spacious, shabby and convenient, with a small garden and garage at the back. We couldn't afford to do much with it. Its most attractive feature was a large front room which caught the morning sun and where Angus and I both worked. Apart from this room, I didn't care for the house greatly. The basement, where domestic life took place, was rather dark and gloomy, and there was an upstairs/downstairs feel which at times depressed me.

I didn't care for the street either. My childhood dislike of the Georgian and Victorian terraces in Edinburgh's New Town and West End survived, and I still found something formidable about the relentless march of stone and neo-classical symmetry. The scale continues to make me uncomfortable. The high ceilings and large doors and windows do not seem designed for ordinary human beings. I now live in a 1930s bungalow where the scale is just right for someone of my modest size. Buckingham Terrace was also formidable in another way. The atmosphere was one of severe respectability, where there were complaints if dustbins were not removed from public view as soon as they were emptied, and children playing in the street were unacceptable. On one occasion two fur-hatted middle-aged ladies, who had previously objected to the children's games, leant over the railings when I was sweeping the area steps and bawled at me about their behaviour. I was astonished and very upset.

We moved into Buckingham Terrace in April 1972. Since the previous August we had been living in Angus's parents' flat just up the road, three floors up with a baby and a four and a six year old. Angus was working on a new book and other freelance assignments, and was soon set to tutor for the Open University. I was struggling with the aftermath of Weidenfeld and Nicolson rejecting *There Must Be a Lone Ranger*. It took a while to get my career back on course, but by Christmas I had another publisher, and also a contract for a new book on women in Victorian fiction. The future was looking brighter and I had re-established a work routine. Then I discovered I was pregnant.

The immediate effect of this was that I became indefinably ill. In the early days of our marriage Angus and I had talked about having four children. But when Gideon was born I knew that he would be the last. In the first weeks of his life I would hold him with an overwhelming sense that I should make the most of the experience of cherishing a tiny baby, because it was not going to happen again. Our family was complete. I needed to turn my attention to other priorities. Now, with Gid not yet two years old, there was a fourth on the way.

I knew even at the time that I became ill because I could not face having another child. I crawled to the doctor but couldn't really identify my symptoms. My pregnancy was confirmed. My doctor, Rosalie Paul, was wonderful, and spent a long time talking me through my options. But to me it seemed I had no option; I felt totally defeated by the prospect of another child and yet making the choice to terminate the pregnancy also seemed beyond me. It was a predicament familiar to thousands of women. I turned to Angus for reassurance that together we could make a sensible decision. His response was to say, I'll support you in whatever you decide. But I wanted him to share the responsibility, and felt let down. A few years later there was a repeat performance when I made the decision to be sterilised. He backed off, saying it was entirely up to me, perhaps thinking that he was sparing me from pressure but in fact making it all much more difficult. The night before I went into hospital for the sterilisation, I cried, and Angus appeared not to understand the problem. I think he was both unable and unwilling to involve himself. The night before I went to have the pregnancy terminated I felt numb, and continued to feel numb and out of touch with humanity for weeks afterwards.

It was hard to tell my parents, but it had to be done. I told very few others. I can't remember now if Mabel and Peter ever knew. I am enormously grateful to Dr Paul and to the Eastern General Hospital; they made the experience less traumatic than it might have been. There was no whiff of criticism in the treatment I received. Since then, the abortion debate has ebbed and flowed. I believe that the emotional blackmail employed by the so-called pro-lifers is hypocritical and spurious, and my own experience has strengthened my conviction that it is an essential right that a woman should be able to control whether or not to go through with a pregnancy. A vast amount of pain, injustice and damage to humanity has grown out of the withholding of that right.

That's not to say that I don't have regrets. Rationally, I know that I made the right decision, for the well-being of myself and my family. Emotionally, I have lived ever since with a ghost child. From time to time as he was growing up Gideon would express the wish for a younger sibling, although he had a surrogate little brother when he shared a house for seven years with his cousin, and I suspect that part of the wish was to escape the fate of being the youngest. Every time he said this the ghost came out of the closet. Paradoxically, the ghost was most present and most frightening when Angus and I parted. Gid was eleven, the ghost child would have been nine.

Late in 1975 my mother had an idea. My father was due to retire and they had always planned to return to Scotland. By this time Liz and her husband Derek had moved from London to Edinburgh and were living just down the street from us. Suppose, my mother suggested, we looked for a large house outside Edinburgh, which could be divided into living space for the three families. We called the scheme 'dream palace'. We spent a lot of time talking the idea over. My main concern was that Angus was up for it; it would mean throwing his lot in with my family to an extent that had never been required before. He and my mother were very fond of each other, and I am sure that influenced his view. I think he was enthusiastic, or reticent about voicing dissent, because it was her idea.

Everyone involved appeared to be keen. I was more than happy to revive the old plan of living in the country. We could all see the benefits of life in an extended family, especially with Liz expecting a child. In the course of 1976 we began seriously to look for somewhere and by the end of the year had found and agreed on Philpstoun House in West Lothian, about fourteen miles from Edinburgh. It was to let, not for sale, but we could get a ten-year lease with an option to break it after seven years.

There was snow on the ground when I first saw the white harled house sitting in the midst of fields and sheltering trees. I fell for it at once, and in spite of all that happened there – the break up of two marriages, the deaths of my mother and Angus's father, and a period of desperate unhappiness – I loved living in the house. There were people, including my brother, who thought the whole escapade was crazy, and in a way they were right. But they were also wrong. It was certainly a risk, but it was also an adventure with huge rewards. The adventure came to an end in 1984, but I often pass the house, and it is always the good things that come to mind when I do. I loved the fact that I could walk out the door with our Border collie Breck into gardens and green fields, that a mile to the north was the Firth of Forth, and to the south the Union Canal, the railway and the shale bings that said so much about West Lothian's past.

For me the benefits were immediate. I had my own study. For the first time in my married life I had a room of my own, a corner room with a window out to the fields in front of the house and another overlooking the formal part of the garden. And there were resident babysitters. We moved in early July. Liz, Derek and Ben, born the previous September, had been there for a couple of months and my parents were due to move up from Sussex a month after us.

It was hard work. Even with the help of Basil, the gardener we inherited from the previous tenants who was lifesaver and liability in equal measure, getting to grips with the extensive garden was a serious challenge. The house was in a poor state of repair, although the full extent of its problems did not materialise until winter when we encountered the tragi-comedy of frozen pipes, floods and a labyrinth of plumbing which was gradually uncovered with each new disaster. We were endlessly grateful for the fact that our nearest neighbour, Archie Ferguson, was a plumber.

We allotted tasks, worked out rotas and defined boundaries. The house was already loosely divided, with three kitchens and several bathrooms. Each family had its own area. The grandest living room, which the kids at once dubbed 'the ballroom', went to my parents. The 'red room' – red wallpaper and frayed red curtains – was ours. At weekends we all ate together in the big kitchen, and took turns cooking. The Aga, once we had mastered it, was a godsend. The paddock in front of the house was let out to a family with horses, and soon the children were learning to ride on an elderly, long-suffering pony called Jester.

That July I was teaching summer school. One night there was a phone call from my father. My mother had been unwell off and on for some time. In May she had been in Edinburgh, but was walking with a stick as she was experiencing pain in her hip. The pain had worsened and spread; a scan revealed extensive cancer. They would try to control it with radiotherapy, but the prognosis was not good. My father had been told that she had six months to live.

They were in the middle of packing for the big move, clearing a large house which they had lived in for fifteen years. My father insisted that neither I nor Liz should go down to Sussex. But he thought that my mother would like to see Rachel, her first grandchild, who, at nearly twelve, was old enough to be of some help. So we put Rachel on a plane to fly down to Gatwick where her grandfather met her. Later Alan went to help with the final stages of the move, and brought Rachel back.

On 2 August my mother and father left Downsview. I went to meet them at the airport, with Rachel and her cousin Davey, who spent his pocket money on a box of chocolates for Grandma. My father appeared at the arrivals gate; he had lost so much weight that his clothes hung off him. My mother came into view in a wheelchair. I hardly recognised her. How could this painfully thin, paper white shadow, with hardly the strength to raise her hand, be my mother? As I helped her into the front seat of the car I felt as if she might disintegrate at my touch. It was a lovely day, flooded with warm August sunshine. As we approached the turning on to the road to Newton I slowed to check for traffic. In front of us was a golden field of barley lit by the afternoon sun. So quietly that I could barely hear her, my mother said, 'I'd forgotten how beautiful it is.' We brought her into the house and sat her in the red room. I said I would make some tea and went out to the kitchen, where I broke down and wept.

Liz and I had planned a special meal that night and had baked a whole salmon. My father helped my mother into bed to rest, but she got up for the meal, and sat at the head of the table in her blue dressing gown. I don't think she ate anything, but she managed to raise her glass and propose a toast: 'to dream palace'. Two days later she died. She had made it to dream palace by sheer will power.

The shock of my mother's death distorted those early months at Philpstoun, but I had already become aware of Angus's unease at our new life. I think he felt cut off from the sustaining milieu of Edinburgh. For a long time before we left the city he had been spending increasing amounts of time out in the evenings, meeting and talking with friends and colleagues. He was also drinking, much more heavily than I was at first aware. His reluctance to give up the city's bars and companionship was intensified, I realised later, by his uncertainty of his place in the new set up. It was a drastic alteration for all of us, and I am sure we all underestimated what was required to adapt. Angus, I believe, made up his mind, consciously or otherwise, not to adapt. He virtually withdrew from shared responsibility. It made it difficult, perhaps impossible, for him to gain anything from the Philpstoun experiment.

I was working on my biography of Stevenson, my third book for Hamish Hamilton. I had had a productive few years and felt more secure professionally, though not financially, than before. I worked happily in my new space, drawing on my father's library as well as my own, spending days in the National Library as required, and continuing my part-time teaching at the university. The extended family meant it was all much easier to handle than before.

In the spring of 1978 a grant from the Scottish Arts Council enabled me to go to Yale to work on the Stevenson material there.

Angus and the children came too. We arrived in New Haven, Connecticut with nowhere to stay and a very limited budget. We were rescued from the Holiday Inn by a friend of a friend who with great kindness and tolerance put us up in her large and comfortable house while we frantically tried to find a place to rent. In the end we struck lucky. There was a house for rent in Indian Neck, an outlying community of Branford, within easy commuting distance of New Haven. It was a comfortable, undemanding house a few minutes from the sea. The children went to local schools (Gideon fell in love with his black teacher, whose name was Mrs Brown) and I went every day to the Beinecke Library. Angus was able to get on with research for his book on the British Empire. For two and a half months we led a quiet, pleasant and productive existence. Angus seemed happier and more relaxed than he had been for a very long time.

We ended our stay in North America with a two-week trip in a camper van, which took us south to Virginia and as far north as Quebec. We crossed the Chesapeake Bay bridge tunnel and visited Jamestown, Williamsburg and Monticello. We drove the length of the Blue Ridge Mountains and on into Pennsylvania and went to Gettysburg, the scene of the battle that marked the turning point of the Civil War and of Abraham Lincoln's address reaffirming commitment to the abolition of slavery. We stayed with the Calders' old friend Jeri Knight, widow of Eric, the creator of *Lassie Come Home*, in her farmhouse near Quakertown. We viewed Niagara Falls and the St Lawrence River, and went to Toronto to visit Diana and Nicky and their two daughters: they had been teaching for several years at Toronto's York University. On our way back south to New York we went to Saranac in the Adirondacks where Stevenson had spent a winter trying to cure the TB he didn't have, and spent a wonderful night in a lakeside campsite where there were baby toads in the showers. We drove down the length of Lake Champlain and the Hudson River. It was a happy two weeks, and in effect the finale of our marriage as a committed and beneficial union.

Was Margaret Drabble right when she said that for women marriage, children and career were not sustainable? I do know of examples that would seem to contradict her (I say seem because this is very private territory, and the internal dynamic of a marriage is rarely what it appears) but by and large I think she probably was right, for the 1960s and '70s. I hope that now it would be harder to make the same comment with conviction, although it is clear that contradictory pressures on women have if anything intensified. The debates continue, but the excuses for men to avoid the same kind of parental commitment as women and to expect to receive one hundred per cent of a woman's attention are diminishing. The political and cultural undervaluing of women is still deeply rooted. Equal opportunities legislation has helped women who work, but not done much for perceptions of the roles of wife and mother or for society's accommodation of children. Because of this undervaluing, it is easy for men to contest, implicitly or directly, the professional and wage-earning activities of women. The working world is still dominated by an ethos which assumes that the details of cleaning and feeding and caring for others are looked after by someone else, usually a woman. In academia an insidious double standard often operates, which allows men simultaneously to parade intellectual feminist credentials and undermine women's achievements, both personal and professional. There are exceptions, of course, and I myself know several.

Everyone concerned in the business of balancing wage-earning and child-raising needs the help that must come not just from changed perceptions, but from the political will to support both the partnership of people who elect to bring up children together and those who from choice or necessity raise children on their own. As long as identity as parent comes (often a long way) second to identity as breadwinner, as long as power is expressed through paid work, the roles of carers and sustainers will be relegated. Legislation is slowly responding to the problem: the provision of paternity leave is an example. Men who hang on to attitudes and behaviours that many of us consider to be anachronistic are still protected by a formidable closing of male ranks. I remember Angus refusing to criticise a philandering male colleague, and I think this was before he himself had joined the ranks of the philanderers.

For me, if one thing had to go, it was always going to be marriage. My commitment to my children and my need for a profession were too great to deny. Of course I believed that my marriage could and should accommodate both: the shock and disillusion when I began to understand that it couldn't were very great. Even when I realised that a crucial factor was Angus's inability to deal with my professional role, I was reluctant to accept the consequences. I never made a calculated decision to relinquish marriage, but that was the way it turned out.

Being mother acquired a new challenge: being a single mother. But it was balanced by a huge sense of release. I no longer had to struggle with a difficult man in a difficult marriage. In the years of long-drawn-out disintegration I often found myself desperate to be alone, to measure myself against the demands of the world, of my job and of my children, without what had become a massive burden. The day that Angus moved out I felt as if a great weight had dissolved. When over a year later I moved into a new house it was with an exhilarating sense of a new beginning. I was, almost, a different person.

CHAPTER NINE

Symbols of Memory

MY FIRST STATED ambition was to be an artist. As a child I spent hours drawing and painting, but my subjects were stories. Pictures were a means of story telling. I wasn't interested in painting what I saw; I wanted to put down on paper what was in my head. By the time I reached my teens I realised I had more skill with words than with images, and my urge to tell stories was increasingly expressed through language. It was hardly surprising. I grew up in a house full of books. There were pictures too, of course, and music, but books dominated. My father was proud of my mother's talent for painting, but at the time I wasn't aware of this. My own interest in art was encouraged and I am sure my parents would both have been happy if I had pursued it as a career, but literature was more compelling.

By the time I went to university, I assumed that I would earn my living through teaching and writing. I had profound reservations about following in my father's footsteps – apart from anything else, I felt I should be more adventurous, that I should avoid the obvious and easy route. I toyed with thoughts of studying the social sciences, and was attracted by philosophy; like literature, the latter was in the blood, as my grandfather had written his doctoral thesis on David

Hume, paradoxical as that might seem for a rabbinical scholar. I am pleased that my son is a philosopher. But literature was insistent, and that's what I studied for five years, although my interests took me into politics and social history, and the wider contexts of writing. Critical theory has never much attracted me.

Literature proved not to be an easy route, and perhaps even as a schoolgirl I knew this. There was a lot of baggage, which I could not ignore. I did not find it too difficult to deal with being a student at the university that employed my father, although I was relieved when he left at the end of my first year to play his part in initiating the University of Sussex. I felt under huge pressure to do well, but that would have been with me wherever I had gone, and possibly whatever I had done. It was in part a pressure of my own creation, for my parents never directly articulated their hopes for my success. Nevertheless, I received a powerful message, just as I had when I was on the threshold of becoming an English schoolgirl. My father's achievements were profoundly important for him as an outsider, which he was at every stage in his career, except perhaps at Sussex, until – and there is considerable irony in this as there had been no place for him in Scotland during all the years he had done so much to re-invigorate the reading and teaching of Scottish literature – his return to Edinburgh in 1977. But his tales of successes at school and university, of prizes and bursaries, the scholarship which took him to Oxford, were markers of aspiration. I knew he passionately wanted his own children to do well, and I passionately wanted this myself.

In the context of high parental expectations many children rebel, strike out on their own, cut themselves off from parental influence. I didn't do any of these things, or at least not in any obvious way. I admired my father, and as I was starting out on what I thought was going to be an academic career I wanted his support and approval. I also wanted to do things differently, intellectually and practically. Some difference was inevitable, simply because I was female and by the age of twenty-three a wife and mother. My father, although he so much wanted me to do well, may have underestimated how important my career was to me. (This wasn't true of my mother.) After my marriage I noticed that he paid more professional attention to Angus than to me, and at times I found this quite hurtful. I am quite sure he did not intend to imply that I was less capable than my husband; it was a common reaction for someone of his generation and his background, and it was also natural for him to be economical with praise. When my first book was published, and with every book I've published since, I have awaited his comment with trepidation. In every case his reaction has been minimal, sometimes almost perfunctory. In this, I think he was replicating the responses of his own father to his achievements. It took me some time to realise that, although reticent in his comment to my face, he enthusiastically celebrated my achievements to others. I have heard him many times singing the praises of my brother and sister and his grandchildren, but never in their presence.

Going to Israel and going to Africa were both attempts at carving out some kind of independence. But in the end, professional independence came accidentally and from an unexpected quarter. When the children were growing up in Edinburgh we took them quite often to the Museum of Antiquities in Queen Street, the National Gallery, the Gallery of Modern Art still at that time at Inverleith House in the Botanic Garden, and the Royal Scottish Museum in Chambers Street. Their favourite was the latter where, like hundreds of other children, they loved the animals and the working models. Every year they entered the RSM's Christmas art competition, and at the age of six Rachel won a second prize for her drawing of an elephant. Gowan usually drew ladies in lovely dresses, and Gideon anything with wheels. It became as essential a part of the Christmas ritual as going to the zoo on Christmas Day. I suspect that it was a more valuable and educational experience than any amount of interactive screens or elaborate gadgetry.

For me, the attraction of museums was the simple pleasure of looking at things. Although there is a general view that museums are, or should be, sources of authoritative information, it was the intrinsic visual attraction and human connection of objects that pulled me in. It is shape, colour, material, and the knowledge that each thing has some direct and intimate connection with an individual, or many individuals, that appeal. The making, using and having of things are quintessential human activities. Museums are profoundly human places, although they do not always seem so because the need to preserve and protect so often distances artefacts from their human dimension.

It never occurred to me to think of working in a museum, but in the summer of 1978, having failed for the fourth time to get a full-time job at Edinburgh University where I had been teaching part-time, a job advertisement in the *Scotsman* caught my eye. The Royal Scottish Museum was looking for a 'Guide Lecturer' to join its Education Department. I felt I had some, but certainly not all, of the experience and qualifications required, and applied for the job. When I was interviewed the questioning focused on the teaching of children, in which I had no experience whatsoever. To my surprise, I was offered the job.

It was not a good time to embark on a change of career. By 1978 I had published eight books on English, American and Scottish literary and historical themes. I thought of myself as a writer first, a teacher second. I had a London agent and London publishers, and was half way through a biography of RL Stevenson. I had just been engaged by Lothian Region and City of Edinburgh Museums to work on an RLS exhibition and conference planned for the summer of 1980. In spite of this, Angus and I were in a situation where our joint freelance earnings were declining, and we had agreed that one of us, if not both, should try for full-time salaried employment. So on 1 November 1978 I climbed the imposing steps in Chambers Street as a member of staff of the Royal Scottish Museum.

It was, in many ways, like stepping back a century. On my first day I was shown around by the Head of Education, and introduced to a bewildering array of curators in airless offices and my fellow education officers who occupied offices on the cast iron spiral stair at the back of the building. The spiral stair has gone, but survives, and always will I suspect, in the memories of all of us who resided there in the late 1970s and early '80s as a place of spirited, at times raucous, debate and excoriation. But to start with I found museum life strangely silent and subdued.

My ear gradually attuned to the language of museums. A quarter of a century ago it was a language of hierarchy, authority and exaggerated respect. Senior staff were never addressed by their first names – indeed, any written communication to me was always to

'Mrs Calder'. Curators would refer reverentially to their heads of department as 'the Keeper'. The Director was always 'the Director', never referred to by name. Many of the warding staff were ex-army, and there was a tendency to address the public as if they were undisciplined civilians.

It was as if the unequivocally Victorian character of the building itself determined the life that went on within it. The Dickensian nature of existence there was underlined by some of the personalities. There was an other-worldliness about some of the older senior staff, who led their professional lives in habitats stacked with books and papers and specimens and looked vaguely puzzled if they were asked to turn their attention to public needs. The director occupied a large, dark office. There were a few books in a glass-fronted bookcase and a large, empty desk, which he considered to be the mark of an efficient operator. His manner was brusque. He liked to provoke argument, and he often lost his temper. One non-museum acquaintance of mine had occasion to discuss a proposed exhibition with him, and was astonished to find himself at the receiving end of a table-thumping tirade. He had a habit of dropping in on staff unannounced and engaging them in conversation which often had nothing to do with museum work; on one occasion he appeared in my office and tried to provoke a political argument, losing patience with me when I refused to respond. He was fascinated by authoritarian figures and referred with admiration to the Thatcherite style of governance. He was extraordinarily patronising to women. When I had my annual appraisal interview with him he told me that although my work had been entirely satisfactory, promotion was irrelevant as there was no career structure for education officers and anyway, I didn't need the money as I was a married woman and obviously worked for love not remuneration.

It seemed to me then, and still does now, that there is something inherent in museums that nurtures time-warped attitudes. Unlike the academic world, I suspect this has less to do with male competitiveness and the identification of women as threatening, and more with a dislocation from most other worlds, whether business, academic or domestic. It is not just that museum material is generally, though not always, of the past. It is something to do with an ethos that is concerned with preservation, and an archival mentality that classifies and arranges. While the academic historian creates a narrative, the museum historian, or curator, creates order out of a process of identification. 'What is it?' is the question that has to be answered first, with 'when?' and 'where?' following close after. For some curators, that is sufficient. The 'why?' and the 'how?', for many the most interesting parts of the story, are left out. This affects the dynamics of museums, which are so often places that collect, identify and preserve, but fail to communicate. It means that the hierarchy of the traditional museum puts the work of the curator at the apex, with all other activities at lower levels, rather than seeing curation as a centre with all other activities radiating outwards. It is only quite recently that the hierarchical structure of museums has begun to be replaced by something more radial. But now there is a new problem, that the existence of collections as a museum's focal point is in danger of being blurred, even threatened, by fashionable notions of management and pressures to court corporate involvement.

Over the last decade or so museums have had a rude awakening and been forced to take more notice of the world in which they operate. There have been some benefits, most notably in the area of public access and accountability, but many difficulties. Government's attitude to museums has been at best ambivalent, and at times hostile. There have been attempts to impose systems of operation and accountability which show little understanding of the nature and purpose of museums. Like universities, museums have been subjected to forms of assessment that focus on quantity rather than quality: how many visitors through the door, how many research papers published, how many mentions in the press. Figures are so much easier to evaluate than the more elusive and subjective criteria of quality and effect on people's lives. It is not difficult to calculate the spend per visitor of a particular exhibition or lecture, or per purchaser of a book. But how do you assess the cultural, intellectual and personal impact of any of these?

Sometimes it is only when, years later, people you meet are still talking about an exhibition that you begin to understand that it worked. Anecdotal evidence and gut feelings are not accommodated in a climate that demands targets and performance that can be measured. Such a climate does not nurture imagination or adventure or even the acquisition of knowledge, all of which are among the stated aims of most museums.

Back in 1978 I wasn't at all sure that I would find a place in this strange world I had entered. It was clear that there was untapped potential for multi-disciplinary approaches to education, and I found this exciting. But problems quickly emerged. Curators could be extraordinarily possessive, often referring to the material held in trust on the public's behalf as 'my collections'. Not only were education officers seen as servants to curators, attempts to cross boundaries were regarded with suspicion.

Rich collections in the arts and sciences were crying out to be brought together, but territories were rigidly defined and jealously patrolled. There were exceptions, and some inspiring multi-disciplinary exhibitions, but there are still pockets of resistance to any approach that takes material out of a traditional and narrowly defined context. This deprives the public from discovering new meanings for themselves by crossing the frontiers so often imposed and perpetuated by scholars. It is hard not to deduce that many scholar-curators are unsure of their authority and become nervous if they cannot control the meaning of the objects in their care. A fourteen-year-old once made a comment to me about one of the Royal Museum galleries: 'I don't like being made to feel that I'm not allowed to understand.'

Twenty years ago, those who were best placed to facilitate the crossing of frontiers were the education staff, and one of the ways we did it was by putting together integrated programmes. Rather than carve up a series of talks into departmentally defined topics – natural history, technology, ethnography, European decorative arts, ancient archaeology, and so on – we began to choose over-arching themes, polar exploration for example, or a straightforward chronologically defined period, which brought disparate material together. Sometimes we ran into trouble: a holiday project for kids on the 1950s had us carpeted by the director. And sometimes curators refused to co-operate. But hindsight suggests that we were part of, even at the forefront of, a process of radical change in the museum community which has brought a much keener awareness of public need and expectation, and much more imaginative ways of responding to them.

For my first two months at the RSM I was instructed to 'get to know the collections' and was not allowed to address an audience. Today that would be unthinkable. New staff are expected to get stuck in at once (though museum educators these days do much less hands-on teaching). But I spent two months in the galleries, asking questions, on occasion being shown material in store, and reading up background material. I found the experience rather isolating, and was eager to join my colleagues in giving talks and taking classes. I was making connections between the appeal of the third dimension and the often extraordinarily rich information which not only shed light on the objects themselves but also on the people associated with them. I wanted to communicate this, and also to recover something of the original Victorian enthusiasm for things and for eclecticism. There was potential for making connections not only in a museum context but with the concerns and aims of other institutions.

The Victorians were not inhibited by ring-fences of specialisation, and Victorian museums reflected this. The open nature of the RSM galleries, linked by expansive archways which enabled visitors to see from one gallery to the next, to look from stuffed animals to sculpture to machines (and also enabled the museum's custodians to observe and check on the behaviour of the public) were a celebration of the diversity and availability of material. The growing Victorian middle classes liked to fill their homes with things, and the museum and the department store were the twin cathedrals where the object was worshipped. There was an excitement in discovering, and imitating, objects from other times, other places. 'Things' were serious, and had their place in the cultural spectrum.

Encountering the world of objects it struck me forcibly that material culture was generally overlooked in examinations of Scotland's past. As academics in Scotland increasingly turned their attention to reawakening an interest in Scottish history and culture, little attention was paid to the artefacts which often offered the most immediate interpretation of the past and definition of 'Scottishness'.

Objects were an add-on. Schoolchildren were taken to the museum as an outing, a treat, not as an integral part of their studies. University courses commonly overlooked museums altogether. Students might study, for example, African history and literature, without an awareness of or any direct encounter with the artefacts which were at the heart of African cultural values. Newly developed literary traditions were measured against long-established old-world literatures rather than being read in the context of their own cultural environment. This becomes a double-bind, since it is partly through the tendency to think of material cultural as having most prominence in traditional and tribal societies that it is undervalued.

It took time to find my feet at the museum. In some ways, I wonder if I ever did. What I wanted most of all was to bring together all my interests, literary, historical and material. I didn't give up my literary concerns. I finished the Stevenson book, which was published in 1980, and continued to write, mainly articles and book reviews. The museum seemed to regard my extra-curricular writing activities with suspicion. The message was that I couldn't expect my reputation as a writer to be a factor in the way I was regarded in the museum. Inevitably I felt I led a divided existence which may have been prejudicial on both fronts. I tried to stay in touch with academic literary life, but wasn't able to keep up to date with new work, even in the very specific fields that were my main concern.

In the museum context, it was not only the lack of opportunity for promotion that frustrated me. It was the fact that there was little scope for contributing directly to exhibitions, temporary or permanent, which were the main outlet for intellectual and creative engagement, and a crucial means of developing new audiences. Now it is common for education staff to be involved at the early planning stages of an exhibition and to play a key role in reaching target audiences, with education officers on occasion proposing, developing and even curating exhibitions. In the 1980s there was one small, specifically educational display in which education officers played a leading role, with the support of one of the younger and more imaginative curators. That was a breakthrough.

There was at this time no exhibitions policy. There was no consistency of presentation or style. There was little thought given to the purpose of an exhibition, or the public it was trying reach. Similarly, for the books and catalogues the RSM published through HMSO, there was no publications policy and no editorial consistency. It was often curators who decided what to write and what to publish and how many copies to print. No one asked why a book was being published. It was unusual for either exhibition texts or books to be edited. It was a situation I found bizarre and disheartening.

In the 1980s education staff were still considered as handmaidens (and they were mainly women) to the curators (mainly men). The curatorial structure allowed for through-grading, which meant that in the natural course of things, unless there were serious deficiencies in their work, curators made their way up the ladder. For education staff there was no through-grading. We were stuck. When the Head of Education retired, all four Guide Lecturers applied for the job, and my colleague Sheila Brock was successful. She was a good friend and well aware of my frustrations, but that couldn't disguise the fact that I was left with nowhere to go. I was also under increasing financial pressure, as by this time Angus and I had parted and my eldest child was soon to enter further education. I applied for a few jobs elsewhere and had several interviews, without success. I felt that by going down the museum education road I had burnt my academic boats. But I was beginning to take on some writing and editing for the museum, and it was this that led me out of a dead-end.

A change in the system meant that the museum and other publicly funded institutions were free to publish directly, without going through HMSO. It was decided that in order to do this the RSM needed an editor, and eventually I got the job, and with it promotion. It was 1987. By this time the institution itself had changed. In 1985 the Royal Scottish Museum amalgamated with the National Museum of Antiquities of Scotland, with the ultimate aim of creating a new museum to house the Scottish collections. It was a time of very mixed feelings among the staff. The RSM was bigger and had a higher profile than NMAS. Not unnaturally, the latter felt they were being taken over, and this was reinforced by the understanding that ultimately the Queen Street building would be vacated. In Chambers Street there were suspicions that the Scottish collections would hog resources, especially if a new building materialised. My own view was very positive. As an education officer I looked forward to extending my concerns to the Scottish collections. I saw it as an opportunity to get to grips with Scottish history and culture. I also saw that the amalgamation expanded the exhibition and publishing potential enormously.

Soon after my appointment, it was decided to shift the publishing operation to Queen Street. I was sorry to leave Chambers Street. One of the abiding pleasures of working there was walking through the glorious Main Hall every morning *en route* to my office, and again at night when I left. I particularly relished the experience late on a winter evening, when the lights were low and there was little sign of human activity. The side galleries took on an atmosphere that was both intimate and mysterious. In Queen Street the publishing section was housed not in the museum but across the road, in the basement of York Buildings. Upstairs were the curators of the Scottish historical and archaeological collections. What York Buildings lost in inspiring architecture it gained in congeniality. I was soon to feel very much at home. It is dislocating now to see the building remade as luxury flats with bathrooms and coffee sold on the ground floor.

Queen Street was very different from Chambers Street. The dynamic was less formal, and there was a flexibility both intellectual and operational. (There were also, as in Chambers Street and just about every institution I've encountered, fierce clashes of both personality and intellect, which could be exasperating but added to the gaiety of nations.) My Scottish literary and historical concerns had a legitimacy in the Queen Street context; I no longer felt compelled to be furtive or apologetic about these interests.

Publishing, however, had its own frustrations and difficulties, and it took several years before it began to move forward with a degree of confidence and institutionally supported purpose. There were several reasons for this, but conflicting aims and priorities were a major inhibition. The National Museums of Scotland, as the amalgamated institution was now called, believed that publishing was an important museum function, but questions of what should be published, for whom, and how publishing should be financed were unresolved. The structure of the publishing unit was itself problematic: there was one editor, three designers (which reflected the emphasis on high design and production values rather than readership), and at first no one to handle marketing, distribution or publicity. It was with painful slowness that the balance was changed.

I believed that publishing was crucial to the NMS effort to reach out to wider audiences. Publicly-funded museums have a responsibility to make information publicly available, and publishing is a very effective way of doing this; books can reach parts that exhibitions can't. I believed that museum publishing should be subsidised, as exhibitions were subsidised, but that there was also commercial potential. Traditionally, museum books were curator and design driven. I wanted to see books that were author and readership driven, but without losing the authority of museum scholarship or the quality of museum design. The trick was to get the mixture right. We were beginning to get there when I moved away from museum publishing in 1997, but achieving that balance is always going to be difficult.

In 1989 the NMS took the first public step in the campaign for a new museum to house the Scottish collections. This took the form of an exhibition called 'The Wealth of a Nation' which featured a strikingly diverse gathering of star Scottish archaeological and historical material, with a book of the same name which I compiled and edited. At the opening of the exhibition Malcolm Rifkind, then Secretary of State for Scotland, announced government support for a new museum. It was an announcement that changed the lives of many people who worked for the NMS, including mine.

Work had already been done to form a picture of the material that would be featured in a new museum, if we ever got it. Almost at once this work intensified. In 1990, I negotiated a short period of unpaid leave to write a book to celebrate the sixtieth anniversary of the National Trust for Scotland. The approach I took was to construct a narrative which showed how NTS properties illuminated aspects of Scottish history, rather than present them as isolated icons of the past. (The NTS were dubious about this approach as they were much more used to stressing the individual and distinctive qualities of their sites and properties, rather than presenting them in a wider context.) Writing the book plunged me into the broad current of Scotland's history, a parallel exercise to the work on the Scottish collections being tackled at the same time by my museum colleagues but in which I myself, at this stage, had no direct involvement. *Scotland in Trust* was published by Richard Drew later that year. The book was quite successful and Richard was encouraging me to think of writing more for him.

I was thinking seriously of returning to a freelance existence when I was asked by Robert Anderson, the museum's director since 1984, if I would take on the task of co-ordinating the initial exhibition brief for the new museum. This was the brief being prepared for the architectural competition. I requested a week to reflect on it: should I go or should I stay? I had mentally and emotionally adjusted to the prospect of full-time writing, helped by the fact that I had so much enjoyed my six weeks' intensive work on *Scotland in Trust*. But it was a financial risk, and I still had a son who had not completed his education. In reality I made up my mind at once: I wanted to be involved in the Museum of Scotland. A day or two's thought confirmed my first reaction, that I couldn't say no; the decision had nothing to do with common sense or caution, or the needs of my family.

For the next six years I divided my time between my publishing activities and working on the new museum. The prospect of a Museum of Scotland was a beneficial development for NMS publishing because it opened the door to change. We took on an additional part-time member of staff on the editorial and marketing side, and so made the first move towards getting a better balance. But all those discussions with Richard Drew about books I might write were still buzzing in my head and I was reluctant to abandon the urge to take on some serious writing. (Richard himself merged his company with W&R Chambers, which was in turn taken over and ceased to have an independent existence. Eventually Richard became a casualty of this process, and I suspect I would have been too. It was probably a lucky escape.) When the opportunity came up to take on a biography of Naomi Mitchison for Virago, I seized it. At that time, late 1991, part of my Museum of Scotland role was to develop displays for the twentieth-century gallery and working on Mitchison would dovetail nicely with this. Then I learnt that the proposal I and colleagues had produced for the twentieth century was being dropped, just when I thought I had finally achieved some kind of synthesis between the museum and my writing. It is a reflection on the management of the project that this decision was never communicated to me directly; I was left to deduce it.

However, a degree of symbiosis did come, in 1994, the centenary year of the death of Robert Louis Stevenson. I had put a proposal forward for an exhibition to mark this event, which was rejected. At that time I didn't know that I had a colleague who was a Stevenson enthusiast. Maureen Barrie had an idea for an exhibition that would celebrate Stevenson in the South Seas and draw on the rich NMS collections of South Pacific material. She asked me to be involved; this time, the proposal was accepted. Working on 'Treasure Islands', both the exhibition and the book that accompanied it, was an enormous pleasure. As always, when the work is both enjoyable and rewarding, it didn't seem all that difficult to find the time for it. Part of the pleasure was the commitment and creative enthusiasm of Maureen herself, who took on the major curatorial responsibility. The result was an exhibition which conveyed a sense of the way Stevenson's literary imagination developed from childhood and responded to his South Sea voyages. Most exhibitions about writers present memorabilia and other objects connected with their lives. *Treasure Islands* used objects to express a writer's work. I would like to try something similar again sometime.

Work on the Museum of Scotland proceeded in fits and starts. The story of the evolution of the building is told in Charles McKean's book *The Creation of the Museum of Scotland* (1999), which makes clear that there was a tension between architectural and curatorial aspirations. Another factor, which profoundly affected my role, was the need to meet public expectation, which had been heightened by the fundraising campaign (government funding was promised for the building, but not for fit out or the exhibitions). We had to make sure we delivered what we promised, and did not promise what we could not deliver.

The proposed museum was from the start freighted with symbolic meaning, of nationhood and of the distinctive nature of Scottish history and cultural expression. This was irrespective of what it would actually contain. At its inception, we did not know that Scotland was moving towards a revived parliament, or that the next decade would see a striking resurgence of interest in Scotland's past. The two things are clearly linked, and equally clearly the Museum of Scotland, both the building and its contents, have made a Scottish identity more visible.

The process of achieving the museum was hugely complex. It involved reconciling three potentially contradictory goals: the need to find appropriate space for Scottish material which in many cases had never been on public display; the need for a distinguished and distinctive building which would take its place in a unique historic townscape; and the need to present material meaningfully to both the people of Scotland and visitors from overseas. There were times when I and my colleagues felt caught in the cross-fire, and times when we had cause to curse thrawn architects, impenetrable management, multiple egocentric agendas, unnecessary aggravation and a vast array of counter-productive manoeuvres. But it was an experience I would not have missed for anything.

Once the several phases and versions of exhibition brief were complete, my role was as 'script co-ordinator', responsible for ensuring that the display texts communicated what was intended in a way that was appropriate and accessible. My main concern was for the script covering Scotland from 1100 to 1914. We aimed for a text that was authoritative and accessible, bearing in mind that different displays would appeal to different audiences. The approach taken in the pre-history area, *Early People*, was rather different from that in the historical galleries. I wasn't very happy with its mingled tones of the colloquial and the academic, but it has proved a popular gallery.

In the historical galleries our brief was to highlight those aspects of the past that are best expressed through material culture, and particularly through the material culture that was held in the NMS collections. We were presenting multiple stories through a thematic approach, not a single narrative with a beginning, a middle and an end. That was something best done through published histories. In many cases our chosen themes provided their own context: the

Medieval Church gallery, for example. In others the material lent itself to a chronological, sequential narrative: telling the Jacobite story was no problem, although the wealth of Jacobite relics (objects relating to the period following defeat rather than the risings themselves) gives the display a rather different emphasis from that in most written histories. The relics vividly demonstrate the continuing hold of Jacobite feeling long after the cause itself was dead. There were some key episodes of Scotland's history which were almost impossible to present through displays but which we knew the public would expect to be there: the Scottish Enlightenment is a good example. How do you use three-dimensional material to express intellectual ideas? These were issues that were strongly debated. And they were issues we wanted the Scottish public to think about. Why do more artefacts survive from society's elite than from the working class? Why are so many of the museum's most resonant objects connected with the church? Why are there so many things relating to the smoking and sniffing of tobacco and to eating and drinking?

And underlying all other questions, implicit but powerful, what is it that makes the Scottish nation distinctive? Or is it distinctive? And if it is not, what other nations does it share experience and character with? And how does Scotland relate to other nations? There are parts of the Museum of Scotland where the issues of identity and influence become quite explicit, especially where the theme is the impact of Scots and Scottish ideas and culture overseas. As has often been said, the focus sometimes becomes clearer and stronger when Scottishness is removed from its home territory. It can also, of course, become distorted.

At an early stage the possibility was discussed of setting aside a gallery that would concern itself head-on with Scottish identity. This was dropped through lack of space rather than as the result of a reasoned decision. But perhaps it would have been redundant. In a sense, identity is the theme of the entire museum, from the examination of the landscape, which is where the story begins, to the temporary twentieth-century gallery which so clearly demonstrates that much of what made twentieth-century life in Scotland different from earlier periods was shared with most of the developed world. Scotland had cars, refrigerators, washing machines, football. The differences were not in kind, but in make, model and colour.

Perhaps what the material culture of the twentieth century shows us is that we, like other nations, began to define ourselves in terms of time rather than place. The speed of change made us aware of how different we were from before rather than from elsewhere. Horses, for example, which had been a dominant feature of travel and of warfare for millennia, disappeared from the streets. When elsewhere provides the criterion, it is generally because elsewhere is in a different, pre-industrial, or now industrial, time zone rather than because it occupies another space. The cultural differences that we become increasingly aware of as incomers make their homes among us are the result of occupying a different time zone. Part of the shock of seeing American bombers in action in Afghanistan is precisely this clash of time zones: Afghan tribesmen may be equipped with modern automatic weapons and sophisticated communication systems, but the relationship between landscape and the life it determines appears timeless.

The 'before and after' criteria make us more aware of those spaces that seem least affected by the speed of change, and we increasingly turn to these in an attempt to recover the defining nature of space. The landscape, however eroded and manipulated by human activity, which itself contributes to its character, remains distinctively 'Scottish', so much so that it is furiously marketed as a tourist attraction. Scotland's washing machines and cars may be no different from those in other 'developed' nations (though I have met Americans who have an image of Scotland as a quaint backwater where sanitation and diet are primitive), but its mountains, lochs and castles are unique. The promotion of tourism is a dangerous contradiction as well as being of equivocal benefit to communities that have come to depend on it. Most tourists want the authentic and unspoilt to be conveniently accessible. How 'authentic' is a landscape with a dual carriageway and a visitor centre? As more people become aware that the best way to connect with Scotland's landscape is to go to places accessible only on foot or by boat, these places, too, will change their nature. Life and the elements mean that change has always been inevitable. We can't stop it, but we need to recognise it and recognise our, disproportionately large, share of responsibility for it.

What is interesting is that very often what new Scots adopt as symbols of a new identity are precisely those old icons that we hang onto in a bid to ensure that the speed of development does not sever our links with the past. If there is now, as there seems to be, a striking resurgence of interest in history, it is surely because of a profound need to maintain connections and continuity. And I think alongside this, part of this, is a reborn interest in place and a wish to rediscover its meanings and its old intimacy. And in Scotland that means re-learning ways of relating to landscape, and reclaiming it from both the tripper's view through the windscreen and the Munro-bagger's trophy counting.

Museums have a critical role to play in ensuring that our links with the past and the people who have gone before are not stretched to breaking point. Part of the function of history museums is to represent a collective memory, especially now that other symbols and vehicles of memory are in decline among the indigenously Scottish population – the church, oral tradition, social cohesion. So many aspects of our lives have lost their distinctiveness. Where we live no longer determines what we eat and what we wear and how we furnish our homes. My visits to Israel in the early 1960s were my introduction to Middle Eastern food, and when I left I was sure I would have to return, if only to eat fellafel again. Now I can buy it in my local supermarket.

This diminishing of distinctiveness may explain the attractions of the past and the burgeoning interest in family history and genealogy. The past can be accessed in all sorts of ways, through documents and documentaries, published accounts and interpretations, film and fiction, reconstructions, monuments and commemorations. What museums offer, at the most basic level, are objects that tell us about the form and texture of life. The substantiality of three-dimensional material is both real and reassuring. No museum can replicate the actual experience of, for example, a collier in a three-foot shaft or a Roman centurion on the Antonine Wall, and arguably should not try, because it can only be a replication. There is an increasing trend towards over-interpretation in museums, in an effort to fulfil fashionable notions of accessibility or often simply as marketing gimmicks. I believe that this can undermine the value of objects and their ability to connect us with the past.

On display in the Museum of Scotland are snowshoes that belonged to an Orcadian Arctic explorer called John Rae. They are beautiful objects in themselves, made from bent birch threaded with sinew. Rae travelled many hundreds of miles on snowshoes, often alone, often in savage conditions. Pause for a moment or two in front of Rae's snowshoes and think about arriving in 1835 at Moose Factory on Hudson Bay after a voyage from Stromness of many weeks. Think about this young Scot observing Cree Indians using snowshoes for their winter travel, and adopting them himself. Think about moving over the snow in them, and also learning how to look after and repair them.

I have no personal link, so far as I am aware, with John Rae, Orkney, or the Hudson's Bay Company which employed him and many other Scots from Orkney and the West Highlands. But these snowshoes are part of a history in which I and millions of others, on both sides of the Atlantic, share. They are intimately connected with an individual who was remarkable for his achievement in exploring and mapping Arctic Canada, and also for his readiness to learn from Canada's aboriginal peoples. The snowshoes are emblems of a collective memory that encompasses the activities of Scots overseas. Very few Scottish families are without a connection overseas. The connection may not be with Canadian winters; nevertheless, John Rae's snowshoes are arguably a more powerful symbol of Scottish character and achievement than tartan or bagpipes.

There are, of course, both tartan and bagpipes in the Museum of Scotland. Neither are unique to Scotland, yet both are recognised as Scottish throughout the world. Snowshoes are not. You need to be provided with a little bit of information to understand the significance of John Rae's snowshoes. You can, apparently, understand tartan and bagpipes without any information. And this is precisely the problem with such icons. They are shortcuts, which bypass most of what is interesting and important about them. 'Tartanry' is denigrated as a cheap and bogus version of Scotland, but the social and cultural history of tartan and its impact illuminates an ambivalent attitude to the Highlands which is a deeply influential current in Scotland's past.

As a child I had little interest in snowshoes although I spent several years in a place of cold winters and plenty snow. I had little interest in museums. The first I remember going to was with my mother, New York's Metropolitan Museum, where I was overawed by echoing rooms and classical statuary. Many museums were designed to inspire awe. The cathedral-like nature of the Royal Museum's Main Hall is no accident. The educational role which was central to so many nineteenth-century foundations was linked with the elevation of learning. The works of nature and the works of humankind were presented as equally wondrous and inspiring. Victorian educators were ambivalent, as they wanted to equip the populace with the skills and information necessary to be productive, but without encouraging the beneficiaries to get above themselves. So to encourage learning in an environment that was not conducive to comfort and informality was desirable. (This attitude may have fuelled the sense of outrage when it was realised that a large public space with a roof provided ideal territory for what was considered inappropriate behaviour between the sexes, a phenomenon which provoked press comment in the late nineteenth century.)

A building that was itself a symbol of national and civic pride filled with material, national and international, demonstrating a commitment to knowledge and instruction was in some respects the ultimate expression of confident identity. There was a long campaign for the museum that was eventually built in Chambers Street in the 1860s, just as there was a long campaign for the museum now standing alongside it. It is easy to forget, especially when an institution becomes a familiar part of the cultural and educational environment, which the Museum of Scotland probably now is, that campaigns and the often agonising process of achieving ambitious goals, in themselves build identities. This affects both the institutions and the people involved in the process. If in 1978 when I joined the RSM I was tentative about what I was doing there, ten years of working on the Museum of Scotland deepened my participation in Scotland's past and present. And participation is a crucial factor in the construction of identity. I understand Scotland, and my ambivalence, better than I did.

CHAPTER TEN

Reinventions

AT THE END of 2001 I reached my sixtieth birthday and retired from my workplace of twenty-three years. Like most people who reach this particular milestone, I had mixed feelings. The last few years of working at the National Museums of Scotland had been particularly rewarding, and yet my tolerance of increasingly convoluted administration and the continuing imbalance of objectives had worn thin. I wasn't overjoyed at having completed six decades, but there was a great deal I wanted to do which only the release from salaried employment would make possible. And I was finding it difficult to give the time I wanted to my elderly father, now living alone.

Some months into retirement I began to feel I had cast off an intellectual straitjacket. All institutions impose their own demands and strictures. The NMS gave me creative scope which I would not have found in academia, but, partly the result of its anachronistic structure, it was an intellectually frustrating environment. Yet my fourth and final job there could hardly have been more appropriate for me, personally and intellectually.

In my last few years on the staff of the National Museums of Scotland, I was again in the position of having no readily identifiable role. I was not a curator, an education officer, an editor. My role developing display scripts for the Museum of Scotland ended when it opened to the public in December 1998. I then became head of a section which came to be called Museum of Scotland International. To solve the problem of form filling, where 'occupation' was asked for, I came up with the designation 'museum officer', which to me conveyed very little apart from the fact that I worked in a museum, but was never queried.

Although I am not keen on labels, they can be a convenient shorthand, and to be without a ready means of defining occupation is a disadvantage. Few people other than my immediate colleagues were aware of what my job entailed, and this made it difficult to explain the section's role as well as my own. The stated aim of Museum of Scotland International was to further understanding of emigration and the activities of Scots overseas. In the context of the history of emigration and its impact, and of the current interest in genealogy and the pursuit of ancestral roots, these aspirations embodied huge potential for generating public interest and institutional partnerships. To carry this through we had a small team of which only two, myself and the project's curator, were full time. Financial resources were limited; we were expected to raise money elsewhere. My work involved tracing surviving material, developing exhibitions, giving lectures and attending conferences, promoting and publicising, and working with other institutions, nationally and internationally. I believed it was necessary to be both strategic and opportunist, although this inevitably generated extra work. I struggled with insufficient resources and pressure to attract outside funding, and with the growing weight of administration which was affecting all the staff. Huge quantities of paper stacked up on my desk, much of which had very little relevance to the job I was trying to do. This is not unusual, of course, but it is extraordinary that so many organisations seem not to grasp that if admin is divorced from executive involvement it will be resisted and resented.

Yet I loved the job, the real job, and felt it was absolutely right for me. I felt I had fallen into it by accident, just as I had fallen into the museum in the first place. But this indefinable job reflected my background and experience, and even the fact that there has never been an easy way of defining who and what I am. My new role was international and cross-cultural. I had myself been part of a Scottish diaspora, and of course I was also part of that first dispersal which had given rise to the word 'diaspora'. Professionally, it brought together my multifarious roles in the museum, and I was able to draw on contacts outwith NMS which had been incidental but in this context became relevant and beneficial. There seemed to be some kind of synchronicity between my divided personal and professional identities.

Over my twenty-three years at the museum I worked for several different line managers and directors. Bosses and colleagues may have very little influence on your day-to-day work, but they have enormous power over your sense of yourself. I have worked with and for men and women who have been overbearing, careless, indifferent, concerned, obsessive, supportive, manipulative. There have been warmth and comradeship, bullying and undermining. I have left work at the end of the day frustrated and diminished, or uplifted and encouraged. I have felt undervalued and ignored; gratified and rewarded. I never wept in the toilets, but I often went home deeply depressed and often lay awake at night wrestling in a state of extreme anxiety with some boss-generated problem. And then of course I was a boss and a colleague myself. How was I affecting the lives of others, their sense of who and what they were? I hope positively, not negatively, but I know the inadvertent and the casual can have unimagined consequences.

There are changing fashions in management as well as in personal styles. In recent years there has been emphasis on teamwork, and I was sent on several team-building courses. Did they achieve anything? At best, they could be quite enjoyable and provide an opportunity of getting to know colleagues a little better. Did I learn anything? Not much. Was I a better team player or team leader as a result? I doubt it. Did I gain a better understanding of my own potential or that of others? Only of those with whom I had not already worked. There are some people incapable of working in a team who will resist all attempts to persuade them into a different *modus operandi*.

Working relationships, like all relationships, depend on good communication and the acknowledgement of the qualities and abilities of others. Many people find these difficult, however good their intentions. There are highly articulate people who cannot make their needs clear and visionaries who cannot transmit their vision. Can bad managers learn to do things differently? I am sure they can if they want to – it's like giving up smoking. The problem is that many are unable to acknowledge there is a problem, and others who are convinced that their own particular management style works.

Are men more likely to resort to strong-arm tactics than women? Probably, but not exclusively. Are women more likely to be caring and uncompetitive? Probably, but I suspect the margin is a narrow one, especially as pressure on women to demonstrate that they are as effective as men in management often results in women adopting macho tactics. It isn't easy to get things right. Adaptability is of the essence. Different circumstances and different personalities need different approaches.

If the working environment is good and the relationships with colleagues positive, the effects of work on personal identity and wellbeing are likely to be benign. In these circumstances it becomes less important to create a barrier between work and home, between the professional and the personal. The destruction of that barrier is, I believe, of particular help to women, especially those who feel under pressure to deny or underplay their domestic and maternal roles in order to demonstrate that they are truly 'professional'. In recent years there has been a trend, particularly for professional women, to dress more and more like men. They wear suits, tailored jackets, dark colours. At the museum I would sometimes find myself in meetings where all the women were wearing black or grey, while the men in bright shirts and ties were much less sombre. Dress is a very complex and very emblematic issue, but I find this trend disturbing, for it indicates that to be taken seriously in the working environment women perceive a need to conform to sartorial and operational styles that are dominated by male conventions.

For many people, work is necessary in order to earn a living but life is another country. For others, work of some kind is an essential part of what they are. They may identify themselves first as a plumber or a teacher, then as husband, wife, parent, football supporter. I am unhappy if deprived of some kind of purposeful activity. That activity does not need to be 'going to work'. It can be digging the garden, reading, writing, walking the dog, painting walls, giving a lecture or cooking a meal. For billions of people, 'purposeful activity' is what they have to do to stay alive. I am lucky. All the activities mentioned above are things I enjoy and provide a great deal of satisfaction. Yes, they may also entail getting wet for the sake of the dog, flogging myself to meet a deadline, driving a hundred icy miles to a lecture engagement, or the intense vexation of computers crashing. There is always the risk of criticism, rejection, failure, as well as discomfort. I can work for months on a book which is never published, or published to total silence. I can spend days preparing a lecture which is then delivered to an audience of half a dozen in a chilly church hall. But I have retained the capacity to believe, most of the time, that I am doing something worthwhile – exercising the dog, myself, my mind, my imagination.

Of all these activities, writing is at the core of my existence. If I go for too long without writing I experience a restless and dissatisfied malaise. I need the physical activity of writing as well as the mental, whether at a keyboard or with a pencil on a scrap of paper. When I am researching a topic I reach a point when ideas start demanding to be put into words and I cannot resist the urge to start writing. Sometimes this is premature but it is never wasted, even if I have to rethink and rewrite at a later stage. I often find writing very difficult. Occasionally it's a breeze and hard to stop.

With retirement, my relationship to my work has changed. I have more choice, the freedom to map out my days with minimal external interference. I am, of course, subject to deadlines and the requirements, and rejections, of publishers, but my early freelance apprenticeship was a good training. It is a way of working with which I feel comfortable. It is solitary but not lonely. Friends and associates are never far away, and their company is all the more enjoyable for the fact that my working life no longer involves incessant interaction, which was sometimes with people who made life unnecessarily difficult. (One of the NMS training courses I didn't attend was on dealing with difficult people.)

Retirement has not deprived me of something essential to my self-image. I can describe myself as 'writer', and do so with much less reticence than in my pre-museum days. Age has its compensations. And if I want to dodge the issue I can simply tick the 'retired' box on those marketing questionnaires that only need to know whether or not you are living on a pension. I have returned to a familiar life as freelance writer on much more favourable terms than before. The grinding pressures of money worries, child care and an unstable emotional life have gone. All this compensates for the bombardment of media images that encourage a public perception of women's anonymity unless they look young and, by implication, sexually vigorous. Grey-haired women don't think, drink, make love or make babies. Women themselves often collude in this, by endeavouring to conform to this stereotype.

For my fiftieth birthday I had thrown a party, cramming a large number of people into my small house in South Queensferry. I decided to mark the next decade more quietly. Arthur and I planned to celebrate my birthday on the island of Gigha, but it was a wild day. Fierce winds drove crashing waves up Loch Fyne and sent spray flying over the road. We ventured out only to watch the storm lash the pier at Ardrishaig and the shore by Inverneil. But the next day was calm and sunny, so we crossed on the ferry to Gigha and walked up Creag Bhan, the little hill in the northern half of the island, from where we had a sparkling view of Islay and the Paps of Jura beyond.

The people of Gigha had recently made a successful bid to buy their island. I have no personal link with the island, but wanted to spend what was a significant date for me in a place that has a significance for Scotland. The changed potential for land ownership is probably the most radical legislation undertaken by the Scottish parliament. Not radical enough, some might argue, but a beginning. I have lived in Scotland for over thirty years. I may still be ambivalent about my place in Scotland, but I have no doubts at all about my commitment to Scotland as a nation and a culture. In childhood Scotland was 'home' emotionally, but alien in practice. Gradually I have got to know the country better, the landscape, the culture, the history and the people. On Gigha I added another little piece of Scotland to that knowledge, a piece that belongs to the people who live there.

My Scottish years have diminished the gulf between the emotional and the intellectual. Literature has helped. My early reading of Scott; writing a biography of Robert Louis Stevenson and then finding that he wouldn't go away; discovering the extraordinarily diverse voices of the twentieth century; these have all been hugely important. Ten years spent working on the Museum of Scotland was valuable not only because it entailed immersion in Scotland's past but because it was a collective and intensely committed effort. But the landscape more than anything else seems to offer an experience of felt connection. On Creag Bhan in the winter sunshine, on the East Lothian cliffs with the Bass Rock rising so astonishingly out of the North Sea, on Beinn an Eoin with the wind howling and the rain obscuring the surrounding mountains, on the sandy Solway shore or the dazzling sands of Harris with the westward pull of the Atlantic, in Rackwick Bay or Crannoch Woods... these are places personal to me, but it is tempting to suggest that the sensation of *feeling* a place is a particularly Scottish phenomenon. Scots have been strikingly effective in expressing a blended physicality and emotional resonance in place, which has created an image of Scotland that has had enduring, if at times illusory, appeal.

When my grandfather arrived in Scotland in 1919 he came as a Jew distant from the land of his birth and even more distant from the land where his people had originated. It was not the romantic appeal of Scotland that drew him, but the intellectual appeal. He was going to make his life in the city of David Hume and the Enlightenment. As rabbi he had a specific job to do on behalf of Edinburgh's Jewish community and of Jews in Scotland generally. But he also saw himself as having a responsibility as citizen of his adopted country. How he identified himself in relation to Lithuania, Poland, Russia and Germany, all of which shaped his upbringing and education, I do not know. But I do know that he identified himself as a Scottish Jew. One identity he was born with, the other he built. My father, growing up in the 'two worlds' he describes in his book with that title, has worn his two identities unambiguously. He has played a key role in re-establishing Scottish literature in world awareness, and although he broke with the orthodoxy of his upbringing he has sustained his Jewish heritage. As I have tried to illustrate in this book, identity has been less clear-cut for the next generation, my generation.

My brother and sister both live in England. Alan has a Scottish wife and retains close connections with Scotland, where he went to school and lived for most of his twenties. Liz also lived in Scotland for several years but now visits only occasionally. As a student Liz went to Israel and worked on a kibbutz. Alan has never been there, nor back to the United States where he was born, although Liz has visited once. They each have their own balance of identities, and neither is the same as mine.

In the next generation the balance shifts again. Two of my children live in Wales. Gowan lives in Scotland but has spent significant periods of time in both the United States and Germany. She has visited Berlin, where her great-grandfather studied, several times. I have never been there. Rachel visited Lithuania specifically to explore and film the connection with her great-grandfather. Work took Gideon there, and shortly afterwards I followed in their footsteps. The fact that they are re-establishing this link, completing the circle in a sense, is of immense importance to me, but its meaning to them is their own. The Jewish strand is there for them to acknowledge to whatever extent they choose. As teenagers, Rachel and Gowan asked their grandfather to teach them some Hebrew. Identities become diluted from one generation to another, but can be recovered or reinvented. They can be willed. They can involve choice as well as birthright.

Maintaining a Jewish identity for the non-practising Jew, and particularly for the non-practising half Jew who is looking for ways of nurturing the Jewish half, is now more complex than ever, for it is not possible to ignore Israel and the appalling distortion of the ideals, that certainly my grandfather subscribed to in the 1920s and '30s, which created the Jewish state. I responded to those ideals when I went to Israel forty years ago. Although I encountered Israeli fear and distrust of their Arab neighbours, and although there were those who, for good reason, genuinely believed that given half a chance those neighbours would obliterate them, I don't think anyone in 1960 could have predicted what is happening now. There are many ghastly ironies in the fact that a country created as a refuge has itself become murderous and that some of the leading promoters of Israel's claim to the lands seized in the Six Day War have not come from Central or Eastern European countries associated with a history of persecution but from North America. I could not go to Israel now, unless it were to ally myself with those voices of protest which seem to be having all too little influence on government.

I wrote the first draft of this chapter on the first night of Pesach, 2002. The previous day I read with approval a piece in the *Guardian* by Suzanne Goldberg suggesting that Jews celebrating the Seder should invite Palestinians to their table in recognition of an oppression that echoes Jewish experience. The day after, on the second day of Pesach, news came through that a suicide bomber had entered a hotel in Netanya, where people were gathered for what is a most joyous ritual with a particular emphasis on welcoming strangers, and blown up himself and them.

My grandfather never contemplated making his life in Palestine (he did not live to see it become Israel). My father did, but in the end chose another direction. I did, but not seriously. Now I have to force myself to read newspaper accounts of the latest bombings and reprisals, the appalling deaths of Palestinian and Israeli youngsters. I find myself wondering which is worse, the manipulation of the young Palestinians who become suicide bombers, or the apparently inevitable brutalisation of Israeli soldiers. It is a terrible thing that Jews, deprived of territory, always uncertain of their welcome, despised and massacred, contributed so much to human creativity and advance, but have now become a symbol of intolerance and human destruction. If I try to dissociate myself from Israel's implosion I deny an essential part of who I am, and collude in the disturbing re-emergence of anti-semitism, which is camouflaged by an understandable condemnation of Israel.

I always wanted to return to America, and that hope was nourished through my interest in American literature and history. All through the English half of my childhood there was a stream of American visitors through our home. It was 1976 before I actually went back, and when I applied for a visa I had to make a decision about citizenship. I could elect for American citizenship and travel on an American passport, or renounce all claim to be an American and stick to my British passport with a visa for the United States. I chose the latter. It was a kind of watershed, but this was the first of many visits to the US which revived my American connections. I feel very much at home in the United States and often miss it. I like the Americans I meet and have often been touched and sustained by their warmth and hospitality. My experience of the American academic and museum environments has been stimulating and regenerating. I always come home buzzing with thoughts and ideas. I continue to read American poetry and fiction. Donna Tartt's *The Little Friend* (2002), though set in Mississippi, returned me to my small-town upstate New York childhood in a tidal rush. Being in the US and reading its literature re-connects me with an American child who never anticipated, however insistent the talk of 'going home', that leaving would be such an abrupt closing of a chapter.

When I first returned to the United States it was a major undertaking. I left Angus and the children for two weeks, flying to New York first, so that I could meet my American publisher, before going on to Laramie, Wyoming, and then a conference on Westerns at Sun Valley, Idaho. I stayed with friends of the Calders in a penthouse apartment on Central Park West. Their lifestyle as high-flying New York professionals I found quite intimidating. They were out of the house at seven in the morning and often not back until late at night. 'Help yourself to the contents of the fridge,' they said, and indicated a huge American refrigerator stuffed with food. Their black housekeeper came in every morning, made herself a gigantic multi-layered sandwich and settled down to watch television.

I explored New York, mainly on foot. I walked down to the Battery, picking my way through the junkies in Washington Square, wandering through the dwarfing Wall Street canyons, and from time to time straying into ominous sidestreets where I felt I shouldn't be. When on one occasion I walked back to the apartment on the park side of the street I was scolded by my hosts. 'Never walk on the park side of the street, even in daylight,' they warned me, and had a tale of an acquaintance who had been recently murdered. They similarly warned against the subway. But two years later, in New York again, I and Gowan went by subway to visit an old university friend living in SoHo, assured by him that it was perfectly safe, as indeed it was.

New York was a place where conspicuous drug addiction rivalled conspicuous consumption, and string quartets on street corners vied with incessant police sirens. There were stunning riches, institutional, cultural and personal, and grim deprivation. People rushed but traffic crawled.

Arriving at Laramie I was met at the airport by Ed Long, history professor and authority on the Civil War, and his wife Barbara, cartographer. They were a memorable example of warm and generous American hospitality, and introduced me to, amongst other things, the Western history holdings of the University of Wyoming, Mexican food, and a bar scarred by the bullets of a recent quarrel over a woman. I travelled on to Salt Lake City by Greyhound bus, through spectacular mountains and descending to a city glowing in the evening sun. The next day I continued on a tiny plane to Sun Valley.

The following few days were an extraordinary mix of movie stars and directors, historians and critics. My contribution was on 'The paradox of the Western hero', and I shared a panel with Clint Eastwood and Warren Oates. The night before in the bar Warren Oates had been heard to mutter, after a drink or two, 'Paradox? Paradox? What the hell's a paradox?' Clint Eastwood was friendly and charming, and if anything larger in life than on screen. He had a physical presence of such magnetism that I have to admit to going rather weak at the knees when I shook his hand. In this melee of personalities I felt very much on the edge, and was glad of the company of the one person I knew, Philip French of *The Observer*. I got up early one morning to walk with him to the grave of Hemingway who had killed himself in Sun Valley in 1961.

My most recent visit to New York was six weeks after 11 September 2001. Two things were unusual. There was a thickness in the air and a pervasive smell, acrid and musty. There was a graininess which you could feel on the skin and could not avoid breathing. It was worst in the vicinity of Ground Zero, but detectable also in Central Park. There was an eerie absence of police sirens; the papers reported a sharp reduction in crime. But the city hadn't gone quiet. The traffic continued through the night as always, and as always it was impossible to sleep. The garbage was noisily collected in the small hours, the only time when trucks could get through the traffic. On Sunday morning in Central Park there were singers and banjo players and a steel band belting out Bob Marley classics to a multi-ethnic crowd clutching the stars and stripes.

In New York I have had taxi drivers who scarcely speak English and have had breakfast coffee in diners where the stream of Italian is only briefly interrupted to serve non-Italophones. On the streets there is a great deal of Spanish, and several oriental languages. I guess Yiddish has probably disappeared; I've certainly never heard it. English voices are quite common, and sometimes Scottish. You often catch Caribbean tones. Shop names echo every European language. Visit Ellis Island and you can almost hear them in the huge halls where thousands were assembled to endure the rigorous inspection process which the authorities imposed on the 'huddled masses' who disembarked there. 'That terrible Ellis Island,' was the way Henry James described it, 'the first harbour of refuge and stage of patience for the million or so of immigrants annually knocking at our official door. Before this door, which opens to them there only with a hundred forms and ceremonies, grindings and grumblings of the key, they stand appealing and waiting, marshalled, herded, divided, sub-divided, sorted, sifted, searched, fumigated...' No doubt among them were members of the Daiches or Levin families.

My grandfather spoke excellent English, with no accent. He spoke and corresponded in several European languages, especially German. Hebrew he had been steeped in from birth, and he had studied Latin and Greek. He came from a Yiddish culture – his birthplace, Vilna, was a vibrant centre of Yiddish literature and music – but did not care to speak it. My Yiddish-speaking great grandfather in Leeds spoke no English. My Highland grandfather spoke English but my grandmother's family spoke Scots. At some point my Mackay antecedents must have been Gaelic speakers. With this polyglot inheritance I should have some facility in languages other than English, but I don't.

There are places where my Scottish and Jewish inheritance meet, areas of shared experience. Like the Jews, the Scots are a migrant people. Perhaps in one of the crowded, echoing halls of Ellis Island a Scottish and a Jewish antecedent stood side by side, waiting their turn to be checked for TB or grilled about their political activities. Thus the USA has the potential to unite disparate currents of origin, although the 'melting pot' may, paradoxically, be a factor in the nation's realigned divisions.

Identities can co-exist seamlessly. There need not be any tension present in the blend of national, religious, occupational, familial and gender identities that most of us live with. But often there is, even when there is no obvious clash. In Scotland, sectarianism is still an issue. Gender still affects potential and achievement. Perhaps as Scotland becomes more confident as a nation the sectarianism and the gender bias will diminish. Oppressed peoples, or peoples who define themselves as oppressed, tend not to be kind to minorities or women.

For me, the tensions continue, and I continue to find them interesting. They are a reason for this book. The fact that I have found my plural identities hard to define and sometimes hard to cope with does not mean I resent them. On the contrary. Life is the richer for them, and although sometimes I envy the ease with which some people define themselves I wouldn't want to be without my own uncertainties. There are contradictions and there have been profound difficulties. Some of these are summed up by the seven years I spent as part of an extended family in Philpstoun House.

It seems to me now that the Philpstoun experiment worked for the women and children, but not for the men. None of the men stayed the course, although for different reasons. Philpstoun was hard work. Maintaining the house and gardens, endless practical difficulties, living with leaky plumbing and rats in the rafters, acres of grass to be cut and weeds to be pulled, dealing with the Hopetoun Estate factor who was at best unhelpful and at worst a bully – all of this demanded a lot of time and effort. My father had never been a practical man, and the death of my mother had left him shattered and emotionally fragile. To our horror, there were people who took advantage of this. When, for example, cowboys turned up at the door offering to resurface the long drive at a cost of several thousand pounds, he was a pushover. The estate refused to contribute although their vehicles used the drive. Our repairing lease meant that the house ate up money.

My father re-married and eventually moved out. His place was taken by Angus's parents. It seemed like a good idea. They had reached their seventies and climbing three flights of stairs to their central Edinburgh flat had become increasingly demanding. Peter was still active in the House of Lords, and joining the extended family meant that Mabel was not alone when he was in London and could play a part in childcare. But neither of them could drive. There was an infrequent bus service. Beyond that, they were dependent for transport on the drivers in the household, and expensive taxis. I think they underestimated the adjustment necessary, and the magnitude of the practical consequences.

But they adjusted rather better than their son. Neither Angus nor Derek, Liz's husband, could cope with the communal dynamic or the responsibilities of a multi-family household in a house that needed a lot of attention. Derek was hugely enthusiastic in theory, but in practice had a habit of being absent when most needed. Angus effectively rejected the whole thing. In his case, perhaps less so in Derek's, it became clear that he could not handle no longer being at the apex of family life. That place was taken by the older generation. For Liz and myself the benefits were obvious. Extended families are good for women with children to look after, especially if women are employed or coping on their own for long periods. First Derek and then Angus made an exit from marriage and the Philpstoun experiment.

Angus's alcohol problem was apparent before Philpstoun, but Philpstoun intensified it. He spent more and more time away from home, and I became used to not knowing exactly where he was. I knew he was drinking, but it was only after we had parted that stories of his excesses began to drift back to me. There was an extraordinarily effective conspiracy of silence concerning both his drinking and his extra-curricular relationships. At home he was often drunk. The practical consequences of Angus's abstention from responsibility were felt by everyone. The emotional and psychological consequences were felt mainly by me. The children, especially Rachel, were aware that things were going wrong, but it was only later that they found themselves having to deal directly with their father's alcohol problem. The collapse of my marriage, fuelled by alcohol as it was, was hugely damaging and left me feeling inadequate and diminished. But also distressing was witnessing the effect of alcohol on personality. The mild-mannered, thoughtful man I had married became after a few drinks explosive and verbally savage, and after more totally self-absorbed and self-pitying. I suspect even now he has little idea of some of the things he said.

The end of a marriage brings more than the loss of one relationship. The loss of friends seems to be almost inevitable, and can be quite bruising. It takes two to maintain contact when circumstances change; with hindsight, I can see that I should have taken the initiative, although that is not easy when confidence has received a beating. One acquaintance, commenting on the divorce of another friend, admitted to feeling threatened and wondering about the security of his own marriage. This may be part of what inhibits people from staying in touch with the recently separated. But I think, also, that many people lack the words and the social skill to deal with divorce. Like death, divorce is territory which we pretend is not ours.

So my social environment changed, but some friendships strengthened, and these were immensely important to me. As a single woman I spent less time with couples, more time with other women like myself. My first serious post-marriage relationship with a man began on a mutually supportive basis but ended with me giving more than I received. I feared this might become a recurring pattern; giving made me feel good, though it wasn't necessarily good for me. With the departure of Gideon for university, the last of the three to leave, I discovered the benefits, and sometimes the exhilaration, of living alone. I had played alone as a child. I had studied alone and worked alone. I had travelled alone. But I was in my early forties before I lived alone. It wasn't difficult. I now believe that it is something everyone should learn at some point in their lives, and probably the earlier the better.

The final year at Philpstoun saw the household reduced to three women and four children, with regular visits from Liz's boyfriend John. It was tough going, although in many ways life for me was easier. We agreed that when the seven year option on the lease came round we would go our separate ways. Mabel was the first to leave, in March 1984, to go into a sheltered flat in Edinburgh. In April I spent two weeks in the United States. It was a significant year for George Orwell studies, and I had been invited to participate in conferences at the Library of Congress and the State University of Ohio. They each paid expenses and a generous fee, and I needed the money. Almost as soon as I got back Liz and her son Ben left to join John in Yorkshire. I had two weeks to vacate Philpstoun House and move to South Queensferry.

The lease required the house to be left in good decorative order (although that was not how it had been when we moved in) and the factor specified which rooms had to be redone. This was a complete waste of time, effort and money as the incoming tenants redecorated the whole house and we suspected that the intention to do so was known beforehand. (It was with great amusement and some considerable *schadenfreude* that we learnt later that the decorators had applied their very expensive wallpaper upside-down.) In those last two weeks I was painting bedrooms, clearing the house with countless trips to the dump and the Salvation Army, packing and trying to ensure that the garden was in reasonable shape. Gowan was in the middle of her Highers. Rachel, who had left school the year before, had an invitation to join her Uncle Nigel and Aunt Lizzie on a sailing trip. The timing was not great, but I did not want her to miss it. She packed up her room before she left. Gideon was nearing the end of his first year at high school and was looking forward to living closer to his school friends.

As I had been away I wasn't able to take much time off work. For two weeks I hardly slept. I lost weight – my clothes were falling off me. There were still uncompleted tasks after the flitting and I had to go back several times to finish the painting and dispose of bulging bin bags. The weather was beautiful. It was strange to drive back to Philpstoun in the early summer evening sunshine, and see the white house empty amidst green fields. I wandered through the echoing rooms. In seven years so much had happened there. I had lost my mother and in a sense my father, as his remarriage had distanced him from my life. My father-in-law had died, and my husband had gone. We had spent seven years cursing the Hopetoun estate factor. We had experienced tragedy and farce, anxiety and exasperation, but those seven years had also been for me productive and often happy. I lingered in those empty rooms, the 'ballroom' which had so suited Mabel's gracious hospitality, the 'yellow room' where we'd played riotous games of Black Maria, the 'red room' where the children had performed their all-singing, all-dancing Christmas shows, the big kitchen where we had gathered for our weekend communal meals. I felt as much regret at leaving as relief.

Every flitting involves casting off at least part of a previous life. I was moving on both from seven years of extended family life and from nineteen years of marriage, and felt ready for a degree of reinvention. But the following year, I had a curious and disturbing experience which reminded me that there were factors influencing my life that were beyond my control. I became aware of a regular attender at the lectures I was then giving at the museum. He sat in the front row and fixed his eyes on me throughout. At around the same time I received two or three letters and cards from a man who signed himself John. He wrote as if he knew me. He said we had been at primary school together in Edinburgh. He also said that I had promised to marry him. I had of course not gone to school in Edinburgh, but at first I thought he had genuinely confused me with someone else.

I destroyed the letters, and cannot now remember the exact sequence of the events that followed, but it was something like this. He phoned me several times, and made himself known to me after one of my lectures (and he was, indeed, the man in the front row). He said that the time had come for me to fulfil my promise. He would meet me after my next lecture, the following week, and we would go off together. I told him this was impossible, that apart from anything else I was already married (although Angus and I had separated we were not yet divorced). Shortly after John spoke to me I received a phone call from his sister; he had informed her that he was going to marry me. She explained that he had a history of mental instability and had recently been discharged from the Royal Edinburgh Hospital, where he was still undergoing treatment. She realised he had embarked on an elaborate fantasy, and asked me to collaborate with the family in having him readmitted. This involved going along with John's plan and agreeing to meet him after my lecture. His sister and brother-in-law would also be there, and would arrange for the police to arrive. I also received a phone call from John's psychiatrist, who explained his condition, in which the sufferer becomes obsessed with someone and convinced that his or her feelings are reciprocated. The objects of affection are more often film stars than museum education officers.

Over the next few days John was frequently in the museum, and I had to ask the staff at the information desk to say that I was not available. They had quickly realised that something was amiss, and were very supportive. I was increasingly concerned that he might discover my home address and stalk me there, but this did not happen. The day of my next lecture duly arrived. There was John in the front row. A couple slipped in late, whom I guessed, correctly, were his sister and brother-in-law. I gave my lecture; I have absolutely no memory of the topic. There were a few questions at the end. John stayed until everyone had left; his sister and her husband stayed in the background, as I recall. I smiled at him duplicitously, knowing that it was important that he believed I was joining him. With perfect timing, two police officers arrived, and quite gently escorted him away, to be sectioned and readmitted. His sister later phoned to say he was back in the Royal Edinburgh, and to thank me.

It was a deeply disconcerting episode. Here was someone insisting, and very convincingly insisting, that I was what I was not. My efforts to persuade him that he had given me a spurious identity made no difference. I didn't feel that he was going to be violent, but had taken the precaution of asking a male colleague to be in the audience, just in case the police arrived late and things got out of hand. But I also felt uncomfortable in colluding with a deception, the result of which was that he was in effect locked up. I had to accept the psychiatrist's view that this was what was best for him. I never learnt what transpired in the end, but for a long time afterwards envisaged him reappearing for a repeat performance.

My elderly aunt sometimes confused me with my mother. Alzheimer's sufferers commonly cannot identify their nearest and dearest, which is one of the manifestations of the condition that members of their families find most distressing. It is important that we are recognised, and recognised as what we think we are. Sometimes, of course, we go to elaborate lengths to project ourselves in a guise other than the way we assume we are normally seen. In ordinary life there is huge scope for both deception and confusion. It is part of the texture of existence. It is at the heart of a vast amount of creative activity.

I have arranged this book under headings that are selective. There are other ways I might have organised my chapters, and there is at least one heading that might be seen as significantly absent. Rather than tease out what was involved in my role as wife, I have written about the consequences of marriage in a number of contexts. The emerging picture probably appears to most readers as negative, so it is perhaps necessary to make it clear that I believe in marriage, although it is for most people an intrinsically difficult arrangement and probably more so now than it has ever been. I believe that a lifelong partnership is possible and potentially of enormous value. I believe that two parents living together are usually, though not always, better for children. I do not regret for one nano-second that I married. As a result of marriage I had experiences of incomparable happiness and immeasurable importance. I had, albeit for a limited period, a valuable and at times inspiring personal and intellectual partnership which gave me the three people who are the most precious to me in the world. But I do not now believe in marriage for myself.

All the other identities I have explored in this book are still with me. In addition there is another layer, which has come inevitably with years. I have joined the almost invisible grey-haired women who travel for nothing on off-peak buses and are kindly addressed as 'dear' by the bus driver. I have become used to being overlooked. I can stand at a bar and watch the bar staff's eyes slide over me. Grey-haired women don't buy drinks. They don't require attention until they reach the stage when they need to be helped across the road. But everything is relative. At the same time as experiencing the curious sensation of vanishing I have an increasing sense of privilege and good fortune.

The ambiguities are all still there. Sometimes one strand becomes more insistent than another. In the wake of the destruction of the World Trade Centre my kinship with America strengthened. I was already expecting to be in New York and New England in the following month; it became even more important for me to go, although around me people were expressing their fears and cancelling trips. With every new Israeli or Palestinian outrage I am forced to examine, increasingly painfully, my Jewishness and, like all Jews, to attempt to define how I can or should relate to what is happening in a part of the world in which I have a personal stake. Similarly, every instance of anti-semitism I come across confirms my Jewish heritage. I still have the urge I had as a ten-year-old to wear a yellow star. I hope to spend the rest of my life in Scotland, though I don't suppose I will ever see myself, or want to see myself, as a one hundred per cent Scot. England may at times feel like a foreign country, but I'll never relinquish the gifts of its literature or the richness of its past. North America will always be a magnet, however deeply distressed I am by its government. As a young woman I became a mother without hesitation, but being a mother hasn't got any easier though its blessings and rewards are manifold. I'll carry on working and travelling until I can't. I will continue to look for synchronicity, and will find it, I am sure, in unexpected places. A constant and sustaining factor in my search for identities has been a friendship that has lasted over fifty years, for much of the time at a distance of 6,000 miles. Underlying everything is the belief in social justice that I think I absorbed with my mother's milk. The more socialism is shunted into history and described as self-evidently an aberration, the more essential it becomes for me to describe myself as a socialist. The same is true of feminism.

Inheritance, accidents and inventions all play a part in identity. Whatever we are born with, we make choices, particularly those of us who live as part of the privileged minority. Most of us have plural identities, which are sometimes fragile and often shifting. My experience of living on a number of margins is not unusual nor need it be negative. I could reinvent myself as a Scot or a Jew, or indeed as a Jewish Scot or Scottish Jew. I could have elected to become a citizen of the United States. I could have chosen not to marry or not to have children, which would almost certainly have made a difference to my career. Sometimes I have longed not to be hybrid. Sometimes I wish I could come up with a straightforward answer when people ask me who I am and where I come from. But straightforward was never an option, and probably isn't for most of us.

Some years ago a new street in Edinburgh was named Daiches Braes. My father and uncle were present at the naming ceremony. 'Daiches' had travelled a long way to be united with a Scots word of Old Norse origins. It's not the end of the journey, but it is a signpost that suggests a shared direction.

Some other books published by **Luath Press**

Scots in Canada
Jenni Calder
1 84282 038 9 PB £7.99

The story of the Scots who went to Canada, from the seventeenth century onwards.

In Canada there are nearly as many descendants of Scots as there are people living in Scotland; almost five million Canadians ticked the 'Scottish origin' box in the most recent Canadian Census. Many Scottish families have friends or relatives in Canada.

Thousands of Scots were forced from their homeland, while others chose to leave, seeking a better life. As individuals, families and communities, they braved the wild Atlantic Ocean, many crossing in cramped under-rationed ships, unprepared for the fierce Canadian winter. And yet Scots went on to lay railroads, found banks and exploit the fur trade, and helped form the political infrastructure of modern day Canada.

...meticulously researched and fluently written... it neatly charts the rise of a country without succumbing to sentimental myths.
SCOTLAND ON SUNDAY

Calder celebrates the ties that still bind Canada and Scotland in camaraderie after nearly 400 years of relations.
THE CHRONICLE AND HERALD, NOVA SCOTIA

Heartland
John MacKay
1 84282 059 1 PB £9.99

This was his land. He had sprung from it and would return surely to it. Its pure air refreshed him, the big skies inspired him and the pounding seas were the rhythm of his heart. It was his touchstone. Here he renourished his soul.

A man tries to build for his future by reconnecting with his past, leaving behind the ruins of the life he has lived. Iain Martin hopes that by returning to his Hebridean roots and embarking on a quest to reconstruct the ancient family home, he might find new purpose.

But as Iain begins working on the old blackhouse, he uncovers a secret from the past, which forces him to question everything he ever thought to be true.

Who can he turn to without betraying those to whom he is closest? His ailing mother, his childhood friend and his former love are both the building – and stumbling – blocks to his new life.

Where do you seek sanctuary when home has changed and will never be the same again?

Heartland will hopefully keep readers turning the pages. It is built on an exploration of the ties to people and place, and of knowing who you are.
JOHN MACKAY

Selected Stories

Dilys Rose

1 84282 077 X PB £7.99

Selected Stories is a compelling compilation by the award-winning Scottish writer Dilys Rose, selected from her three previous books.

Told from a wide range of perspectives and set in many parts of the world, Rose examines everyday lives on the edge through an unforgettable cast of characters. With subtlety, wit and dark humour, she demonstrates her seemingly effortless command of the short story form at every twist and turn of these deftly poised and finely crafted stories.

Praise for Rose's other work:

Dilys Rose can be compared to Katherine Mansfield in the way she takes hold of life and exposes all its vital elements in a few pages.
TIMES LITERARY SUPPLEMENT

Although Dilys Rose makes writing look effortless, make no mistake, to do so takes talent, skill and effort.
THE HERALD

The true short-story skills of empathy and cool, resonant economy shine through them all. Subtle excellence.
THE SCOTSMAN

Lord of Illusions

Dilys Rose

1 84282 076 1 PB £7.99

Lord of Illusions is the fourth collection of short stories from award-winning Scottish writer Dilys Rose.

Exploring the human condition in all its glory – and all its folly – *Lord of Illusions* treats both with humour and compassion.

Often wry, always thought-provoking, this new collection offers intriguing glimpses into the minds and desires of a diverse cast of characters; from jockey to masseuse, from pornographer to magician, from hesitant transvestite to far-from-home aid worker. Each of these finely crafted stories, with their subtle twists and turns, their changes of mood and tone, demonstrate the versatile appeal of the short story, for which Dilys Rose is deservedly celebrated.

Praise for Rose's other work:

A born professional
MURIEL SPARK

Rose is at her best – economical, moral and compassionate.
THE GUARDIAN

Driftnet

Lin Anderson

1 84282 034 6 PB £ 9.99

Introducing forensic scientist Dr Rhona MacLeod...

A teenager is found strangled and mutilated in a Glasgow flat.

Leaving her warm bed and lover in the middle of the night to take forensic samples from the body, Rhona MacLeod immediately perveives a likeness between herself and the dead boy and is tortured by the thought that he might be the son she gave up for adoption seventeen years before.

Amidst the turmoil of her own love life and consumed by guilt from her past, Rhona sets out to find both the boy's killer and her own son. But the powerful men who use the Internet to trawl for vulnerable boys have nothing to lose and everything to gain by Rhona MacLeod's death.

A strong player on the crime novel scene, Lin Anderson skilfully interweaves themes of betrayal, violence and guilt. In forensic investigator Rhona MacLeod she has created a complex character who will have readers coming back for more.

Lin Anderson has a rare gift. She is one of the few able to convey urban and rural Scotland with equal truth... Compelling, vivid stuff. I couldn't put it put it down.
ANNE MACLEOD, author of *The Dark Ship*

Torch

Lin Anderson

1 84282 042 7 PB £9.99

Arson-probably the easiest crime to commit and the most difficult to solve.

A homeless girl dies in an arson attack on an empty building on Edinburgh's famous Princes Street.

Forensic scientist Rhona MacLeod is called over from Glasgow to help find the arsonist. Severino MacRae, half Scottish/half Italian and all misogynist, has other ideas. As Chief Fire Investigator, this is his baby and he doesn't want help – especially from a woman. Sparks fly when Rhona and Severino meet, but Severino's reluctance to involve Rhona may be more about her safety than his prejudice. As Hogmany approaches, Rhona and Severino play cat and mouse with an arsonist who will stop at nothing to gain his biggest thrill yet.

The second novel in the Dr Rhona MacLeod series finds this ill-matched pair's investigation take them deep into Edinburgh's sewers – but who are they up against? As the clock counts down to midnight, will they find out in time?

I just couldn't put it down. It's a real page-turner, a nail-biter – and that marvellous dialogue only a script-writer could produce. The plot, the Edinburgh atmosphere was spot on – hope that Rhona and Severino are to meet again – the sparks really fly there.
ALANNA KNIGHT

Outlandish Affairs

Edited by Evan Rosenthal and Amanda Robinson

1 84282 055 9 PB £9.99

A plethora of bizarre and unusual questions arise when writers from both sides of the Atlantic – inspired by the multicultural nature of society – try to tackle the age old question of love.

When is a country singer gay and when is he straight?

Have you ever truly loved a seal?

Will *West Side Story* inspire the music of love to blossom?

Does an Icelandic strongman, semi-naked in a New York diner, do it for you?

Can Saddam Hussein be Prince Charming?

Have you ever dated anyone from another country, culture, world?

And if so, did sparks fly?

Discover in these stories what might happen when amorous encounters cross boundaries.

The Blue Moon Book

Anne MacLeod

1 84282 061 3 PB £9.99

Love can leave you breathless, lost for words.

Jess Kavanagh knows. Doesn't know. Twenty four hours after meeting and falling for archaeologist and Pictish expert Michael Hurt she suffers a horrific accident that leaves her with aphasia and amnesia. No words. No memory of love.

Michael travels south, unknowing. It is her estranged partner sports journalist Dan MacKie who is at the bedside when Jess finally regains consciousness. Dan, forced to review their shared past, is disconcerted by Jess's fear of him, by her loss of memory, loss of words.

Will their relationship survive this test? Should it survive? Will Michael find Jess again? In this absorbing contemporary novel, Anne MacLeod interweaves themes of language, love and loss in patterns as intricate, as haunting as the Pictish Stones.

As a challenge to romantic fiction, the novel is a success; and as far as men and women's failure to communicate is concerned, it hits the mark.
PETER BURNETT, SCOTLAND ON SUNDAY

High on drama and pathos, woven through with fine detail.
THE HERALD

Luath Press Limited
committed to publishing well written books worth reading

LUATH PRESS takes its name from Robert Burns, whose little collie Luath (*Gael.*, swift or nimble) tripped up Jean Armour at a wedding and gave him the chance to speak to the woman who was to be his wife and the abiding love of his life. Burns called one of *The Twa Dogs* Luath after Cuchullin's hunting dog in *Ossian's Fingal*. Luath Press was established in 1981 in the heart of Burns country, and is now based a few steps up the road from Burns' first lodgings on Edinburgh's Royal Mile. Luath offers you distinctive writing with a hint of unexpected pleasures.

Most bookshops in the UK, the US, Canada, Australia, New Zealand and parts of Europe, either carry our books in stock or can order them for you. To order direct from us, please send a £sterling cheque, postal order, international money order or your credit card details (number, address of cardholder and expiry date) to us at the address below. Please add post and packing as follows: UK – £1.00 per delivery address; overseas surface mail – £2.50 per delivery address; overseas airmail – £3.50 for the first book to each delivery address, plus £1.00 for each additional book by airmail to the same address. If your order is a gift, we will happily enclose your card or message at no extra charge.

Luath Press Limited
543/2 Castlehill
The Royal Mile
Edinburgh EH1 2ND
Scotland
Telephone: 0131 225 4326 (24 hours)
Fax: 0131 225 4324
email: gavin.macdougall@luath. co.uk
Website: www. luath.co.uk